THE RICH . . . THE ROYAL . . . THE RUINED . . .

In Venice an Australian heiress is about to marry the prince of her dreams when, the night before the wedding, he elopes with the best man.

In Geneva, beneath a red-and-white-striped marquee, princesses, baronesses, and businessmen wildly overbid and overpay for the jewels and love tokens of the late Duchess of Windsor.

In New York City a brilliant and controversial photographer who has taken the sexual experience to the limits in his work enjoys his last showing at the Whitney Museum of American Art.

In a great house in the South of France an alluring countess becomes a mythic figure on the French Riviera . . . when it is rumored that she's killed all four of her husbands.

In a quiet garden in Jordan the beautiful, intelligent Queen Noor al Hussein, the American fourth wife of King Hussein, contemplates the precariousness of her throne since the advent of the Gulf War.

THE MANSIONS OF LIMBO

"Awesome . . . If you missed any of these [in *Vanity Fair*], or even if you didn't, buy this book now. Don't put it off. . . . This book is a key to America. It has a Renaissance intensity. It shows us the Wheel of Fortune, the Wages of Hubris. It points out the horrid and satisfying truth that the higher you climb, the more inexorably you fall."
—*New York Newsday*

"Captures the greed, egomania and personal excesses that ripped away at America's social fabric during those long 10 years."
—*Buffalo News*

"Highly entertaining and razor-sharp."
—Liz Smith

THE MANSIONS
OF LIMBO

DOMINICK
DUNNE

BANTAM BOOKS
NEW YORK · TORONTO · LONDON · SYDNEY · AUCKLAND

This edition contains the complete text
of the original hardcover edition.
NOT ONE WORD HAS BEEN OMITTED.

THE MANSIONS OF LIMBO

A Bantam Book / published in association with Crown Publishers, Inc.

PRINTING HISTORY
Crown edition published 1991
All of the articles in this book were
previously published in Vanity Fair

Bantam edition / July 1992

ISBN 0-553-29075-4

Published simultaneously in the United States and Canada

Bantam Books are published by Bantam Books, a division of Bantam Doubleday Dell Publishing
Group, Inc. Its trademark, consisting of the words "Bantam Books" and the portrayal of a rooster,
is Registered in U.S. Patent and Trademark Office and in other countries. Marca Registrada.
Bantam Books, 666 Fifth Avenue, New York, New York 10103.

PRINTED IN THE UNITED STATES OF AMERICA

RAD   0   9   8   7   6   5   4   3   2   1

To Tina Brown
who held out her hand,
with thanks and love

CONTENTS

INTRODUCTION

❧

YEARS AGO, reading a book whose title I no longer remember, I came across a sentence in which the words "the mansions of limbo" appeared. I was struck by those words. I loved the sound of them, and they have always stayed with me. In my Catholic youth, I learned that limbo was a blissful repository for the souls of infants who died before they were baptized, a community whose perfection was marred only by the fact that they were denied the sight of God. As I grew older, the meaning of limbo broadened to signify a state of privileged oblivion with a missing ingredient. When I began to put together the pieces from *Vanity Fair* that make up this collection, I tried to find a unifying factor in the kind of people and situations I write about, and the words that I read so long ago returned to me. However, I could never find the book in which I read them. Neither could scholarly friends or *Bartlett's Quotations* reveal their source. So I have simply usurped the words to make up the title of this book.

Not all, but most of the people I write about here soared in the decade of the eighties, a period in which the fortunes of the rich seemed limitless, and our information about them equally limitless. We knew, often with their cooperation, everything there was to know about them: how much money they were worth, how much they paid for their houses, their paintings, their curtains, their dresses, their centerpieces, and their parties. They acquired and acquired, and climbed and climbed. One man earned $550 million in a single year. The cost of another man's new house reached nearly $100 million. Perhaps it was bliss for them, but, certainly, it was bliss with a missing ingredient. Toward the end, some of the luminous figures went to jail for fiscal irregularities. The marriages of others began to disentangle. And a horrible new disease was killing the innocent in appalling numbers. Then the decade ended.

Has any other decade ever ended so promptly? On the twelfth stroke of midnight on December 31, 1989, it was over, finished, done with, history. The sixties, as they will always be remembered, were reluctant to go. The sixties continued to dance to the music of time until the fourth year of the seventies, before allowing that patient decade to define itself. But people were sick of the eighties, sick of the criminal improprieties of Wall Street, sick of the obeisance to money while the homeless occupied more and more sidewalk space in our cities. People wanted the eighties to be finished. And yet, for as long as it lasted, there was a hilariously horrifying fascination in watching the people who overindulged in extravagance, especially the ones who fell so resoundingly from grace and favor. Twice I went to prisons, one in Lucca, Italy, the other in Bern, Switzerland, to interview financial figures whose life-styles and careers had only recently blazed on the social and financial pages. In Venice an Australian heiress almost married a prince in an international social event, but the heiress was not really an heiress and the prince turned out to be a steward on Qantas Airlines, who eloped with his best man the night before the wedding. In Geneva I watched rich people, mad for instant heritage, stand on chairs and wildly overbid and overpay for the late Duchess of Windsor's jewels at an auction staged by Sotheby's in a circus atmosphere worthy of P. T. Barnum. Once I was the lone American on a sailing ship of English aristocrats and minor royals on a cruise through several tropical islands in the Caribbean, a nobleman's odyssey culminating in a bizarre costume ball on the sands of an island mansion where grand ladies wore tiaras and men adorned themselves with plumes, pearls, and white satin. On Lake Lugano, the beauty queen fifth wife of the man with the second largest art collection in the world, after that of the Queen of England, brought about the transfer of her husband's famed artworks from Switzerland to her native Spain in hopes of obtaining the title of duchess from the Spanish king. In New York, a great photographer, who recorded with acute precision the dark side of the netherworld as it has never been recorded before, took my picture only a short time before he died. In a Beverly Hills mansion, a film mogul and his wife were brutally slain gangland style, and, seven months later, their two handsome and privileged sons were arrested for the crime, after a massive spending spree with their new inheritance.

All the pieces do not fit into the pattern of the late decade. There are the eternal figures like the singer Phyllis McGuire, once the mistress of the gangster Sam Giancana, in her Las Vegas mansion, and the actress Jane Wyman, the only divorced wife of a United States president, who have defied time and continue to fascinate. There is Lady Kenmare, the chatelaine of a great house in the South of France, who flourished in international society in the thirties, forties, and fifties as the rumored murderess of her four husbands. And, finally, there is the beautiful and highly intelligent Queen Noor of Jordan, the American fourth wife of King Hussein, who sits on a precarious throne between Israel and Iraq during the war that will define the new decade.

Dominick Dunne
New York, 1991

THE MANSIONS
OF LIMBO

NIGHTMARE
ON
ELM DRIVE

ON A RECENT New York–to–Los Angeles trip on MGM
Grand Air, that most luxurious of all coast-to-coast flights,
I was chilled to the bone marrow during a brief encounter
with a fellow passenger, a boy of perhaps fourteen, or fifteen, or maybe even sixteen, who lounged restlessly in a
sprawled-out fashion, arms and legs akimbo, avidly reading
racing-car magazines, chewing gum, and beating time to
the music on his Walkman. Although I rarely engage in
conversations with strangers on airplanes, I always have a
certain curiosity to know who everyone is on MGM Grand
Air, which I imagine is a bit like the Orient Express in its
heyday. The young traveler in the swivel chair was returning to California after a sojourn in Europe. There were
signals of affluence in his chat; the Concorde was mentioned. His carry-on luggage was expensive, filled with
audiotapes, playing cards, and more magazines. During the
meal, we talked. A week before, two rich and privileged
young men named Lyle and Erik Menendez had been arrested for the brutal slaying of their parents in the family's
$5 million mansion on Elm Drive, a sedate tree-lined street

that is considered one of the most prestigious addresses in Beverly Hills. The tale in all its gory grimness was the cover story that week in *People* magazine, many copies of which were being read on the plane.

"Do you live in Beverly Hills?" I asked.

"Yes."

"Where?"

He told me the name of his street, which was every bit as prestigious as Elm Drive. I once lived in Beverly Hills and knew the terrain well. His home was in the same general area as the house where Kitty and Jose Menendez had been gunned down several months earlier in a fusillade of fourteen twelve-gauge shotgun blasts—five to the head and body of the father, nine to the face and body of the mother—that left them virtually unrecognizable as human beings, according to eyewitness reports. The slaying was so violent that it was assumed at first to have been of Mafia origins—a hit, or Mob rubout, as it was called, even in the *Wall Street Journal*. The arrest of the two handsome, athletic Menendez sons after so many months of investigation had shocked an unshockable community.

"Did you ever know the Menendez brothers?" I asked the teenager.

"No," he replied. They had gone to different schools. They were older. Lyle was twenty-two, Erik nineteen. In that age group, a few years makes an enormous difference.

"A terrible thing," I said.

"Yeah," he replied. "But I heard the father was pretty rough on those kids."

With that, our conversation was concluded.

Patricide is not an altogether new crime in the second echelon of Southland society. Nor is matricide. On March 24, 1983, twenty-year-old Michael Miller, the son of President Ronald Reagan's personal lawyer, Roy Miller, raped and clubbed to death his mother, Marguerite. In a minimally publicized trial, from which the media was barred, Miller was found guilty of first-degree murder but was acquitted of the rape charge, presumably on the technicality that the rape had occurred after his mother was dead. The judge then ruled that young Miller, who had been diagnosed as schizophrenic, was legally innocent of murder by reason of insanity. "Hallelujah," muttered Michael Miller after the verdict. He was sent to Patton State Hospital, a mental institution in California.

On July 22, 1983, in a Sunset Boulevard mansion in Bel-Air, twenty-year-old Ricky Kyle shot his father, millionaire Henry Harrison Kyle, the president of Four Star International, a television-and-movie-production firm, in the back after awakening him in the middle of the night to tell him there was a prowler in the house. Several witnesses testified that Ricky had confided in them about a long-standing desire to kill his father, who was alleged to have been physically and mentally abusive to his son. The prosecution argued that Ricky was consumed with hatred for his father and greed for his fortune, and that, fearing that he was about to be disinherited, he plotted the ruse of the prowler. With the extraordinary leniency of the Southern California courts for first-time murderers, young Kyle was sentenced to five years for the slaying. Expressing dismay with the verdict, Ricky's mother told reporters she had hoped her son would be spared a prison term. "I think he has suffered enough," she said. Ricky agreed. "I feel like I don't deserve to go to prison," he said.

And then there were the Woodman brothers, Stewart and Neil, accused of hiring two assassins to gun down their rich parents in Brentwood. Tried separately, Stewart was convicted of first-degree murder. To escape the death pen-

alty, he incriminated his brother. Neil's trial is about to
start.

Further elaboration is not necessary: the point has been
made. One other case, however, on a lesser social stratum
but of equal importance, under the circumstances, should
be mentioned: the Salvatierra murder, which received international attention. In 1986, Oscar Salvatierra, the Los
Angeles–based executive of a newspaper called *Philippine
News,* was shot while he was asleep in bed, after having
received a death threat that was at first believed to be tied
to the newspaper's opposition to former Philippine president Ferdinand Marcos. Later, Arnel Salvatierra, his seventeen-year-old son, admitted sending the letter and killing
his father. In court, Arnel Salvatierra's lawyer convinced
the jury that Arnel was the victim of a lifetime of physical
and psychological abuse by his father. The lawyer, Leslie
Abramson, who is considered to be the most brilliant Los
Angeles defense lawyer for death-row cases, compared
Arnel Salvatierra to the tragic Lisa Steinberg of New York,
whose father, Joel Steinberg, had been convicted of mur-
dering her after relentlessly abusing her. "What happens if
the Lisa Steinbergs don't die?" Abramson asked the jury.
"What happens if they get older, and if the cumulative
effect of all these years of abuse finally drives them over the
edge, and Lisa Steinberg pulls out a gun and kills Joel
Steinberg?" Arnel Salvatierra, who had been charged with
first-degree murder, was convicted of voluntary manslaugh-
ter and placed on probation.

This story is relevant to the Menendez case in that the
same Leslie Abramson is one-half the team defending the
affluent Menendez brothers. Her client is Erik Menendez,
the younger brother. Gerald Chaleff, with whom she frequently teams, is representing Lyle. On an earlier burglary
case involving the brothers, Chaleff, who gained promi-

nence in criminal law as the defender of the Hillside Strangler, represented Erik. It is rumored that Abramson and Chaleff are each being paid $700,000. Psychological abuse is a constant theme in articles written about the brothers, and will probably be the basis of the defense strategy when the case comes to trial. There are even whispers—shocker of shockers—of sexual abuse in the Menendez family.

Jose Enrique Menendez was an American success story. A Cuban émigré, he was sent to the United States by his parents in 1960 at age fifteen to escape from Castro's Cuba. His father, a onetime soccer star, and his mother, a former champion swimmer, stayed behind until their last properties were seized by Castro. Young Jose, who excelled in swimming, basketball, and soccer, won a swimming scholarship to Southern Illinois University, but he gave it up when he married Mary Louise Andersen, known as Kitty, at the age of nineteen and moved to New York. He earned a degree in accounting at Queens College in Flushing, New York, while working part-time as a dishwasher at the swank "21" Club in Manhattan, where, later, successful and prosperous, he would often dine. Then began a career of astonishing ascendancy which took him through Hertz, where he was in charge of car and commercial leasing, to the record division of RCA, where he signed such high-earning acts as Menudo, the Eurythmics, and Duran Duran. By this time he and Kitty had had two sons and settled down to a graceful life on a million-dollar estate in Princeton, New Jersey. The boys attended the exclusive Princeton Day School and, urged on by their father, began developing into first-rate tennis and soccer players. Their mother attended every match and game they played. When Jose clashed with a senior executive at RCA in 1986, after having been passed over for the executive vice presidency of RCA Records, he uprooted his family, much to the distress of Kitty, who loved her life and house in Princeton, and moved to Los Angeles. There he leapfrogged to I.V.E., International Video Entertainment, a video distributor which eventually became Live Entertainment, a division of the hugely successful Carolco Pictures, the company that produced the Rambo films of Sylvester Stallone as well as some of Arnold Schwarzenegger's action films. Jose Menendez's success at Live Entertainment was dazzling. In 1986 the company lost $20 million; a year later, under Menendez, Live earned $8 million and in 1988 doubled that. "He was the perfect corporate executive," I was told by one of his lieutenants. "He had an incredible dedication to business. He was focused, specific about what he wanted from the business, very much in control. He believed that whatever had to be done should be done—with no heart, if necessary."

The family lived at first in Calabasas, an upper-middle-class suburb of Los Angeles, inland beyond Malibu, where they occupied one house while building a more spectacular one on thirteen acres with mountaintop views. Then, unexpectedly, almost overnight, the family abandoned Calabasas and moved to Beverly Hills, where Jose bought the house on Elm Drive, a six-bedroom Mediterranean-style house with a red tile roof, a courtyard, a swimming pool, a tennis court, and a guesthouse. Built in 1927, rebuilt in 1974, the house had good credentials. It had previously been rented to Elton John. And Prince. And Hal Prince. And a Saudi prince, for $35,000 a month. Erik Menendez, the younger son, transferred from Calabasas High to Beverly Hills High, probably the most snobbish public school in America. Lyle was a student at Princeton University, fulfilling one of the many American dreams of his immigrant father.

They were the ideal family; everyone said so. "They were extraordinarily close-knit," an executive of Live Entertainment told me. "It was one big happy family," said John E. Mason, a friend and Live Entertainment director. They did things together. They telephoned one another several times a day, about tennis matches and girlfriends and the results of exams. They almost always had dinner together, which, in a community where most parents go to parties or screenings every night and leave their children to their own devices, is a rare thing. They talked about world events, as well as about what was happening in Jose's business. On the day before the catastrophic event, a Saturday, they chartered a boat called *Motion Picture Marine* in Marina del Rey and spent the day together shark-fishing, just the four of them.

On the evening of the following day, August 20, 1989, the seemingly idyllic world that Jose Menendez had created was shattered. With their kids at the movies in Century City, Jose and Kitty settled in for a comfortable evening of television and videos in the television room at the rear of their house. Jose was in shorts and a sweatshirt; Kitty was in a sweatshirt, jogging pants, and sneakers. They had dishes of strawberries and ice cream on the table in front of the sofa where they were sitting. Later, after everything happened, a neighbor would report hearing sounds like firecrackers coming from the house at about ten o'clock, but he took no notice. It wasn't until a hysterical 911 call came in to the Beverly Hills police station around midnight that there was any indication that the sounds had not been made by firecrackers. The sons of the house, Lyle and

Erik, having returned from the movies, where they said they saw *Batman* again after they couldn't get into *License to Kill* because of the lines, drove in the gate at 722 North Elm Drive, parked their car in the courtyard, entered the house by the front door, and found their parents dead, sprawled on the floor and couch in the television room. In shock at the grisly sight, Lyle telephoned for help. "They shot and killed my parents!" he shrieked into the instrument. "I don't know . . . I didn't hear anything . . . I just came home. Erik! Shut up! Get away from them!"

Another neighbor said on television that she had seen one of the Menendez boys curled up in a ball on the lawn in front of their house and screaming in grief. "I have heard of very few murders that were more savage," said Beverly Hills police chief Marvin Iannone. Dan Stewart, a retired police detective hired by the family to investigate the murders, gave the most graphic description of the sight in the television room. "I've seen a lot of homicides, but nothing quite that brutal. Blood, flesh, skulls. It would be hard to describe, especially Jose, as resembling a human that you would recognize. That's how bad it was." According to the autopsy report, one blast caused "explosive decapitation with evisceration of the brain" and "deformity of the face" to Jose Menendez. The first round of shots apparently struck Kitty in her chest, right arm, left hip, and left leg. Her murderers then reloaded and fired into her face, causing "multiple lacerations of the brain." Her face was an unrecognizable pulp.

The prevalent theory in the days following the murders was that it had been a Mob hit. Erik Menendez went so far as to point the finger at Noel Bloom, a distributor of pornographic films and a former associate of the Bonanno organized-crime family, as a possible suspect. Erik told police and early reporters on the story that Bloom and his father

had despised each other after a business deal turned sour.
(When questioned, Bloom denied any involvement whatsoever.) Expressing fear that the Mob might be after them as
well, the brothers moved from hotel to hotel in the aftermath of the murders. Marlene Mizzy, the front-desk super-
visor at the Beverly Hills Hotel, said that Lyle arrived at
the hotel without a reservation two days after the murders
and asked for a two-bedroom suite. Not liking the suites
that were available on such short notice, he went to another
hotel.

Seven months later, after the boys were arrested, I visited the house on Elm Drive. It is deceptive in size, far
larger than one would imagine from the outside. You enter
a spacious hallway with a white marble floor and a skylight
above. Ahead, to the right, is a stairway carpeted in pale
green. Off the hallway on one side is an immense drawing
room, forty feet in length. The lone piece of sheet music on
the grand piano was "American Pie," by Don McLean. On
the other side are a small paneled sitting room and a large
dining room. At the far end of the hallway, in full view of
the front door, is the television room, where Kitty and Jose
spent their last evening together. On the back wall is a
floor-to-ceiling bookcase, filled with books, many of them
paperbacks, including all the American-history novels of
Gore Vidal, Jose's favorite author. On the top shelf of the
bookcase were sixty tennis trophies—all first place—that
had been won over the years by Lyle and Erik.

Like a lot of houses of the movie nouveau riche still in
their social and business rise, the grand exterior is not
matched by a grand interior. When the Menendez family
bought the house, it was handsomely furnished, and they
could have bought the furniture from the former owner for
an extra $350,000, but they declined. With the exception
of some reproduction Chippendale chairs in the dining

room, the house is appallingly furnished with second-rate pieces; either the purchase price left nothing for interior decoration or there was just a lack of interest. In any case, your attention, once you are in the house, is not on the furniture. You are drawn, like a magnet, to the television room.

Trying to imagine what happened that night, I found it unlikely that the boys—if indeed it was the boys, and there is a very vocal contingent who believe it was not—would have come down the stairs with the guns, turned right, and entered the television room, facing their parents. Since Jose was hit point-blank in the back of the head, it seems far more likely that the killers entered the television room through the terrace doors behind the sofa on which Kitty and Jose were sitting, their backs to the doors, facing the television set. The killers would probably have un-locked the doors in advance. In every account of the murders, Kitty was said to have run toward the kitchen. This would suggest, assuming she was running away from her assailants, that they had entered from behind.

Every person who saw the death scene has described the blood, the guts, and the carnage in sick-making detail. The furniture I saw in that room was replacement furniture, rented after the murders from Antiquarian Traders in West Hollywood. The original blood-drenched furniture and Oriental carpet had been hauled away, never to be sat on or walked on again. It is not farfetched to imagine that splat-terings of blood and guts found their way onto the clothes and shoes of the killers, which would have necessitated a change of clothing and possibly a shower. There is no way the killers could have gone up the stairs, however; the blood on their shoes would have left tracks on the pale green stair carpet. The lavatory beneath the stairs and adja-cent to the television room does not have a shower. What probably happened is that the killers retreated out the same terrace doors they had entered, and went back to the guest-house to shower and change into clothes they had left there. The guesthouse is a separate, two-story unit beyond the swimming pool and adjacent to the tennis court, with a sitting room, a bedroom, a full bath, and a two-car garage opening onto an alley.

There is also the possibility that the killers, knowing the carnage twelve-gauge-shotgun blasts would cause, wore boots, gloves, and overalls. In that event, they would have only had to discard the clothes and boots into a large gar-bage bag and make a dash for it. One of the most interest-ing aspects of the case is that the fourteen shell casings were picked up and removed. I have been told that such fastidiousness is out of character in a Mafia hit, where a speedy getaway is essential. There is a sense of leisurely time here, of people not in a hurry, not expecting anyone, when they delay their departure from a massacre to pick the shell casings out of the bloody remains of their victims' bodies. They almost certainly wore rubber gloves to do it.

Then they had to get rid of the guns. The guns, as of this writing, have still not been found. We will come back to the guns. The car the killers left in was probably parked in the guesthouse garage; from there they could make their exit unobserved down the alley behind the house. Had they left out the front gate on Elm Drive, they would have risked being observed by neighbors or passersby. Between the time the killers left the house and the time the boys made the call to the police, the bloody clothes were proba-bly disposed of.

On the day before the fishing trip on the *Motion Picture Marine,* Erik Menendez allegedly drove south to San Diego and purchased two Mossberg twelve-gauge shotguns in a Big 5 sporting-goods store, using for identification the stolen driver's license of a young man named Donovan Goodreau. Under federal law, to purchase a weapon, an individual must fill out a 4473 form, which requires the buyer to provide his name, address, and signature, as well as an identification card with picture. Donovan Goodreau had subsequently said on television that he can prove he was in New York at the time of the gun purchase in San Diego. Goodreau had once roomed with Jamie Pisarcik, who was, and still is, Lyle Menendez's girlfriend and stalwart supporter, visiting him daily in jail and attending his every court session. When Goodreau stopped rooming with Jamie, he moved into Lyle's room at Princeton, which was against the rules, since he was not a student at the university. But then, Lyle had once kept a puppy in his room at Princeton, and having animals in the rooms was against the rules, too.

What has emerged most significantly in the year since the murders is that all was not what it seemed in the seemingly perfect Menendez household. There are people who will tell you that Jose was well liked. There are more people by far who will tell you that he was greatly disliked. Even despised. He had made enemies all along the way in his rise to the high middle of the entertainment industry, but everyone agrees that had he lived he would have gone right to the top. He did not have many personal friends, and he and Kitty were not involved in the party circuit of Beverly Hills. His life was family and business. I was told that at the memorial service in Los Angeles, which preceded the funeral in Princeton, most of the two hundred people who attended had a business rather than a personal relationship with him. Stung by the allegations that Jose had Mob connections in his business dealings at Live Entertainment, allegations that surfaced immediately after the murders, the company hired Warren Cowan, the famed public-relations man, to arrange the memorial service. His idea was to present Menendez as Jose the family man. He suggested starting a Jose Menendez scholarship fund, a suggestion that never came to fruition. It was also his idea to hold the memorial service in an auditorium at the Directors Guild in Hollywood, in order to show that Jose was a member of the entertainment community, although it is doubtful that Jose had ever been there. Two people from Live Entertainment gave glowing eulogies. Brian Andersen, Kitty's brother, spoke lovingly about Kitty, and each son spoke reverently about his parents. One person leaving the service was heard to say, "The only word not used to describe Jose was 'prick.' "

Although Jose spoke with a very slight accent, a business cohort described him to me as "very non-Hispanic." He was once offended when he received a letter of congratulations for having achieved such a high place in the business world "for a Hispanic." "He hated anyone who knew anything about his heritage," the colleague said. On the other hand, there was a part of Jose Menendez that secretly wanted to run for the U.S. Senate from Florida in order to free Cuba from the tyranny of Fidel Castro and make it a U.S. territory.

Kitty Menendez was another matter. You never hear a bad word about Kitty. Back in Princeton, people remember her on the tennis courts with affection. Those who knew her in the later years of her life felt affection too, but they also felt sorry for her. She was a deeply unhappy woman, and was becoming a pathetic one. Her husband was flagrantly unfaithful to her, and she was devastated by his infidelity. There has been much talk since the killings of Jose's having had a mistress, but that mistress was by no means his first, although he was said to have had "fidelity in his infidelity" in that particular relationship. Kitty fought hard to hold her marriage together, but it is unlikely that Jose would ever have divorced her. An employee at Live Entertainment said, "Kitty called Jose at his office every thirty minutes, sometimes just to tell him what kind of pizza to bring home for supper. She was a dependent person. She wanted to go on his business trips with him. She had June Allyson looks. Very warm. She also had a history of drinking and pills." Another business associate of Jose's at Live said, "I knew Kitty at company dinners and cocktail parties. They used to say about Kitty that she was Jose with a wig. She was always very much at his side, part of his vision, dedicated to the cause, whatever the cause was."

A more intimate picture of Kitty comes from Karen Lamm, one of the most highly publicized secondary characters in the Menendez saga. A beautiful former actress and model who was once wed to the late Dennis Wilson of the Beach Boys, Lamm is now a television producer, and she and her partner, Zev Braun, are developing a mini-series based on the Menendez case. Lamm is often presented as Kitty's closest friend and confidante. However, friends of Erik and Lyle decry her claims of friendship with Kitty, asserting that the boys did not know her, and asking how she could have been such a great friend of Kitty's if she was totally unknown to the sons.

Most newspaper accounts say that Karen Lamm and Kitty Menendez met in an aerobics class, but Lamm, who says she dislikes exercise classes, gave a different account of the beginning of their friendship. About a year before the murders, she was living with a film executive named Stuart Benjamin, who was a business acquaintance of Jose Menendez. Benjamin was a partner of the film director Taylor

Hackford in a production company called New Visions Pictures, which Menendez was interested in acquiring as a subsidiary for Live Entertainment. During the negotiation period, Benjamin, with Lamm as his date, attended a dinner party at the Menendez house on Elm Drive. Lamm, who is an effusive and witty conversationalist, and Kitty spent much of the evening talking together. It was the beginning of a friendship that would blossom. Lamm described Kitty to me as being deeply unhappy over her husband's philandering. She claims that Kitty had tried suicide on three occasions, the kind of at-home suicide attempts that are more cries for help than a longing for death. Kitty had once won a beauty contest and could still be pretty on occasion, but she had let her looks go, grown fat (her autopsy report described her as "fairly well-nourished" and gave her weight as 165), and dyed her hair an unbecoming blond color that did not suit her. Lamm suggested that she get back into shape, and took her to aerobics classes, as well as offering her advice on a darker hair color. During the year that followed, the two women became intimate friends, and Kitty confided in Lamm, not only about Jose's infidelity but also about the many problems they were having with their sons.

Lamm said she met the boys three times, but never talked to them in the house on Elm Drive. She told me, "Those kids watched their mother become a doormat for their father. Jose lived through Lyle. Jose made Lyle white bread. He sent him to Princeton. He gave him all the things that were not available to him as an immigrant." Lamm finally talked with Kitty's sons at the memorial service at the Directors Guild. She was introduced to Lyle, who, in turn, introduced her to Erik as "Mom's friend." She said that Lyle had become Jose overnight. He radiated confidence and showed no emotion, "unless it was a convenient moment." Erik, on the other hand, fell apart.

Over the previous two years, the handsome, athletic, and gifted Menendez sons had been getting into trouble. Although a great friend of the boys dismissed their scrapes as merely "rich kids' sick jokes," two events occurred in Calabasas, where the family lived before the move to Beverly Hills, that were to have momentous consequences for all the members of the family. The brothers got involved in two very serious criminal offenses, a burglary at the home of Michael Warren Ginsberg in Calabasas and grand theft at the home of John Richard List in Hidden Hills. In total, more than $100,000 in money and jewels was taken from the two houses—not an insignificant sum.

Jose dealt with his sons' transgressions the way he would deal with any prickly business problem, said a business associate, by "minimizing the damage and going forward, fixing something that was broken without actually dealing with the problem." He simply took over and solved it. The money and jewels were returned, and $11,000 in damages was paid. Since Erik was underage, it was decided that he would take the fall for both brothers, thereby safeguarding Jose's dream of having Lyle study at Princeton. Jose hired the criminal lawyer Gerald Chaleff to represent Erik—the same Gerald Chaleff who is now representing Lyle on the charge of murdering the man who once hired him to represent Erik on the burglary charge. Everything was solved to perfection. Erik got probation, no more. And compulsory counseling. And for that, Kitty asked her psychologist, Les Summerfield, to recommend someone her son could go to for the required number of hours ordered by the judge. Les Summerfield recommended a Beverly Hills psychologist named Jerome Oziel, who, like Gerald Chaleff, continues his role in the Menendez saga right up to the present.

Prior to the thefts, Erik had made a friend at Calabasas High School who would also play a continuing part in the story. Craig Cignarelli, the son of a prominent executive in the television industry, is a Tom Cruise look-alike currently studying at the University of California in Santa Barbara. Craig was the captain of the Calabasas High School tennis team, and Erik, who had recently transferred from Princeton Day, was the number-one singles player on the team. One day, while playing a match together, they were taunted by two students from El Camino High School, a rival school in a less affluent neighborhood. Menendez and Cignarelli went out to the street to face their adversaries, and a fight started. Suddenly, a whole group of El Camino boys jumped out of cars and joined the fray. Erik and Craig were both badly beaten up. Erik's jaw was broken, and Craig received severe damage to his ribs. The incident sparked a close friendship between the two, which would culminate in the co-writing of a movie script called *Friends,* in which a young man named Hamilton Cromwell murders his extremely rich parents for his inheritance. One of the most quoted passages from this screenplay comes from the mouth of Hamilton Cromwell, speaking about his father: "Sometimes he would tell me that I was not worthy to be his son. When he did that, it would make me strive harder . . . just so I could hear the words 'I love you, son.' . . . And I never heard those words." To add to the awful irony, Kitty, the loving mother who could not do enough for her sons, typed the screenplay in which her own demise seems to have been predicted. In the embarrassing aftermath of the burglaries, the family moved to the house on Elm Drive in Beverly Hills. Jose told people at Live Entertainment that he was upset by the drug activity in

Calabasas and that the tires of his car had been slashed, but it is quite possible that these stories were a diversionary tactic, or smoke screen, created to cover the disgrace of his son's criminal record.

A further setback for the family, also partly covered up, had occurred the previous winter, when Lyle was suspended from Princeton after one semester for cheating in Psychology 101. Taken before a disciplinary committee, he was told he could leave the university voluntarily or be expelled. He chose to leave. This was a grave blow to Jose, who loved to tell people that he had a son at Princeton. Again taking over, he tried to talk the authorities at Princeton into reinstating his son, but this time the pressure he applied did not work. The suspension lasted a year. In a typical reaction, Jose became more angry at the school than he was at his son. He urged Lyle to stay on in Princeton rather than return to Beverly Hills, so that he would not have to admit to anyone that Lyle had been kicked out.

But Lyle did return, and worked briefly at Live Entertainment, where he showed all the worst qualities of the spoiled rich boy holding down a grace-and-favor job in his father's company. He was consistently late for work. His attention span was brief. He worked short hours, leaving in the afternoon to play tennis. He was unpopular with the career-oriented staff. "The kids had a sense of being young royalty," said an employee of the company. "They could be nasty, arrogant, and self-centered." But, the same person said, Jose had a blind spot about his sons. And tennis held the family together. Once, Jose took the Concorde to Europe just to watch Lyle play in a tennis tournament, and then came right back. However, for all the seeming closeness of the family, the sons were proving to be disappointments, even failures, in the eyes of their perfection-demanding father. Jose had apparently come to the end of financing his recalcitrant sons' rebellion, and there are indications that he planned to revise his will.

After the Calabasas debacle, Erik transferred to Beverly Hills High School for his senior year. His classmates remember him chiefly as a loner, walking around in tennis shorts, always carrying his tennis racket.

"A girl I was going out with lusted after him," a student told me. "She said he had good legs."

"Was he spoiled?"

"Everyone at Beverly High is spoiled."

Like his father, Lyle is said to have been a great ladies' man, which pleased Jose, but several of Lyle's girlfriends, mostly older than he, were not considered to be suitable by his parents, and clashes occurred. When Jose forbade Lyle to go to Europe with an older girlfriend, Lyle went anyway. A person extremely close to the family told me that another of Lyle's girlfriends—not Jamie Pisarcik, who has been so loyal to him during his incarceration—was "manipulating him," which I took to mean manipulating him into marriage. This girl became pregnant. Jose, in his usual method of dealing with his sons' problems, moved in and paid off the girl to abort the child. The manner of Jose's interference in so personal a matter—not allowing Lyle to deal with his own problem—is said to have infuriated Lyle and caused a deep rift between father and son. Lyle moved out of the main house into the guesthouse at the back of the property. He was still living there at the time of the murders, although Erik continued to live in the main house.

Karen Lamm told me that in her final conversation with Kitty, three days before the killing and one day before the purchase of the guns in San Diego, Kitty told her that Lyle had been verbally abusive to her in a long, late-night call from the guesthouse to the main house.

•   •   •

From the beginning, the police were disinclined to buy the highly publicized Mafia-hit story, on the grounds that Mafia hits are rarely done in the home, that the victim is usually executed with a single shot to the back of the head, and that the wife is not usually killed also. The hit, if hit it was, looked more like a Colombian drug-lord hit, like the bloody massacre carried out by Al Pacino in the film *Scarface,* which, incidentally, was one of Lyle's favorite movies.

Months later, after the arrests, the Beverly Hills police claimed to have been suspicious of the Menendez brothers from the beginning, even from the first night. One detective at the scene asked the boys if they had the ticket stubs from the film they said they had just seen in Century City. "When both parents are hit, our feeling is usually that the kids did it," said a Beverly Hills police officer. Another officer declared, two days after the event, "These kids fried their parents. They cooked them." But there was no proof, nothing to go on, merely gut reactions.

Inadvertently, the boys brought suspicion upon themselves. In the aftermath of the terrible event, close observers noted the extraordinary calm the boys exhibited, almost as if the murders had happened to another family. They were seen renting furniture at Antiquarian Traders to replace the furniture that had been removed from the television room. And, as new heirs, they embarked on a spending spree that even the merriest widow, who had married for money, would have refrained from going on—for propriety's sake, if nothing else—in the first flush of her mourning period. They bought and bought and bought. Estimates of their spending have gone as high as $700,000. Lyle bought a $60,000 Porsche 911 Carrera to replace the Alfa Romeo his father had given him. Erik turned in his Ford Mustang 5.0 hardtop and bought a tan Jeep Wrangler, which his girl-friend, Noelle Terelsky, is now driving. Lyle bought $40,000 worth of clothes and a $15,000 Rolex watch. Erik hired a $50,000-a-year tennis coach. Lyle decided to go into the restaurant business, and paid a reported $550,000 for a cafeteria-style eatery in Princeton, which he renamed Mr. Buffalo's, flying back and forth coast to coast on MGM Grand Air. "It was one of my mother's delights that I pursue a small restaurant chain and serve healthy food with friendly service," he said in an interview with *The Daily Princetonian,* the campus newspaper. Erik, less successful as an entrepreneur than Lyle, put up $40,000 for a rock con-cert at the Palladium, but got ripped off by a con-man partner and lost the entire amount. Erik decided not to attend U.C.L.A., which had been his father's plan for him, but to pursue a career in tennis instead. After moving from hotel to hotel to elude the Mafia, who they claimed were watching them, the brothers leased adjoining condos in the tony Marina City Club Towers. "They liked high-tech sur-rounds, and they wanted to get out of the house," one of their friends said to me. Then there was the ghoulish sense of humor another of their friends spoke about: Sitting with a gang of pals one night, deciding what videos to rent for the evening, Erik suggested *Dad* and *Parenthood.* Even as close a friend as Glenn Stevens, who was in the car with Lyle when he was arrested, later told the *Los Angeles Times* that two days after the murders, when he asked Lyle how he was holding up emotionally, his friend replied, "I've been waiting so long to be in this position that the transi-tion came easy." The police were also aware that Lyle Me-nendez had hired a computer expert who eradicated from the hard disk of the family computer a revised will that Jose had been working on. Most remarkable of all was that, unlike the families of most homicide victims, the sons of Jose and Kitty Menendez did not have the obsessive interest in the police search for the killers of their parents that usually supersedes all else in the wake of such a tragedy.

As the C.E.O. of Live Entertainment, Jose Menendez earned a base pay of $500,000 a year, with a maximum bonus of $850,000 based on the company's yearly earnings. On top of that, there were life-insurance policies. An interesting sidebar to the story concerns two policies that were thought to have been taken out on Menendez by Live Entertainment. The bigger of the two was a $15 million keyman policy; $10 million of which was with Bankers Trust and $5 million with Credit Lyonnais. Taking out a keyman life-insurance policy on a top executive is common practice in business, with the company being named as beneficiary. Live Entertainment was also required to maintain a second policy on Menendez in the amount of $5 million, with the beneficiary to be named by him. Given the family's much-talked-about closeness, it is not unlikely that Kitty and the boys were aware of this policy. Presumably, the beneficiary of the insurance policy would have been the same as the beneficiary of Jose's will. In the will, it was stated that if Kitty died first everything would go to Jose, and if Jose died first everything would go to Kitty. In the event that both died, everything would go to the boys.

The murders happened on a Sunday night. On the afternoon of the following Tuesday, Lyle and Erik, accompanied by two uncles, Kitty's brother Brian Andersen and Jose's brother-in-law Carlos Baralt, who was the executor of Jose's will, met with officials of Live Entertainment at the company's headquarters to go over Jose's financial situation. At that meeting, it became the difficult duty of Jose's

successor to inform the heirs that the $5 million policy
with beneficiaries named by Jose had not gone into effect,
because Jose had failed to take the required physical exami-
nation, believing that the one he had taken for the $15
million policy applied to both policies. It did not. A person
present at that meeting told me of the resounding silence
that followed the reception of that information. To expect
$5 million, payable upon death, and to find that it was not
forthcoming, would be a crushing disappointment. Finally,
Erik Menendez spoke. His voice was cold. "And the $15
million policy in favor of the company? Was that in order?" he asked. It was. Jose had apparently been told that
he would have to take another physical for the second policy, but he had postponed it. As an officer of the company
said to me, "That anything could ever happen to Jose never
occurred to Jose."

The news that the policy was invalid caused bad blood
between the family and the company, especially since the
immediate payment of the $15 million keyman policy gave
Carolco one of its biggest quarters since the inception of
the company. One of Jose's former employees in New York,
who was close enough to the family to warrant having a
limousine sent to take him from a suburb of New York to
the funeral in Princeton, said to me, "The grandmother?
Did you talk to her? Did she tell you her theory? Did she
tell you the company had Jose taken care of for the $15
million insurance policy?" The grandmother had not told
me this, but it is a theory that the dwindling group of
people who believe in the innocence of the Menendez boys
cling to with passion. The same former employee continued, "Jose must have made a lot of money in California. I
don't know where all that money came from what I've been
hearing about and reading about."

Further bad feelings between the family and Live Entertainment have arisen over the house on Elm Drive, which, like the house in Calabasas, is heavily mortgaged: Approximately $2 million is still owed on the Elm Drive house, with estimated payments of $225,000 a year, plus $40,000 a year in taxes and approximately $40,000 in maintenance. In addition, the house in Calabasas has been on the market for some time and remains unsold; $1.5 million is still owed on it. So, in effect, the expenses on the two houses are approximately $500,000 a year, a staggering amount for the two sons to have dealt with before their arrest. During the meeting on the Tuesday after the murders, when the boys were told that the $5 million life-insurance policy had not gone into effect, it was suggested that Live Entertainment might buy the house on Elm Drive from the estate, thereby removing the financial burden from the boys while the house was waiting to be re-sold. Furthermore, Live Entertainment was prepared to take less for the house than Jose had paid for it, knowing that houses where murders have taken place are hard sells, even in as inflated a real-estate market as Beverly Hills.

Ads have run in the real-estate section of the *Los Angeles Times* for the Elm Drive house. The asking price is $5.95 million. Surprisingly, a buyer did come along. The unidentified person offered only $4.5 million, a bargain for a house on that street, and the offer was hastily accepted. Later, however, the deal fell through. The purchaser was said to have been intimidated by the event that occurred there, and worried about the reaction neighborhood children would have to his own children for living in the house.

The arrangement for Live Entertainment to purchase the property from the estate failed to go into effect, once the police investigation pointed more and more toward the boys, and so the estate has had to assume the immense cost of maintaining the properties. Recently, the Elm Drive house has been leased to a member of the Saudi royal family—not the same prince who rented it before—for $50,000 a month to allay expenses.

Carolco, wishing to stifle rumors that Live Entertainment had Mob connections because of its acquisition of companies like Strawberries, an audio-video retailing chain, from Morris Levy, who allegedly has Genovese crime-family connections, and its bitter battle with Noel Bloom, hired the prestigious New York firm of Kaye, Scholer, Fierman, Hays & Handler to investigate the company for underworld ties. The 220-page report, which cynics in the industry mock as a whitewash, exonerated the company of any such involvement. The report was read at a board meeting on March 8, and the conclusion made clear that the Beverly Hills police, in their investigation of the Menendez murders, were increasingly focusing on their sons, not the Mob. An ironic bit of drama came at precisely that moment, when a vice president of the company burst in on the meeting with the news that Lyle Menendez had just been arrested.

Concurrently, in another, less fashionable area of the city known as Carthay Circle, an attractive thirty-seven-year-old woman named Judalon Rose Smyth, pronounced Smith, was living out her own drama in a complicated love affair. Judalon Smyth's lover was a Beverly Hills psychologist named Jerome Oziel, whom she called Jerry. Dr. Oziel was the same Dr. Oziel whom Kitty Menendez's psychologist, Les Summerfield, had recommended to her a year earlier as the doctor for her troubled son, after the judge in the burglary case in Calabasas had ruled that Erik must have counseling while he was on probation. During that brief period of court-ordered therapy, Jerome Oziel had met the entire Menendez family. Judalon Smyth, however, was as unknown to Lyle and Erik as they were to her, and yet, seven months from the time of the double murder, she would be responsible for their arrest on the charge of killing their parents.

On March 8, Lyle Menendez was flagged down by more than a dozen heavily armed Beverly Hills policemen as he was leaving the house on Elm Drive in his brother's Jeep Wrangler, accompanied by his former Princeton classmate Glenn Stevens. Lyle was made to lie on the street, in full view of his neighbors, while the police, with drawn guns, manacled his hands behind his back before taking him to the police station to book him for suspicion of murder. The arrest came as a complete surprise to Lyle, who had been playing chess, a game at which he excelled, until two the night before at the home of a friend in Beverly Hills.

Three days earlier, Judalon Smyth had contacted the police in Beverly Hills and told them of the existence of audiotapes in the Bedford Drive office of Dr. Oziel on which the Menendez brothers had allegedly confessed to the murders of their parents. She also told police that the brothers had threatened to kill Oziel if he reported them. Lastly, she told them that the two twelve-gauge shotguns had been purchased at a sporting-goods store in San Diego. All of this information was unknown to the Beverly Hills police, after seven months of investigation. They obtained a subpoena to search all of Oziel's locations. The tapes were found in a safe-deposit box in a bank on Ventura Boulevard.

Lyle's arrest was reported almost immediately on the local Los Angeles newscasts. Among those who heard the news was Noel Nedli, a tennis-team friend from Beverly Hills High who was Erik Menendez's roommate in a condominium that Erik was leasing for six months at the Marina City Club Towers, next to the condominium that his brother had leased with his girlfriend, Jamie Pisarcik. Erik was playing in a tennis tournament in Israel, where he had been for two weeks, accompanied by Mark Heffernan, his $50,000-a-year tennis coach. By a curious coincidence, Erik happened to telephone Nedli at almost the same moment Nedli was listening to the report of Lyle's arrest on the radio. It was merely a routine checking-up-on-everything call, and Nedli realized at once that Erik did not know about Lyle's arrest. He is reported to have said to Erik, "I hope you're sitting down." Then he said, "Lyle was just arrested."

"Erik became hysterical. He was crying, the whole nine yards," said a friend of Nedli's who had heard the story from him. This friend went on to say that the immediate problem for Erik was to get out of Israel before he was arrested there. Accompanied by Heffernan, who was not aware of the seriousness of the situation, the two got on a plane without incident, bound for London. There they split up. Heffernan returned to Los Angeles. Erik flew to Miami, where several members on the Menendez side of the family reside. An aunt advised him to return to Los Angeles and turn himself in. Erik notified police of his travel plans and gave himself up at Los Angeles International Airport, where he was taken into custody by four detectives. He was later booked at the Los Angeles County Men's Central Jail on suspicion of murder and held without bond.

According to Judalon Smyth, and the California Court of Appeals decision, she had stood outside the door of Dr. Oziel's office and, unbeknownst to the Menendez brothers, listened to their confession and threats. Dr. Oziel has denied this.

. . .

Approximately a year before any of the above happened, Judalon Smyth told me, she telephoned Jerome Oziel's clinic, the Phobia Institute of Beverly Hills, after having heard a series of tapes called *Through the Briar Patch,* which had impressed her. She was then thirty-six, had been married twice, and was desirous of having a relationship and a family, but she tended to choose the wrong kind of men, men who were controlling. The *Briar Patch* tapes told her she could break the pattern of picking the wrong kind of men in five minutes.

She says Oziel began telephoning her, and she found him very nice on the phone. She felt he seemed genuinely interested in her. After Oziel's third call, she sent him a tape of love poems she had written and called *Love Tears.* She also told him she was in the tape-duplicating business. She found his calls were like therapy, and she began to tell him intimate things about herself, like the fact that she had been going to a professional matchmaker she had seen on television. "I was falling in love over the phone," she said. "You don't think someone's married when he calls you from home at night."

Eventually, he came to her house with two enormous bouquets.

"The minute I opened the door I was relieved," she said. "I wasn't attracted to him. He was shorter than me, blond, balding, with a round face." She told me she was attracted to men who looked like the actor Ken Wahl or Tom Cruise. Oziel was forty-two at the time. "He kept trying to get physical right away. I said, 'Look, you're not my type. I'm not attracted to you.' He said he just wanted a hug. I said, 'Just because you know all this intimate stuff about me doesn't mean . . .' "

"Finally I gave in. It was the worst sex I ever had in my life. To have good sex you either have to be in love or in lust. I wasn't either. It was also awful the second time. The third time was better. I broke off with him four or five times between September and October. Then Erik Menendez came."

Although Dr. Oziel had not seen any members of the Menendez family since Erik's counseling had ended, when news of the murders was announced in August 1989, according to Smyth, he became consumed with excitement at his proximity to the tragedy. "Right away, he called the boys and offered his help." At the time, the boys were hiding out in hotels, saying they thought the Mafia was after them. "Jerry would go to where the boys were. He was advising them about attorneys for the will, etc. He had an I'll-be-your-father attitude."

At the end of October, Smyth told me, Oziel got a call from Erik, who said he needed to talk with him. Erik came at four on the afternoon of Halloween, October 31, to the office at 435 North Bedford Drive. There is a small waiting room outside the office, with a table for magazines and several places to sit, but there is no receptionist. An arriving patient pushes a button with the name of the doctor he is there to see, and a light goes on in the inner office to let the doctor know that his next patient has arrived. Off the waiting room is a doorway that opens into a small inner hallway off which are three small offices. Oziel shares the space with several other doctors, one of them his wife, Dr. Laurel Oziel, the mother of his two daughters.

Once there, Erik did not want to talk in the office, so he and Oziel went for a walk. On the walk, according to Smyth, Erik confessed that he and his brother had killed their parents. Lyle, who was at the Elm Drive house at the time, did not know that Erik was seeing Oziel for that purpose. Lyle did not know either that Erik had apparently also confessed to his good friend Craig Cignarelli, with whom he had written the screenplay called *Friends.*

When Smyth arrived at the office, Erik and Oziel had returned from their walk and were in the inner office. According to Smyth, Oziel wanted Erik to tell Lyle that he had confessed to him. Erik did not want to do that. He said that he and Lyle were soon going to the Caribbean to get rid of the guns and that he would tell him then. The plan, according to Erik, Judalon Smyth told me, was to break down the guns, put them into suitcases, and dump the bags in the Caribbean. On the night of the murders, the boys had hidden the two shotguns in the trunk of one of their parents' cars in the garage. The police had searched only the cars in the courtyard in front of the house, not the cars in the garage. Subsequently, the boys had buried the guns on Mulholland Drive. Smyth says Dr. Oziel convinced Erik that the boys would certainly be caught if they were carrying guns in their luggage. He also persuaded him to call Lyle and ask him to come to the office immediately.

It took ten minutes for Lyle to get to the office from the house on Elm Drive. Smyth says he did not know before he got there that Erik had confessed. When he walked into the waiting room, he picked up a magazine and chatted briefly with Smyth, assuming that she was another patient. "Been waiting long?" he asked her. He also pushed the button to indicate to Oziel that he had arrived. Oziel came out and asked Lyle to come in.

According to the California Court of Appeals decision, Smyth says she listened through the door to the doctor's meeting with the boys and heard Lyle become furious with

Erik for having confessed. She told me he made threats to Oziel that they were going to kill him. "I never thought I believed in evil, but when I heard those boys speak, I did," she said.

The particulars of the murders she is not allowed to discuss, because of an agreement with the Beverly Hills police, but occasionally, in our conversation, things would creep in. "They did go to the theater to buy the tickets," she said one time. Or, "The mother kept moving, which is why she was hit more." Or, "If they just killed the father, the mother would have inherited the money. So they had to kill her too." Or, "Lyle said he thought he committed the perfect murder, that his father would have had to congratulate him—for once, he couldn't put him down."

Judalon went on to say, and it is in the opinion of the California Court of Appeals, that she was frightened that she might be caught listening if the boys came out of the office. She went back to the waiting room. Almost immediately, the door opened. "Erik came running out, crying. Then Lyle and Jerry came out. At the elevator, I heard Jerry ask if Lyle was threatening him. Erik had already gone down. Lyle and Jerry followed." From a window in the office, Smyth could see Lyle and Oziel talking to Erik, who was in his Jeep on Bedford Drive.

According to Smyth, Erik knew, from his period of therapy with Oziel after the burglaries, where the doctor lived in Sherman Oaks, a suburb of Los Angeles in the San Fernando Valley. Fearing the boys might come after him, Oziel called his wife and told her to get the children and move out of the house. "Laurel and the kids went to stay with friends," said Smyth. Oziel then moved into Smyth's apartment, the ground floor of a two-family house in the Carthay Circle area of Los Angeles.

In the days that followed, Smyth told several people

what she had heard. She has her own business, an audio-video duplicating service called Judalon Sound and Light, in the Fairfax section of Los Angeles. Behind her shop, in which she also sells crystals, quartz, and greeting cards, there is a small office which she rents to two friends, Bruce and Grant, who also have a video-duplicating service. As self-protection, she told them that the Menendez boys had killed their parents. She also told her mother and father and her best friend, Donna.

Then Oziel set up another meeting with the boys. He told them on the second visit that everything they had told him was taped. According to Smyth, the original confession, on October 31, was not taped. What was taped was Oziel's documentation of everything that happened in that session and subsequent sessions with the boys, giving times and dates, telling about the confession and the threat on his life, "a log of what was happening during the time his life was in danger." Smyth further contends that, as time went on, the relationship between the doctor and the boys grew more stable, and the doctor no longer felt threatened.

She said that Oziel convinced the boys "he was their only ally—that if they were arrested he would be their only ally. He was the only one who knew they were abused children, who knew how horrible their home life was, who knew that Jose was a monster father, who knew that Kitty was an abused wife. He convinced them that if they had any hope of ever getting off, they needed him."

Meanwhile, the personal relationship between Smyth and Oziel deteriorated. In a lawsuit filed in the Superior Court of the State of California by Judalon Rose Smyth against L. Jerome Oziel, Ph.D., on May 31, three months after the arrest of the Menendez brothers, it is charged that while Smyth was receiving psychiatric and psychological counseling from defendant Oziel he "improperly maintained Smyth on large doses of drugs and, during said time periods, manipulated and took advantage of Smyth, controlled Smyth, and limited Smyth's ability to care for herself . . . creating a belief in Smyth that she could not handle her affairs without the guidance of Oziel, and convincing Smyth that no other therapist could provide the insight and benefit to her life that Oziel could." In the second cause of action in the suit, Smyth charges that on or about February 16, 1990, defendant Oziel "placed his hands around her throat attempting to choke her, and pulled her hair with great force. Subsequently, on the same day, Defendant Oziel forced Smyth to engage in an act of forcible and unconsented sexual intercourse." According to the California Court of Appeals decision, approximately three weeks after the alleged attack, Smyth contacted the police in Beverly Hills to inform them about the confession she said the Menendez brothers had made to Oziel.

Oziel's lawyer, Bradley Brunon, called Smyth's allegations "completely untrue," and characterized her behavior as "an unfortunate real-life enactment of the scenario in *Fatal Attraction*. . . . She has twisted reality to the point where it is unrecognizable."

"The boys are *adorable*. They're like two foundlings. You want to take them home with you," said the defense attorney Leslie Abramson, who has saved a dozen people from death row. She was talking about the Menendez brothers. Leslie Abramson is Erik's lawyer. Gerald Chaleff is Lyle's.

"Leslie will fight to the grave for her clients," I heard from reporters in Los Angeles who have followed her career. "When there is a murder rap, Leslie is the best in town."

Abramson and Chaleff have worked together before.

"We're fifty-fifty, but she's in charge," Chaleff said in an interview. They like each other, and are friends in private life. Abramson met her present husband, Tim Rutten, an editorial writer for the *Los Angeles Times,* at a dinner party at Chaleff's home.

During the arraignment in the Beverly Hills courthouse, I was struck by the glamour of the young Menendez brothers, whom I was seeing face-to-face for the first time. They entered the courtroom, heads held high, like leading actors in a television series. They walked like colts. Their clothes, if not by Armani himself, were by a designer heavily influenced by Armani, probably purchased in the brief period of their independent affluence, between the murders and their arrest. Their demeanor seemed remarkably light-hearted for people in the kind of trouble they were in, as they smiled dimpled smiles and laughed at the steady stream of Abramson's jocular banter. Their two girlfriends, Jamie Pisarcik and Noelle Terelsky, were in the front row next to Erik's tennis coach, Mark Heffernan. Everyone waved. Maria Menendez, the loyal grandmother, was also in the front row, and aunts and uncles and a probate lawyer were in the same section of the courtroom. Several times the boys turned around and flashed smiles at their pretty girlfriends.

They were told to rise. The judge, Judith Stein, spoke in a lugubrious, knell-like voice. The brothers smiled, almost smirked, as she read the charges. "You have been charged with multiple murder for financial gain, while lying in wait, with a loaded firearm, for which, if convicted, you could receive the death penalty. How do you plead?"

"Not guilty, Your Honor," said Erik.

"Not guilty," said Lyle.

Later I asked a friend of theirs who believes in their innocence why they were smiling.

"At the judge's voice," she replied.

Leslie Abramson's curly blond hair bounces, Orphan Annie style, when she walks and talks. She is funny. She is fearless. And she is tough. Oh, is she tough. She walked down the entire corridor of the Beverly Hills courthouse giving the middle finger to an NBC cameraman. "This what you want? You want that?" she said with an angry sneer into the camera, thrusting the finger at the lens, a shot that appeared on the NBC special *Exposé*, narrated by Tom Brokaw. Her passion for the welfare of the accused murderers she defends is legendary. She is considered one of the most merciless cross-examiners in the legal business, with a remarkable ability to degrade and confuse prosecution witnesses. "She loves to intimidate people," I was told. "She thrives on it. She knows when she has you. She can twist and turn a witness's memory like no one else can." John Gregory Dunne, in his 1987 novel *The Red White and Blue,* based the character Leah Kaye, a left-leaning criminal-defense attorney, on Leslie Abramson.

"Why did you give the finger to the cameraman?" I asked her.

"I'll tell you why," she answered, bristling at the memory. "Because I was talking privately to a member of the Menendez family, and NBC turned the camera on, one inch from my face. I said, 'Take that fucker out of my face.' These people think they own the courthouse. They will go to any sleazoid end these days. So I said, 'Is this what you want?' That's when I gave them the finger. Imagine, Tom Brokaw on a show like that.

"I do not understand the publicity of the case," she continued, although of course she understood perfectly. "I mean, the president of the United States wasn't shot."

Before I could reply with such words as "patricide," "matricide," "wealth," "Beverly Hills," she had thought over what she had said. "Well, I rate murder cases different from the public." Most of her cases are from less swell circumstances. In the Bob's Big Boy case, the only death-penalty case she has ever lost, her clients herded nine employees and two customers into the restaurant's walk-in freezer and fired shotguns into their bodies at close range. Three died and four were maimed. One of those who lived had part of her brain removed. Another lost an eye.

"What's the mood of the boys?" I asked.

"I can't comment on my clients," she said. "All I can say is, they're among the very best clients I've ever had, as far as relating. Both of them. It's nonsense, all this talk that there's a good brother and a bad brother. Lyle is wonderful. They're both adorable."

In the avalanche of media blitz that followed the arrest of the Menendez brothers, no one close to Lyle and Erik was the object of more intense fascination and scrutiny than Craig Cignarelli, Erik's tennis partner, with whom he had written the screenplay *Friends.* A family spokesperson told me that in one day alone Craig Cignarelli received thirty-two calls from the media, including "one from Dan Rather, 'A Current Affair,' 'Hard Copy,' etc., etc. I can't remember them all. We had to hire an attorney to field calls." The spokesperson said that "from the beginning it was presumed that Craig knew something."

Craig, clearly enjoying his moments of stardom following the arrests of his best friend and best friend's brother, talked freely to the press and was, by all accounts of other friends of the brothers, too talkative by far. In articles by Ron Soble and John Johnson in the *Los Angeles Times,* Craig said he was attracted to Erik by a shared sense that they were special. He recalled how they would drive out to

Malibu late at night, park on a hilltop overlooking the ocean, and talk about their hopes for the future, about how much smarter they were than everyone else, and about how to commit the perfect crime. They had nicknames for each other: Craig was "King," and Erik was "Shepherd." "People really looked up to us. We have an aura of superiority," he said.

As the months passed, it was whispered that Erik had confessed the murders to Craig. This was borne out to me by Judalon Smyth. But he confessed them in an elliptical manner, according to Smyth, in a suppose-it-happened-like-this way, as if planning another screenplay. It was further said that Craig told the police about the confession, but there were not the hard facts on which to make an arrest, such as came later from Judalon Smyth.

Craig's loquaciousness gave rise to many rumors about the two boys, as well as about the possibility that a second screenplay by them exists, one that parallels the murders even more closely. Craig has since been requested by the police not to speak to the press.

At one point, Cignarelli was presumed to be in danger because of what he knew, and was sent away by his family to a place known only to them. An ongoing story is that a relation of the Menendez brothers threatened Craig after hearing that he had gone to the police. The spokesperson for Craig wanted me to make it clear that, contrary to rumors, Craig "never approached the police. The police approached Craig. At a point Craig decided to tell them what he knew." When I asked this same spokesperson about the possibility of a second screenplay written by Craig and Erik, he said he had never seen one. He also said that the deputy district attorney, Elliott Alhadeff, was satisfied that all the information on the confession tapes was known to Craig, so in the event that the tapes were ruled inadmissible by the court he would be able to supply the information on the stand.

Sometime last January, two months before the arrests, the friendship between the two boys cooled. That may have been because Erik suspected that Craig had talked to the police.

Earlier that month, during a New Year's skiing vacation at Lake Tahoe, Erik had met and fallen in love with Noelle Terelsky, a pretty blond student at the University of California in Santa Barbara from Cincinnati. The romance was instantaneous. "Erik's not a hard guy to fall for," said a friend of Noelle. "He's very sweet, very sexy, has a great body, and is an all-around great guy." Noelle, together with Jamie Pisarcik, Lyle's girlfriend, visits the brothers in jail every day, and has been present at every court appearance of the brothers since their arrest. Until recently, when the house on Elm Drive was rented to the member of the Saudi royal family, the two girls lived in the guesthouse, as the guests of Maria Menendez, the proud and passionate grandmother of Lyle and Erik, who believes completely in the innocence of her grandsons. Maria Menendez, Noelle, and Jamie are now living in the Menendezes' Calabasas house, which has still not been sold.

Five months had passed since the arrest. Five months of hearings and deliberations to see whether the audiotapes of Dr. Jerome Oziel were admissible in the murder trial of Lyle and Erik Menendez. Police seizure of therapy tapes is rare, because ordinarily conversations between patients and therapists are secret. But there are occasional exceptions to the secrecy rule, one being that the therapist believes the patient is a serious threat to himself or others. Only the defense attorneys, who did not want the tapes to be heard, had been allowed to participate in the hearings. The prosecution, which did want them to be heard, was barred. Oziel had been on the stand in private hearings from which the family, the media, and the public were barred. Judalon Smyth had also been on the stand for two days in private sessions, being grilled by Leslie Abramson. The day of the decision had arrived.

There was great tension in the courtroom. Noelle and Jamie, the girlfriends, were there. And Maria, the grandmother. And an aunt from Miami. And a cousin. And the probate lawyer. And others.

Then the Menendez brothers walked in. The swagger, the smirks, the smiles were all gone. And the glamour. So were the Armani-type suits. Their ever-loyal grandmother had arrived with their clothes in suit bags, but the bags were returned to her by the bailiff. They appeared in V-necked, short-sleeved jailhouse blues with T-shirts underneath. Their tennis tans had long since faded. It was impossible not to notice the deterioration in the appearance of the boys, especially Erik. His eyes looked tormented, tortured, haunted. At his neck was a tiny gold cross. He nodded to Noelle Terelsky. He nodded to his grandmother. There were no smiles that day.

Leslie Abramson and Gerald Chaleff went to Judge James Albracht's chambers to hear his ruling on the admissibility of the tapes before it was read to the court. The brothers sat alone at the defense table, stripped of their support system. "Everybody's staring at us," said Erik to the bailiff in a pleading voice, as if the bailiff could do something about it, but there was nothing the bailiff could do. Everybody did stare at them. Lyle leaned forward and whispered something to his brother.

The fierce demeanor of Leslie Abramson when she returned to the courtroom left no doubt that the judge's ruling had not gone in favor of the defense. As the judge read his ruling to the crowded courtroom, Abramson, with her back to the judge, kept up a nonstop commentary in Erik Menendez's ear.

"I have ruled that none of the communications are privileged," said the judge. There was an audible sound of dismay from the Menendez family members. The tapes would be admissible. The judge found that psychologist Jerome Oziel had reasonable cause to believe that Lyle and Erik Menendez "constituted a threat, and it was necessary to disclose the communications to prevent a danger." There was no doubt that this was a serious setback to the defense.

Abramson and Chaleff immediately announced at a news conference that they would appeal the judge's ruling. Abramson called Oziel a gossip, a liar, and "less than credible." Neither Judalon Smyth's name nor her role in the proceedings was ever mentioned.

A mere eight days later, in a stunning reversal of Judge Albracht's ruling, the 2nd District Court of Appeals blocked the release of the tapes, to the undisguised delight of Abramson and Chaleff. Prosecutors were then given a date by which to file opposing arguments. Another complication occurred when Erik Menendez, from jail, refused to provide the prosecution with a handwriting sample to compare with the handwriting found on forms for the purchase of two shotguns in San Diego, despite a warning by the court that his refusal to do so could be used as evidence against him. In a further surprise, Deputy District Attorney Elliott Alhadeff, who won the original court ruling that the tapes would be admissible, was abruptly replaced on the notorious case by Deputy District Attorney Pamela Ferrero.

·   ·   ·

Since their arrest in March, Lyle and Erik Menendez have dwelt in the Los Angeles County Men's Central Jail, in the section reserved for prisoners awaiting trial in heavily publicized cases. The brothers' cells are not side by side. They order reading material from Book Soup, the trendy Sunset Strip bookshop. Erik has been sent *The Dead Zone,* by Stephen King, and a book on chess. They have frequent visits from family members, and talk with one friend almost daily by telephone. That friend told me that they have to pay for protection in jail. "Other prisoners, who are tough, hate them—who they are, what they've been accused of. They've been threatened." He also told me they feel they have lost every one of their friends. Late in August, when three razor blades were reportedly found in Erik's possession, he was put in solitary confinement, deprived of visitors, books except for the Bible, telephone calls, and exercise. That same week, Lyle suddenly shaved his head.

Los Angeles District Attorney Ira Reiner stated on television that one motive for the murders was greed. Certainly it is possible for a child to kill his parents for money, to wish to continue the easy life on easy street without the encumbrance of parental restrictions. But is it really possible for a child to kill, for merely financial gain, in the manner Kitty and Jose Menendez were killed? To blast holes into one's parents? To deface them? To obliterate them? In the fatal, *coup de grâce* shot, the barrel of one shotgun touched the cheek of Kitty Menendez. You wonder if her eyes met the eyes of her killer in the last second of her life. In this case, we have two children who allegedly participated in the killing of each parent, not in the heat of rage but in a carefully orchestrated scenario after a long gestation period. There is more than money involved here.

There is a deep, deep hatred, a hatred that goes beyond hate.

The closest friend of the Menendez brothers, with whom I talked at length on the condition of anonymity, kept saying to me over and over, "It's only the tip of the iceberg." No amount of persuasion on my part could make him explain what the iceberg was. Months earlier, however, a person close to the situation mouthed but did not speak the word "incest" to me. Subsequently, a rich woman in Los Angeles told me that her bodyguard, a former cop, had heard from a friend of his on the Beverly Hills police force that Kitty Menendez had been shot in the vagina. At a Malibu barbecue, a film star said to me, "I heard the mother was shot up the wazoo." There is, however, no indication of such a penetration in the autopsy report, which carefully delineates each of the ten wounds from the nine shots fired into Kitty Menendez's body. But the subject continues to surface. Could it be possible that these boys were puppets of their father's dark side? "They had sexual hatred for their parents," one of the friends told me. This same person went on to say, "The tapes will show that Jose molested Lyle at a very young age."

Is this true? Only the boys know. If it is, it could be the defense argument that will return them to their tennis court, swimming pool, and chess set, as inheritors of a $14 million estate that they could not have inherited if they had been found guilty. Karen Lamm, however, does not believe such a story, although it is unlikely that Kitty would have revealed to her a secret of that dimension. Judalon Smyth was also skeptical of this information when I brought up the subject of sexual abuse. She said she had heard nothing of the kind on Halloween afternoon when, according to the California Court of Appeals decision, she listened outside Dr. Oziel's office door as Lyle and Erik talked about the murders. She said that last December, almost two months after the October 31 confession to Oziel, which was not taped, the boys, feeling that the police were beginning to suspect them, voluntarily made a tape in which they confessed to the crime. In it, they spoke of their remorse. In it, apparently, they told of psychological abuse. But sexual abuse? Judalon Smyth did not hear this tape, and by that time Dr. Oziel was no longer confiding in her.

October 1990

QUEENS
OF
THE ROAD

⟭

JUST WHEN you thought you knew all there was to know about the highly publicized Collins sisters, Joan and Jackie, or Jackie and Joan, comes the news that big sister Joan, the soap-opera superstar, whose divorces and romantic exploits have been making tabloid headlines for thirty years, has turned literary in her fifty-fifth year and is moving in on the printed-page turf of her little sister Jackie, the superstar novelist, whose eleven-volume *oeuvre* has sold 65 million copies in thirty languages throughout the world over the last two decades. Yes, friends, Joan Collins, between takes as the beloved bitch Alexis Carrington Colby on "Dynasty," has written her *own* novel, called *Prime Time,* about a top-rated soap opera on American television, with eight or ten characters, all of them actors and actresses, and a leading lady who has overcome obstacles, both personal and financial, to regain her stardom.

And as if that weren't enough, Joan's literary agent, the legendary Irving "Swifty" Lazar, a superstar in his own right, has sold Joan's book for a million bucks to, you guessed it, Jackie's publisher, Simon and Schuster, where her editor is another superstar, Michael Korda, a novelist in his own right, who—hang on to your hat—also happens to be Jackie's editor. (Lazar sold it abroad for an additional $2 million—$1 million in England alone—without showing one written word.)

"I get along very well with both of them," said Korda. "I'm very fond of them."

There are those who will tell you that Jackie isn't happy with the proximity, and neither is her superstar agent, Morton Janklow, who long ago moved in on Swifty Lazar's turf as the agent who got the most bucks for his writer clients. As a reaffirmation of Simon and Schuster's warm feeling for its massive money-maker, Michael Korda signed Jackie up for two additional books after the completion of her current contract.

"I don't like to talk figures," said Jackie Collins in her Beverly Hills home about her new deal, "but I will say it's a record-breaking contract."

Michael Korda, from his New York office, added, "If this isn't the largest amount of money in American book publishing, it sure ought to be. It's about the same size as the Brazilian national debt." Then he added, almost as an afterthought, "But I also bought two more books from Joan."

"Is there a feud going on between them?" I asked.

"Probably so, at some level," he answered. "Jackie can't help but feel that Joan is crowding her territory."

Said Irving Lazar, "Certainly, there is sibling rivalry at times."

Said Joni Evans, formerly of Simon and Schuster, now publisher of Random House, "Of course, there has to be."

Said Morton Janklow, "Yes, Jackie and Joan have flare-ups, but since Simon and Schuster has both books, Irving and I can see to it that they don't come out head to head. So both sisters will have a couple great months."

The Collins sisters themselves are quick to tell you that there is no trouble between them at all, although their publicist, Jeffrey Lane, who is actually Joan's publicist, best pal, and traveling companion, but who doubled as Jackie's publicist for this article, laid down some ground rules for me to abide by, namely that if Jackie's name was used first in one sentence, then Joan's must be used first in the next, and that there was to be equal copy on each sister. Like that.

The fact is, I know both of these ladies. The first time I ever saw Joan was in 1957. She walked up off the beach in Santa Monica, California, where I was renting a beach house, wearing a bikini before anyone I knew was wearing a bikini, and asked if she could use the bathroom. She was then in the first of her two stardoms, the one that didn't last. Of course she could use the bathroom. In my scrapbooks I have pictures of her from the sixties, at parties my wife and I had in Beverly Hills: with Mia Farrow, before she married Frank Sinatra; with Ryan O'Neal, after he split from Joanna Moore; with Michael Caine, long before he married Shakira; and with Natalie Wood, after her first marriage to Robert Wagner. Joan was then in the second of her four marriages, to the English star Anthony Newley. In every picture she is having a good time.

Jackie I met much later. We sat next to each other at one of Irving Lazar's Academy Awards parties at Spago. It struck me then how alike the sisters are, and also how different. Last year at the Writers' Conference in Santa Barbara, Jackie and I were both speakers, along with Thomas McGuane, Irving Stone, William F. Buckley, Jr., and others. Jackie arrived only minutes before she was scheduled to speak, in a stretch limousine with a great deal of video equipment to record her speech. Only, she didn't make a speech the way the rest of us did. The conference provided her with an interviewer, and the interviewer asked her questions. There wasn't an empty seat in the hall. "Can you give the writers here some advice?" the interviewer asked. "Write only about what you know," she told them. Later, when the floor was thrown open to questions from the audience, the audience was told in advance by the interviewer, "Miss Collins will answer no questions about her sister." Her sister was, at the time, involved in the highly publicized extrication from her fourth marriage.

"It's nonsense," said Jackie when I asked her about the rumors of a rift. "We're very amicable together."

"I don't have a rivalry with my sister," said Joan when I asked her. "People are always saying I have rivalries— particularly with Elizabeth Taylor and Linda Evans. I've never said a bad word about another actress, at least in print. And now they're saying I have this rivalry with Jackie. It's not true."

"Let me put it this way," said Jackie. "We're not in each other's pockets, but we're good friends. We're not the kind of sisters who call each other every day, but she knows I'm there for her."

"Jackie lives a totally different life from me," said Joan. "If I get five days off from work, I take off. I like Los Angeles, but I'm more European than she is in my outlook. I like staying up late. I like sleeping late. I like two-hour lunches, with wine. I do not like tennis, golf, lying by the pool. What I like doing here is to work very hard and then leave."

"We have a lot of the same friends," said Jackie. "Roger and Luisa Moore, Dudley Moore, Michael and Shakira Caine. Then Joan has *her* whole group of friends, and I have *my* whole group."

"I like getting on planes and going on trips," said Joan.

"*Hollywood Wives* gave me a high profile," said Jackie. "Before that, in England, I was always Joan's little sister. I was lucky to have made it in America before Joan hit in 'Dynasty.' What I love about Joan is that she's one of the great survivors. She did things ahead of her time that have since become accepted. She always lived her life like a man. She was a free spirit. If she saw a guy she wanted to go to bed with, she went after him, and that was unacceptable behavior at the time."

"Oh, God, Jackie, that's great," said Joan, touching the emerald of a borrowed necklace her sister was wearing for the shoot. "Is it yours?"

Jackie laughed. "No, darling."

"You should buy it for yourself," said Joan. "You can afford it."

Joan Collins is the embodiment of the kind of characters that Jackie Collins writes about. She is beautiful, famous, rich, was once a movie star, has been what is known in Hollywood as on her ass, meaning washed up and nearly broke, and then resurrected herself as a greater television star than she ever was a movie star. Jackie flatly denies that her character Silver Anderson in *Hollywood Husbands* was based on her sister, although Silver Anderson is a washed-up, middle-aged star who makes it back, bigger than ever, in a soap opera, who "wasn't twenty-two and didn't give a damn," and who "had a compact, sinewy body, with firm breasts and hard nipples."

Joan has been married and divorced four times. "I've always left my husbands," she said, about Maxwell Reed, Anthony Newley, the late Ron Kass, and the recent and unlamented Peter Holm, who asked for, but didn't receive, a divorce settlement of $80,000 a month. Her host of romances over the years, which she delineated in detail in her autobiography, *Past Imperfect,* have included Laurence Harvey, Warren Beatty, Sydney Chaplin, Ryan O'Neal, and Rafael Trujillo, the son of the dictator of the Dominican Republic, an affairette masterminded in the fifties by Zsa Zsa Gabor. She currently lives in a house that Joan Crawford might have lived in at the height of her fame. Built by Laurence Harvey but redone totally by Joan, it has a marble entrance hall and white carpets and white sofas and a peach bedroom with an Art Deco headboard and a spectacular view of the city of Los Angeles. She has posed for more than five hundred magazine covers, and many of them are framed on the walls of her office. She has diamonds for all occasions, and Bob Mackie and Nolan Miller design the glittering evening gowns she favors for her public appearances. Swifty Lazar says, "Joan is addicted to the precept that life is for fun and having a great time. She throws caution to the wind. It has brought her troubles at times. She has been broke when she didn't have to be. She is much less cautious than Jackie. She worries much less about what's going to happen in ten years. She lives totally in the present."

Known as a great hostess, she loves having parties as much as she loves going to them. She gives Sunday lunches, seated dinners for eighteen, and buffet suppers for forty, and recently she tented over her swimming pool and had several hundred of her nearest and dearest friends, mostly famous, in for a black-tie dinner dance, with, according to Swifty Lazar, "great music, great wines, and place cards," the kind of party that people in Hollywood always say they used to give out here but don't give anymore. She loves nightlife, and one of her complaints about Hollywood, where she has lived on and off since the 1950s, is that everyone goes to bed too early. As often as possible, every three weeks or so, she is on a plane to London for four or five days, because her three children are there. Tara and Sacha, twenty-five and twenty-three, by her marriage to Anthony Newley, are living on their own. Her other daughter, Katyana, called Katy, by Ron Kass, who died in 1986, is the child she literally willed back to life after she was struck by a car and hovered between life and death for weeks in an intensive-care unit when she was eight. Katy, now fifteen, attends school in London and lives in a rented flat with Joan's longtime English secretary and a nanny. Although Joan is said to party nonstop during her London weekends, it is to see her children that she travels there so often, and not to see her latest love, Bill Wiggins, known as Bungalow by the English tabloids because he has "nothing upstairs and everything down below." As of this writing he is no longer her latest love but just "a dear friend." "She loves it there," said Douglas Cramer, an executive producer on "Dynasty." "Next to the Queen, she's the queen."

"How do the producers feel about your traveling so much to England while the show is in production?" I asked Joan.

"They're quite accommodating, actually, because they want me back next season," said Joan.

"Are you coming back next season?"

"I would only do it on my terms. I would not want to be in every episode."

• • •

While Joan is known as a great hostess, Jackie is known as a great housekeeper. She cooks. She markets. She dusts. She has no live-in servants, only a cleaning woman three times a week, and her children have their household chores. At Christmastime, she presided over a family dinner for seventeen, including Joan, which she cooked and served herself, urging seconds and thirds on everyone, and then organized charades. She is a very concerned family person.

Like her sister, she has a tremendous drive to be on top. "Being number one in America means being number one in the world," she said. She has been married for over twenty years to Oscar Lerman, who co-owns discotheques in London and Los Angeles. Ad Lib, his famous London club of the sixties, was a favorite hangout of the Beatles and the Stones. It was there Jackie conceived the idea for her about-to-be-released novel, *Rock Star.* Tramp, the Los Angeles branch of his London disco, is a hangout for young stars like Sean Penn and Timothy Hutton. Jackie goes there one night a week to watch the action and store away information. She married for the first time at the age of nineteen, but the marriage ended tragically when her husband overdosed on drugs. Her oldest daughter, Tracy, is from that marriage, and she has two more daughters by Oscar, Tiffany, twenty, and Rory, eighteen, who are not, absolutely not, she will tell you, "Hollywood kids," which will be the subject of the book after *Lady Boss,* which will be the book after *Rock Star.* All three girls live at home, in a deceptively large white house in the flats of Beverly Hills which Carroll Baker once bought with her *Baby Doll* earnings. It is definitely not the kind of house where Joan Crawford would have lived, but rather a house that screams family and family life. There are so many cars in the driveway it looks like a parking lot: Jackie's '66 Mustang and her two Cadillacs, Oscar's Mercury, her daughters' cars, and sometimes their boyfriends' cars. Every room has bookcases brimming over with books, most of them best-sellers of the Harold Robbins and Sidney Sheldon school, and so many paintings that they are stacked against the walls. Pictures of movie stars at movie-star parties, all taken by the famous author herself, who never goes to a party without her camera, line the walls of her powder room.

On my first visit to Jackie's home, two large yellow Labradors were flaked out on the white sofas in the living room, and she did not tell them to move. "Poor old thing, he's fifteen," she said about one of the dogs, and we moved to another room rather than disturb them.

When the doorbell rang later, the dogs charged for the door. Joan Collins, in a fox coat, had stopped by to have tea with her sister.

"Am I going to be jumped on by these wild animals?" she screamed from the front hall. All Joan's entrances are entrances. The day before, she had walked down a stairway wearing a—for her—demure dress. "This is my *jeune fille* look," she said in greeting. "Still trying after all these years."

"Joan's not crazy about dogs," Jackie explained to me, rising to take the dogs elsewhere. It occurred to me that Silver Anderson in *Hollywood Husbands* is not crazy about dogs either.

The sisters greeted each other with a kiss on each cheek. One had tea. One had coffee. They talked about movies they had seen the night before. They always see movies in friends' projection rooms or at studio screenings. Jackie had seen *The Last Emperor* at Roger Moore's house.

Joan had seen *Baby Boom* at someone else's house. "It's my favorite movie. Diane is so good," she said about Diane Keaton. "She had one of the best scenes I ever saw." She then re-enacted it while Jackie watched. Whatever you hear about these two sisters having a feud, just remember this. They like each other. They laugh at each other's stories. They listen to each other, and they're proud of each other's success.

"We are the triumph of the immigrant," said Joan. "That's what America's all about. People dream that the streets are paved with gold, and my sister and I showed that they are. If only Mummy had lived to see the two of us now, she would have been so proud."

Their father, now in his eighties, they remember as aloof, strict, and austere when they were children. "English men are rather cool and into themselves," Joan said. He was a theatrical agent with Lew Grade, later Sir Lew Grade, now Lord Grade. But it was their mother, who died in 1962, whom both sisters spoke of in the most loving terms, as being affectionate and feminine and protective of them. There are pictures of her in both sisters' houses.

"We wish our mother was alive to see what's happened to us. She would have enjoyed this more than anyone," said Jackie.

Joan said it was not true, as I had heard, that she was so broke in 1981 that Aaron Spelling had to pay her grocery bills before she could return to California to do "Dynasty." "Where do these stories start?" she asked.

In a large album of color photographs on the tea table, there is a picture of Joan, taken by Jackie, at the party Joan gave to celebrate her recent divorce from Peter Holm, the toy-boy husband who almost made Joan look foolish, but didn't, because she laughed at herself first. In the photograph, she is wearing a T-shirt that says, "HOMEless," a gift from her friend David Niven, Jr. She is laughing, but behind her mascara'd eyes there is the unmistakable look, at once gallant and sad, of the Hollywood survivor.

When I asked her about Peter Holm, who is rumored to be writing a book called *Joan and Me,* she began to sing. It is a topic she is thoroughly sick of. "I wonder what's happened to him," she said finally.

"Do you care?" I asked.

She shrugged her shoulders.

"One of these days I just know I'm going to meet somebody with whom I would like to share my life," she said.

Later, as I was leaving, she called after me a variation on that line in *Tea and Sympathy,* "When you write about this, and you will, be kind!"

Jackie Collins is a high-school dropout and was a self-confessed juvenile delinquent at age fifteen. "I'm glad I got all of that out of my system at an early age," she said. She arrived in Hollywood at sixteen to visit her sister, then a contract player at Twentieth Century-Fox. Joan was just leaving to go on location for a film, and she tossed her sister the keys to her apartment. "Learn how to drive" was her only L.A. advice. Jackie said she started out her Hollywood life with Joan's famous friends and the friends she made herself—kids who pumped gas and waited on tables. She still draws on the latter group for inspiration. In all her books, there are characters who embody the underlying hostility of the have-nots for the haves. Chauffeurs and gardeners urinate in movie stars' swimming pools; hired waiters steal cases of liquor at A Group parties where they serve; butlers sell their employers' secrets to the trash press.

Jackie's style is different from Joan's, but it's style.

Watch her walk into Le Dome for lunch, a superstar in action. Le Dome, on the Sunset Strip, is the hot hot hot spot for the in movie crowd to lunch these days. Outside the front door, fans with cameras wait for the stars. "Look this way, Miss Collins," they yell when we arrive, and she obliges, adjusting her head to the perfect angle, smiling the friendly but not too friendly smile that celebrities use for their fans. Inside, Michael Yhuelo, one of the owners, greets her with open arms and gives her an air kiss near each cheek. Waiters turn to look at her as if she were a film star rather than a novelist. She walks through the terrace room and makes a turn into the dining room to the table she has asked for in the far corner. "Hi, Michelle," she calls to Michelle Phillips on the way. "Hi, Jack," she calls to the columnist Jack Martin.

"I really love L.A.," she said. "In England, I grew up reading Harold Robbins, Mickey Spillane, and Raymond Chandler." L.A. to Jackie means strictly Hollywood, which she affectionately calls the kiss-ass capital of the world. She loves the picture business, the television business, the record business, and the people in them, the stars, celebrities, directors, and producers. She is also a great partygoer, but more in the role of observer than participant, someone doing research. Like all seasoned Hollywood people, she refers to Hollywood as "this town." "One of the reasons I've gotten along here is that I've never needed this town, or anything from anyone here." As she said at the writers' conference last summer, "Write about what you know." And what this lady knows about is Hollywood. Sue Mengers, the famed Hollywood actors' agent, now in semiretirement, called *Hollywood Husbands* the definitive book about Hollywood in the eighties. "Jackie got the feeling of this town better than anyone ever caught it. She understands it."

"I love what I do," said Jackie. "I fall in love with my characters. They become me, and I become them. They're part of me forever, even when I'm finished with them."

Her writing schedule is rigid. She works seven days a week, writing in longhand in spiral notebooks in a room she calls her study. On a good day she can write twenty pages. On a bad day she knocks off ten. When she gets to about seven hundred pages, she starts to bring the novel to an ending. She does not type; a secretary transfers her longhand to a word processor. Jackie is aware that her grammar is not always perfect, but that is the way she wants it. Once she asked her secretary to change anything she thought was wrong, and she then realized that her work lost in the translation to correct grammar.

"I never show *anything* to my publishers until after I finish writing the entire book," said Jackie. At the time I talked with her in December, she had not yet submitted *Rock Star* to Simon and Schuster, although it was coming out in April. Most books are not published until eight or ten months after submission. Confirming this, Michael Korda diplomatically said, "I would rather not have it this way." Only someone who has shown the same consistent success year after year could command that kind of leverage with a publisher.

Finally we get around to the subject of Joan Collins the novelist.

"Everybody wants to write a book once in their life," said Jackie about Joan's book, which she has not read. "If Joan can do it, good luck to her. She does everything well." She looked at her menu and continued: "I don't see Joan as becoming a novelist. I see it as a diversion for her. I've been a published novelist for twenty years. All eleven of my books have never been out of print." She thought over what she had said. "Of course, the fact that I've been offered the lead in a soap opera has nothing to do with her book!"

Joan Collins is the kind of woman you expect women to hate, but they don't. When her friends talk about her, they use the adjectives "indomitable" and "indefatigable." Her former agent, Sue Mengers, who handled the crème de la crème of Hollywood stars when she was still in the picture business, confirmed for me a story that Joan had told me. During Joan's down years, when the movie offers had stopped coming, Sue took Joan, whom she truly liked, out to lunch and told her she had to face up to the fact that after forty it was tough for actresses. "You have to realize that nothing more may happen in your career. Go home and concentrate on real life." Mengers went on to say that Joan cried a little that day, but she refused to give up. "Never," she said. "I'm so happy she proved me wrong," said Mengers. "Even Aaron Spelling, when he cast Joan in the part of Alexis, could not have imagined how strongly the public would take to her—especially women. The femme fatale number she plays is in good fun. In her own life, she has more women friends than any woman I know."

Joan Collins can carry on a conversation with you on the set of "Dynasty" at the same time she is being pinned up by one person, powdered by another, and having her hair sprayed by a third. She continues her conversation while she looks in a mirror that someone holds for her, checks her left side, checks her right, and makes a minute readjustment of a curl. She has been on movie sets since she was seventeen, and she retains the figure of a teenager and a bosom so superb that she recently had to threaten to sue the London *Sun* and *News of the World* after they reported that she had had a breast implant. She hadn't had a breast implant at all, and she got a retraction.

"Actually, I started writing novels when I was seven or eight," said Joan, about her new career as a novelist. " 'The Little Ballerinas,' 'The Gypsy and the Prince.' That kind of thing."

She is called to the set to shoot a scene with Linda Evans, a variation of half a hundred other confrontation scenes between Alexis and Krystle that have been shot in the six years that she has been on "Dynasty." Joan, as Alexis, paced back and forth in her office, reading a stock report, and Linda Evans, as Krystle Carrington, entered.

ALEXIS: What do you want, Krystle?

KRYSTLE: To go over a few things with you.

ALEXIS: Such as?

KRYSTLE: Your life.

ALEXIS: Is this some sort of joke?

KRYSTLE: I'm getting closer and closer to the truth of who and what you really are.

ALEXIS: I'm going to call security.

The director yelled, "Cut!" Joan returned to where we had been talking, and picked up the conversation as if a scene had not just been filmed. "I write in bed, on planes, under the hair dryer, on the set. Sometimes I write twelve to fifteen hours a day for a week, and then I don't touch it for a while. It's erratic, because it's a second career for me."

"Most of her manuscript comes in on the most extraordinary pieces of paper," says Michael Korda, who is working closely with her on her novel, as he did on her autobiography. "But every word is from her. Every revision. There is no ghostwriter, no helper, no hidden person. Her concentration is remarkable, given all the things going on in her life." Korda, the nephew of Sir Alexander Korda, the film producer, is an old acquaintance of Joan's from their teenage years in London. He remembers that when he was nineteen he took her to a party for Sonny Tufts at the house of Sir Carol Reed, but he adds that Joan did not remember this early date when he reminded her of it.

He thinks that when the two books come out the media will manufacture a rivalry between Joan and Jackie. "But if the time should ever come when the two of them are neck and neck on the *New York Times* best-seller list," he says, "I'm going to have a hot time of it."

March 1988

Teardown

TEARDOWN is the new word on everyone's lips in what has become known as the Platinum Triangle, the prestigious residential area of Los Angeles that encompasses Beverly Hills, Holmby Hills, and Bel-Air, and teardowns are rampant on almost every one of its fashionable streets. Sounds of hammering and drilling fill the air, and the once-quiet drives are jammed with cement mixers, cherry pickers, trucks, and lunch wagons as one of the greatest and most expensive building booms in real-estate history takes place. If *teardown* is a new word to you, it means buying a house, very often a beautiful house, for a great deal of money, and tearing it down in order to build a bigger house, for a great deal more money, on the same piece of land, a process that results, very often, in the construction of houses that are vastly overscaled for the size of the property on which they sit. The value of the land alone is so high that people are paying $3 million and up for an acre.

"We're in a renaissance out here. There's nothing like it in the world," said the enormously successful realtor Bruce Nelson as he drove me around the various high-priced areas in his pale yellow Rolls Corniche, in which the telephone never stopped ringing. "Excuse me," he said at one point, stopping in the middle of a sentence to answer the phone and discuss a deal with a possible buyer for the house of a Saudi Arabian prince, which the prince had bought a few years earlier from the shipping and real-estate magnate D. K. Ludwig, reportedly the richest man in America until recent business reversals in the Amazon region of Brazil toppled him from that lofty perch to a current net worth of a mere $550 million.

"All the great homes here were built in the thirties," Nelson continued after he hung up. "At that time, two-acre lots went for $15,000 or $20,000. Now the same property goes for between $7 million and $10 million, but without the house." Nelson was not exaggerating. In fact, a few days later the *Los Angeles Times* reported in its real-estate column that a two-acre vacant lot in Beverly Hills had been sold by the film and record producer David Geffen for $7.45 million. Geffen had bought the land only a year and a half earlier for $3.85 million, and after having plans for a house drawn up had decided against building it. Even more amazing was the story of a young couple who had purchased eight acres in the Pacific Palisades for $6.5 million. Only two of the eight acres were flat; the rest was downhill. Yet even before the couple started to build, they had an offer of $24 million in cash for the land. And they refused it!

Real-estate agent Thelma Orloff, who was a show girl in the great days of the MGM musicals, holds court in the coffee shop of the Beverly Hills Hotel at 8:30 every morning, before leaving for her office. Still statuesque, she arrives each day to a chorus of "Hello, Thelma" from the regular breakfasters at the counter. Thelma Orloff has been around a long time, first as a show girl, then as an actress, wife, and mother, and now—stardom at last—as a real-estate agent *extraordinaire*. She recently celebrated fifty years of friendship with her best pal, Lucille Ball. She used to swim in Fanny Brice's pool in Holmby Hills, and can tell you every person who's lived in that house since Fanny died and what he paid. It is said that Thelma Orloff made the former television gossip celebrity Rona Barrett rich by turning over Beverly Hills real estate for her. As she drove me through the streets in her sleek black Cadillac, her comments on the houses of the famous were like an oral history of the area. "That's Eva Gabor's house, which is now up for sale; she bought it from Henry Berger after Anita Louise died. That's Betsy Bloomingdale's house, and up there next to it there used to be a one-story house that burned down; this developer bought it and has built a $7.8 million spec house, using every square inch of the land. Over there's Bonita Granville Wrather's house, which is about to come on the market. I went to Ann Warner with an offer of $30 million for her house, but she said, 'Forget it.' " Ann Warner is the widow of Jack Warner, of Warner Brothers, and her magnificent house, set on nine prime Beverly Hills acres, is considered one of the great estates of the area. Mrs. Warner, who lives in virtual seclusion in a few upstairs rooms in the house, has turned down offer after offer for her mansion. One real-estate agent told me she would probably accept $25 million for it on the condition that she have the right to live there for the rest of her life, with everything as it is.

In my early days in Hollywood, the grandest house of all to get into, once you had arrived socially, was the white Georgian mansion belonging to the late William and Edith Mayer Goetz. A famed Hollywood wit as well as a distinguished film producer, Bill Goetz was one of the earliest major art collectors in the film colony. His wife, Edie, the

sion, has said of it, "It's mind-boggling, the space. Just beautiful." Four different real-estate agents told me that "some Japanese" had secretly gone through the Spelling house and offered $52 million for it.

"Do you mean the Spelling house is for sale?" I asked.

"No, no, of course it isn't for sale. But everything out here is for sale."

The mode of upscale spending is bewildering to longtime residents of Beverly Hills, who shake their heads in sadness at the evaporation of their once-charming community with its side-by-side potpourri of architectural styles. There is no remembrance of things past. "Beverly Hills has been destroyed. It's gone," one resident told me. New people moving in can't tear down fast enough. "New money wants new houses," said Stan Herman, a Beverly Hills realtor with eighteen agents working under him in an elegant office that sports a bar. Herman, who has a press agent and a press kit that lists the names of 131 famous people "who have lived in Stan Herman's homes," used to be married to Linda Evans of "Dynasty," and he moves in the fast lanes of Beverly Hills and Malibu life. Over the years he has bought many houses, redone them, and then resold them at enormous profit. He bought, for instance, the house Frank Sinatra lived in during his brief marriage to Mia Farrow in the 1960s, redid it entirely, even adding one of his trademarks, a wall urinal in the marble master bathroom, and then resold it to the theatrical producer James Nederlander and his wife for over $4 million. Herman says that if he had just held on to it until the teardown period started, he wouldn't have had to bother to do it over; he could have sold it for the same price without doing one thing. "There's megabucks here today. The Australians, the Japanese, people from Hong Kong. The Taiwanese money isn't here yet, but it's coming, and, of course, the French and the Italians. These people build enormous kitchens, the size of commercial kitchens, but they never cook, because they go out every night, and only the maids cook their own dinners in them." The big question everyone wants answered is, Who *are* these people who are knocking down all the houses and building new ones, putting as many square feet of house on the property as they can? Stan Herman said, "You'd think you would know, or should know, who someone is who has $10 million to spend on a house, but these days you don't."

KEEP OUT signs are posted everywhere to prevent the curious multitudes from staring in. Any sign of unauthorized entry brings a foreman yelling "Uh-uh" in no uncertain terms, meaning *"Out!"* and the grander places under construction have uniformed security guards. However, by arriving on the sites in Bruce Nelson's yellow Corniche and using "attitude," as Nelson calls it, I was able to gain entry to a surprising number.

Four of the most extraordinary new houses that I visited are being built by men in their early forties, most of them self-made men who acquired their fortunes during the Reagan years and who have probably been influenced by the flamboyance of Donald Trump's highly publicized life-style. In one instance, two houses on adjoining lots were torn down to build one 24,000-square-foot home for the couple and their three children, three nannies, and four maids. In another, two houses on adjoining lots were gutted, rebuilt, and joined together as one, encircled by a miniature railroad for the owners' two young sons. "You're only this age once. You may as well do it," one architect quoted his client as saying.

"We're talking all cash in these houses. There are no

loans on any of them," said Bruce Nelson. "Vast fortunes have been coming into the Los Angeles area for years now, but very quietly."

Standing in the curve of a sweeping staircase, looking out over the marble-columned hallway, I said, "My God, these people could give a dance in this hall."

The contractor who had let me in answered, "They don't have to. There's a discotheque downstairs."

"Who is the owner?" I asked.

"He is not anyone you ever heard of," said the contractor.

Whoever these people are, they have not only a grand style in mind for their houses but also a grand style for the lives they intend to live in their houses once they are complete. In one *petit palais* under construction that I entered, the architect told me that the owner, described only as being "in airplane parts," had been so impatient to show off his vast new structure that he had increased the already large work staff of masons and bricklayers and agreed to pay them double and triple time to face the front of the mansion with red brick before Christmas so that he could give an outdoor party in the courtyard and let his friends see his work in progress.

"This is the only place in the world where real-estate agents become stars. I'm writing a novel about it," said real-estate agent Elaine Young. "What I'd really like to have is a three- or four-minute segment on the news dealing with real estate. When I first went into the business thirty years ago, there were only men in real estate, and older women. Real-estate people have been getting better- and better-looking. We just hired three new people in our office, two gorgeous girls and one handsome man. A man buying a $5 million house would rather buy from a beautiful woman than a homely one. It's such a personal business —we're in people's houses, in their bedrooms and their bathrooms. I love what I do. I could have gone into show business, but I ended up making a lot more money than some of the producers I've dated. We're sort of the periphery of show business."

A glamorous figure, Elaine Young lunches daily at the same table in the Polo Lounge of the Beverly Hills Hotel. An hour before I talked with her, she had been interviewed by another writer for another magazine. She was once married to the late film star Gig Young, who, years later, in the third week of a subsequent marriage, shot and killed his bride and himself in an unexplained mystery. Her hair is very very blond, her dress is very very pink, and her glasses have white frames. People turn to look at Elaine Young. "It's awesome," she said about the boom. "Every year I've said it can't go up any more, and then it does. Nothing hurts California real estate. Nothing. The rest of the country can get into a recession and California doesn't know. Even the earthquakes don't stop it. Did you feel the earthquake last night? I slept right through it."

Four or five times during the hour we spent together, the captain in the Polo Lounge brought her a remote-control telephone. "I told them not to put calls through," she said each time, and then took the call and transacted some business. "The Burt Reynolds house is up for sale for $6 million, and I've got some people interested," she said. "Burt's moving to Florida lock, stock, and barrel. It's the Japanese who are driving up the prices. They don't want anything over five years old. Even an older house redone they're not interested in. That's why there's so many teardowns. The Koreans are pretty much the same. I don't believe the prices! I have rentals for $40,000 a month. And there's no end in sight. Oh, God, here's another call. I told them not to put calls through."

In Europe, in the fifteenth century, laws called sumptuary laws were created to limit the excesses of the rich: the tower of a castle could be only so high, the length of a jeweled train only so long. "These people don't know when to stop," said Bruce Nelson about the new builders. "There are only two or three really great architects working in all this boom. What you're getting mostly is schlock. Look at this house. French balustrades and Corinthian columns. Everything is overbuilt. They don't know that the essence of elegance is simplicity. It's hard for them to stop. Now water is the new status symbol. I don't just mean Jacuzzis and very, very large swimming pools. Waterfalls are becoming very popular, and lakes."

At this point we drove into the courtyard of a $30 million spec house. I had been reminded by one real-estate agent to explain that a spec house did not mean a spectacular house, although it might very well be spectacular. A spec house is a house built on speculation, for sale to anyone with the necessary bucks. This $30 million spec house was being built right next door to an almost matching house. They were being built by two former business partners who reportedly no longer speak. Each house has a tennis court that is cantilevered out over Coldwater Canyon. The houses can be seen for miles around, and have caused outrage in the neighborhood. One Beverly Hills society figure, who lives directly below them, said, "I know it's terrible to talk about money, but my husband had to have $50,000 worth of shrubbery put in our lawn to block out those two monstrosities." The one I was allowed to enter has more gigantic marble columns than Hadrian's

Villa. The master suite has his-and-her bathrooms of un-paralleled luxury, with Jacuzzis, sunken tubs, and etched-glass doors. The floor of the dining room has clear glass panels that reveal an indoor swimming pool below. Leaving through the front door, which is eighteen feet high, the real-estate agent pointed to the house next door and said to me, "Imagine spending $30 million on this house and having that ugger right on top of you."

"Do you think this will sell?" I asked.

"Hell, yes," he said. "We're at the beginning of this boom. We're not at the end of it. No matter what happens to the economy, these people won't be affected."

The real big shots are taken by helicopter to look at property. That includes the very rich Japanese, members of the Saudi royal family, and agents representing the Sultan of Brunei's family. "I sold one house to a man from Hong Kong," said Bruce Nelson. "It always surprised me that he never wanted to see it when he was in town. Then I was told it was a subterfuge for the brother of the Sultan of Brunei. He paid $15 million for the house, but he's never moved in."

Brooks Barton, the patrician real-estate broker who is the first vice president of Coldwell Banker, spent hours in the air showing places to Sir James Goldsmith, the international financier, before Goldsmith abandoned the idea of living in Los Angeles and settled on Mexico instead. "The economy of Southern California is incredible, and growing all the time," Barton told me as he pointed out the Jerry Perenchio estate below. Although any spread with two acres is referred to as an estate by most brokers, there are only four major estates left that have not been broken up into smaller lots. One of them is the aforementioned Ann Warner estate. Another is the former Conrad Hilton estate in Bel-Air, which, like the Warner place, has nine acres.

Now owned by the tremendously rich widower David Murdock, who is listed by *Forbes* magazine as being worth "well over $900 million," the property was described by one broker as "the perfect estate. You can't see it from the road. The driveway goes into a proper courtyard. The house opens onto the gardens." Another is the Knoll, considered by many to be the most beautiful house in Beverly Hills. The Knoll was built in the 1950s and lived in for many years by a Doheny heiress, Lucy Doheny Battson, whose family at one time owned four hundred acres in Beverly Hills. In 1975 Mrs. Battson sold the house for what was considered at the time the astronomical price of $2 million to the Italian film producer Dino De Laurentiis, who sold it six years later to the country-western star Kenny Rogers for $13 million. Rogers in turn sold it three years later to the Denver oil billionaire Marvin Davis for $20-plus million. Davis, who owned Twentieth Century-Fox Studios briefly and then sold it, and owned the Beverly Hills Hotel briefly and then sold it, and his popular wife, Barbara, are cutting a wide social swath in both the film community and the group that hovers around former president Reagan and Mrs. Reagan. The Davises' annual Christmas party in their new house is said to outdo for sheer splendor and movie star attendance any other party in the community in years and years. The last of the four great estates is the Bel-Air showplace known as the former Kirkeby house, which became well known around the world as the house in the television series "The Beverly Hillbillies." Driven to despair by the constant tourist traffic past the place, the late Carlotta Kirkeby very much regretted ever having let the house be used. The French-château-style mansion is now owned by Jerry Perenchio, the former talent agent turned sports promoter who was later partners with television mogul Norman Lear until he sold his interests to Coca-Cola for $485 million. Perenchio paid $13.5 million for the estate, then bought the house on each side for an additional $7 million in order to protect his property. He is living in one of them until the big house is finished; he tore down the other to build a new driveway. Perenchio is doing what in real-estate circles is called a total gut job on the elegant mansion, keeping the shell of the house but realigning and opening up the inside—all under the supervision of Henri Samuel, the great Parisian decorator, who also guided to completion the magnificent apartment of the socially visible John and Susan Gutfreund in New York.

Move over, Aaron Spelling. Someone with even grander plans than yours is moving in on your turf, and the only way to get an idea of the extent of this envisioned Shangri-la is to see the property from the air: 157 acres of Beverly Hills land called Benedict Canyon Mountain, purchased about twelve years ago by Princess Shams for her brother the Shah of Iran as the site for a palace for his years in exile. Fate, however, had plans for the Shah other than retirement in Beverly Hills. Now the property is owned by Merv Griffin, the former big-band vocalist turned talk-show host and game-show entrepreneur, who sold his interest in "Wheel of Fortune" to Coca-Cola for $250 million plus. He then bought the Beverly Hilton Hotel for $100 million, and has subsequently built a greater fortune in radio stations and real estate, even vying with the formidable Donald Trump for supremacy in the Resorts International chain. At present Griffin lives in a handsome gray stone Georgian mansion in Beverly Hills, which is on the market for $20 million. The new pool pavilion for this temporary house was inaugurated with a lunch party for Mrs. Ronald Reagan, at which Griffin's great friend Eva Gabor acted as hostess. "It's a shame we had to back the gates with canvas," said Waldo Fernandez, who decorated the house and designed the pavilion, "but there were too many people looking in and taking pictures." Fernandez was also the architect for the very large weekend house Griffin built in Palm Springs, which burned to the ground the week it was completed and then had to be completely rebuilt. But nothing, absolutely nothing, can compare with the about-to-be-started house on the top of Benedict Canyon Mountain.

I was driven there in the black Bentley of Waldo Fernandez, who also decorated the Bel-Air home of Elizabeth Taylor. Fernandez, fortyish, mustached, stylishly dressed by Giorgio Armani, will design Griffin's mountaintop palace with views in all directions. Fernandez's aide followed the Bentley in a Land Rover, and when we got to what will be the entry gates of the estate, we got out of the Bentley and into the Land Rover in order to negotiate the terrain. Fernandez was in charge of grading the mountaintop to the present seventeen flat acres, at a cost of $4 million. Three lakes are being built on it. At one point, the driveway will pass between two of the lakes. There will be two sets of gates for security, with armed guards at each. All cars will be stopped for clearance at both. There will be a guest parking area for ninety cars. There will be a helicopter pad. Permission to build the helicopter pad was secured only with the understanding that Griffin's helicopter would service the hills in case of fire. And there will be all the other requisites of the good life: a theater, tennis courts, a gymnasium with a pool, not to be confused with the other pool by the pool pavilion. "We didn't want to see the courts or the pool from the house," said Fernandez. "There will be trails to those areas." He pointed to another area. "The vineyards will be there."

The house, which will take from two and a half to three years to build, will be 60,000 square feet, 4,000 square feet larger than the Spelling house. It will be Palladian in style, with an atrium fifty feet by fifty feet by fifty feet in the middle. The facing will be limestone; the roof, red tile. The estimated cost of the building: $50 million.

"I'll soon be going to Europe to tag furniture for the house," said Fernandez.

"It all sounds very Hearstian," I said, referring to San Simeon, the palace William Randolph Hearst completed in 1939.

"It is," said Fernandez. Looking over the beautiful acreage, he said, "It's a dream of a job."

Despite all the hoopla connected with the Griffin estate, several highly placed people among the real-estate cognoscenti believe the house will never be built. "He's got ten in it now," they say, meaning $10 million. "You can buy Merv's land and Waldo Fernandez's blueprints for the house for $25 million."

But not to worry. There's always Robert Manoukian, an international figure of Armenian descent, who is a trusted friend of the Sultan of Brunei, and who also acts as his emissary. He negotiated to buy the Beverly Hills Hotel from Marvin Davis for the Sultan. Manoukian's new house, which is in the planning stages, is being designed by Budd Holden. It is to be built on 3.75 acres, on three descending lots, one of which was the old James Coburn estate, and, depending on whose version you believe, is going to be 58,000 square feet, 60,000 square feet, or 70,000 square feet. Fit for a king.

"Which is the Reagans' house?" I asked Brooks Barton in the helicopter.

"There," he answered, pointing down.

"Where?"

"There, that one."

"That little thing?"

"Yes."

Spoiled now by mansions of all sizes, styles, and shapes, I peered down critically at the modest ranch-style structure that is the new home of the former president of the United States and Mrs. Reagan—modest, at least in comparison with the houses in the neighborhood. It is a one-story, three-bedroom house of about 7,300 square feet (roughly the size of Candy Spelling's dressing room and closets), with pool, which friends of the Reagans bought for them for $2.5 million. Local rumor has it that Nancy Reagan does not enjoy having the house described as ranch-style. A block away on one side is the elaborate spec house designed by Budd Holden on 1.9 acres which recently sold for $15 million to the man from Hong Kong. On the other side is Jerry Perenchio's French château.

April 1989

HIGH ROLLER

The Phyllis McGuire Story

ONE DAY several years ago I was lunching at Le Cirque, arguably New York's most fashionable noontime restaurant, when my attention was drawn from my companions to three vaguely familiar-looking ladies of a certain age whom I at first mistook for triplets, since they were dressed identically in beige Chanel suits with matching bags, bracelets, pins, and honey-colored hairdos and were all speaking at the same time in an animated fashion. Seated at one of the very best tables, they were not unaware of the stir they were creating as they received the kind of deferential treatment from the sometimes haughty Le Cirque staff that Mrs. Astor or Mrs. Rockefeller might receive. The limitless curiosity of the socially inquisitive traveled from table to table: "Who are they?" And the answer came back, "The McGuire Sisters." A snap of the fingers—of course! The McGuire Sisters, the beautiful trio from Middletown, Ohio, who had had thirty hit records and given command performances for five presidents and the Queen Mother of England. One of the most popular singing groups of the fifties, discovered and made famous by Arthur Godfrey, they had by then been long out of circulation.

"Which one is Phyllis?" I asked the captain.

"In the middle," he answered.

"Wasn't she the—?"

Before I could finish my sentence, he nodded, *Yes, she was.* If I *had* finished my sentence that day at Le Cirque, it would have been, "Wasn't she the girlfriend of Sam Giancana?" Giancana, for decades one of the Mafia's most notorious and highly publicized figures, was also renowned for his role in the CIA plot to assassinate Fidel Castro, for his friendship with Frank Sinatra, and for his carrying on a love affair with Judith Campbell Exner at the same time she was having an affair with John F. Kennedy, the president of the United States.

Phyllis McGuire met Sam Giancana, according to legend, in Las Vegas in 1960, when the McGuire Sisters were performing there four times a year and pulling down $30,000 a week. Sam was a widower of fifty-two, and Phyllis, barely thirty, had already divorced Neal Van Ells, a radio/television announcer from Dayton, Ohio. Like many another Vegas performer, Phyllis had taken a liking to the gaming tables and had run up a hefty marker. As the story goes, Sam, spotting her, and liking her, went to Moe Dalitz, who ran the Desert Inn, and asked him how much the McGuire girl owed. Moe told him $100,000, a large marker at any time but enormous then. Sam is alleged to have said to Moe, "Eat it," meaning, in gangland parlance, erase the debt, which is different, of course, from paying the debt, but nonetheless it was a gesture not without charm and romantic appeal, especially since Sam followed it up with a suiteful of flowers. They fell in love.

For a time, the romance remained a well-kept secret, but wherever the trio traveled, Sam was there. In 1962, when the sisters were appearing at a nightclub in London, they were photographed there with their hairdresser, Frederic Jones, and Sam Giancana was also in the picture, with his arm wrapped around Phyllis. The photograph was flashed around the world, with enormous repercussions. The press and the public expressed a sense of outrage that the popular singer would associate with a person like Sam Giancana. In a tearful interview with the late gossip columnist Dorothy Kilgallen, Phyllis McGuire denied the rumors that she and Sam had been secretly married in Sweden, and also swore that she was never going to see Sam again. In 1968, the McGuires performed for the last time as a trio on "The Ed Sullivan Show," broadcast from Caesars Palace in Las Vegas. Since then, Phyllis has occasionally appeared as a solo act, as well as in musicals around the country, most recently in *Applause!* in Atlantic City.

Sam Giancana's life was ended in 1975, while he was cooking Italian sausage in the basement kitchen of his Oak Park, Illinois, home, by a shot from a High-Standard Duromatic .22 target pistol, with a silencer attached, fired into the back of his head. That shot was followed by a second, fired into his mouth after he fell to the floor, and then by a third, fourth, fifth, sixth, and seventh, which were fired upward into his chin, shattering his lower jaw, ripping through his tongue, and lodging in the back of his skull. The FBI believes to this day that the deliverer of the blasts was a friend of many years, who still lives in the Chicago area, and that Sam was murdered because he had refused to cut the Chicago Mob in on the gambling empire he had set up outside the United States, in Iran, Haiti, and Central and South America, as well as on five gambling ships he ran in the Caribbean. Furthermore, Sam had become old, he was in poor health, and it was time for a change.

Long before then, Phyllis and Sam had ceased being lovers, but they had remained friends and she had visited him on numerous occasions during his eight-year exile in Mexico. Both the Mob nobility and the show-business greats with whom Sam had hobnobbed snubbed his Chicago funeral. Only Phyllis McGuire and Keely Smith, who had once sung with Louis Prima, arrived to pay their respects to Giancana's three daughters and to say farewell to Sam in his $8,000 silver casket.

For several years the McGuire Sisters have been planning a nightclub comeback. In February they performed at Rainbow & Stars in New York, and shortly after that, I made arrangements to interview Phyllis McGuire. "Don't mention Sam Giancana to her," people warned me, but not mentioning Sam Giancana when writing about Phyllis McGuire would be like not mentioning Richard Burton when writing about Elizabeth Taylor, or, in a more parallel situation, like not mentioning Nicky Arnstein when writing about Fanny Brice. As it turned out, I didn't have to bring up Sam's name, because Phyllis McGuire brought it up first. Their story has all the stuff of which myths are made.

I arrived in Las Vegas with elaborate directions for how to get from the airport to Rancho Circle, the exclusive enclave behind a guarded gate where she has lived for years. "Past the Lit'l Scholar Schoolhouse," I read from my instruction sheet, but the driver said he didn't need any instructions. "Everybody in Vegas knows where Phyllis McGuire lives."

From outside, the place looked like a suburban ranch-style house built in the fifties, but all resemblance to ranch-style life ended at the front door, which was opened by a man wearing a gun in a holster under his open suit jacket. Paul Romines has been her bodyguard for fourteen years. I stood for a moment in the hallway. To the right was a dining room with a mirrored floor. Through a door was a men's lavatory with two wall urinals side by side. Ahead was a replica of the Arc de Triomphe, which separated the hall from the living room. The living room was one of the largest I have ever been in, so large that a forty-four-foot-high replica of the Eiffel Tower did not seem to cramp the space. Beyond that was a vast area which included the formal dining room and, to the right of it, a bar with twelve bar chairs. To the left was an area identified by the bodyguard as the Chinese area, and to the right an area he designated as the French area. The windows, he informed me, were all bulletproof and could take a magnum shot, and at the touch of a button steel doors would drop from the eaves over all the windows, securing the house completely, fortress-style.

The floor of the living room was black and white marble. The rugs in the French area were Aubusson and Tabriz, and the walls were covered in rose damask. The chandeliers and sconces were Bavarian, with amber light bulbs. The mirrors on the walls were Venetian, and the chairs and sofas were all French, in multiple groupings, so many chairs that I lost count at sixty. That was when Phyllis McGuire came in.

She was dressed in a nautical style, with white flannel trousers and a white cashmere sweater with naval insignia on it. Her earrings were anchors. She was not at all what I was expecting, and from the moment she spoke I liked her. She was friendly, funny, gracious, utterly enthusiastic, constantly up, with boundless energy. And pretty, very pretty.

"Did anyone offer you a cup of coffee?" she asked. "Or anything?" She flung up her hands in mock exasperation and called into the kitchen, "Enice, take care of Mr. Dunne. And I'll have some coffee too. And some Perriers."

She asked me, "Did you meet Enice? Enice Jobe? She's been with me for thirty-three years."

We sat on French chairs in the French area. "Is the music too loud?" she asked. "I can turn it down. Turn it down, Enice, will you, and put the coffee right here on this table."

I asked about the sisters, Dorothy and Christine, and she said, "We've been singing together since I was four years old. We sang in the car, using the windshield wiper for a metronome. My sisters are the most incredible harmony singers. I can start in any key, and they pick it up." The sisters got their start singing in the First Church of God in Middletown, Ohio, where their mother, an ordained minister, was an associate pastor.

"We were middle class," she said. "My father worked for forty-six years for Armco Steel. He made steel before there were jet furnaces, working at an open hearth, shoveling in the pig iron. He wore safety shoes and long thick underwear, safety shirts and gloves, and a hard hat. At night after work, his clothes were coated with salt from his sweat. When my sisters and I started making money, we asked our parents what they owed, and we paid off everything. We made my father retire, and ordered a custom-made Cadillac with a gold plaque on it that said, FOR ASA AND LILLIE MCGUIRE, FROM DOROTHY, CHRISTINE, AND PHYLLIS. We sent them all over the world."

Looking around the French area, she said, "Some of this furniture is very valuable, and some is just personal to me. That Aubusson should be hanging on the wall rather than be on the floor. A lot of the furniture and the paneling came from the house of Helen Bonfils in Denver, Colorado. Her father was the editor and publisher of the *Denver Post*. She was one of the finest women I ever knew. That desk belonged to Helen's father."

One thing I'll say about Phyllis McGuire, she's not hard to converse with. Raise any topic—with few exceptions—and she will talk away. She told me that one of the newspapers had called her a motor-mouth.

"Do you want to see everything?" she asked.

"Sure."

She took me through the house and grounds. There are eight acres and two guesthouses. "That's where my sisters stay when they come here to rehearse. The rest of the time they live in Arizona. They came to Vegas during the week and went home on weekends while we were getting ready for the comeback. We worked six to eight hours a day. We worked out and did stretching exercises in the mornings and did three hours each afternoon with Jim Hendricks, our pianist. One night I had Altovese and Sammy Davis over to hear the act. Chris and Dorothy each have their own bedroom and television set, and they share the living room and kitchen."

Sister Dorothy is no stranger to romantic headlines herself, having engaged in 1958 in a steamy love affair with fellow Arthur Godfrey singing star Julius La Rosa, which resulted in a public scolding on-air by Godfrey. Although the choirgirl image was tarnished, that affair caused no lessening of the group's popularity.

Behind the main house, we came to a moatlike area where Phyllis's twenty-three swans swim. "Those are the black Australian swans there," she said. "That one is about ready to hatch." Pointing to her tennis court, she said, "That's where Johnny Carson learned how to play tennis. It needs to be swept," she added, shaking her head.

"Someone told me all the flowers in your garden are fake," I said. She laughed and said, "Honey, I keep five gardeners."

In the pool house, noticing a crack in one of the windows, she picked up the telephone and called the main house. "Enice, tell maintenance there's a crack in the window of the pool house. Have him replace it, will you?" A bit farther on, she said, "Over there's my putting green. My waterfalls aren't on today—sorry."

Back in the house, she took me downstairs. "This is my nightclub. It even has a neon sign. The carpet rolls up and it's a dance floor underneath. The dance floor is in the shape of a piano. There have been lots of parties in this room. Over here is a blackjack table. Moe Dalitz gave me this table as a gift. I've taught more people how to play blackjack here at this table."

There is a beauty salon in the house, with several chairs and dryers so that the sisters, or houseguests, can have their hair done at the same time. In the health club, next to the beauty salon, are three changerooms and three massage tables next to one another, where three masseurs can work on three guests at the same time. "The steam room is always ready," she said, peering into a window of the steam room.

Her huge bathtub is part of her bedroom, and her closets are enormous. "This is all Chanel," she said, pointing to one area. "Over there, it's all Galanos, and there in that room is all Pauline Trigère." It was a tour she was used to giving. "This is for my furs. The lynx, ermine, and sable are here. The older furs are over there. I keep a record of everything I wear so that I don't ever repeat with the same people. All my clothes are on a computer. So are all the books in my library, and all the furniture. They're all on video as well."

She picked up a model airplane. "This was my G-II," she said. "It had a sign saying, WELCOME ABOARD THE PHYLLIS SPECIAL. I've decorated the interiors of three planes. Do you feel like lunch?"

"Sure."

The mail had arrived. "Enice, I don't want to see the tabloids. The Searles across the street said there was something in them about us. Don't show me." We sat in the small dining room, and Enice, having given the mail to a secretary, brought in the lunch. "I have the greatest kitchens in the world," Phyllis said. "I don't cook, but I always have great chefs. And some of my maids have been with me for fourteen or seventeen years."

"How many people work for you in this house?" I asked, having noticed several in the background.

She began to count, looking up, looking over at Enice for verification, placing the forefinger of her left hand against the pinkie finger of her right hand, then against the ring finger, then the center finger, then against the other forefinger, and then repeating the process, at the same time reeling off a seemingly endless list of names—maids, cooks, guards, gardeners, drivers, secretaries.

"Twenty-eight," she said finally.

She thinks a great deal about security. "My limo driver carries a gun," she said. "But if they want to get you, they're going to get you. For me, it's the most secure feeling in the world when those steel doors are down."

Phyllis McGuire has a more elaborate lifestyle than most television and nightclub performers of the fifties whose stars have dimmed with time and the fickle musical tastes of the public, and nowhere is her wealth more visible than in her wondrous jewelry. No one who knows about jewels has not heard about her fantastic collection, which ranks among the best in the world, right up there with the famous collections of Elizabeth Taylor, Imelda Marcos, Candy Spelling, Mrs. Marvin Davis, and the fifth Baroness Thyssen. Harry Winston, the great jeweler, once said to her, "If ever there was a lady meant to wear jewels, it's you." She told me, "There was a time when I was purchasing millions of dollars' worth of jewelry. I was one of Harry Winston's best customers." She paused for a moment and then added, "Maybe some Saudis were ahead of me. Jewels really turned me on then, and they still do. I wear the jewels, they don't wear me."

On the day I was in her house, most of her jewels had been put in the vault because she was leaving imminently for a singing engagement with her sisters at the Moulin Rouge in Chicago. But a few were still at hand. "Enice," she called out, "bring in the canaries." The canaries consisted of a forty-two-carat yellow diamond set in a ring, surrounded by smaller diamonds, and some loose yellow diamonds which she was planning to have made into earrings. She examined her stones like a jeweler. "I'm not sure I like the way they put the diamonds around the canary," she said, "but I'm trying it this way." From the same package she pulled a twenty-eight-carat marquise-shaped diamond ring, which she called "one of the babies" because of its small size—small, at least, in comparison with some of her other rings. The canaries brought to mind a fairly recent drama in her life.

In 1979, she said, she took a D-flawless-diamond ring to Harry Winston's to have it cleaned and to have the prongs checked. When the ring was returned to her, it didn't seem to have the same sparkle it had had previously. Even now, a decade later, recounting the story, she held her hand up and examined her ring finger as if she were looking at the ring in question. She said that she had said at the time, "This can't be my ring. It doesn't sparkle the same." She said she had begun to question her own sanity. "I said to Enice, 'Is this my ring, Enice?' and she said, 'I think it is, Miss Phyllis.' But there is a process called cubic zirconia, where a fake diamond can be cut exactly to match a real diamond. I knew that my ring had been switched. I turned in one to be cleaned, and they gave me back another. I sued Winston for $60 million. They countersued me for $100 million." At the time, a spokesman for Winston denied the allegations "absolutely."

"I was only trying to recover my jewels," she continued. "I deposed for three days at Foley Square in New York. I discovered the diamond wasn't mine at Christmas of '79, and the case was settled in '82." She seemed to be finished with her story.

"But what happened?" I asked.

"I'm not allowed to discuss the outcome of the suit. That's part of the agreement," she said, giving a helpless shrug, but neither her smile nor her attitude indicated any discontent with the outcome.

A spokesman for Winston told me the company had no comment to make.

Her conversation is peppered with the names of the very rich and very famous, with whom she has spent most of her time over the last twenty-five years. "I met Imelda Marcos at a party at Adnan Khashoggi's," she told me, and she and her sisters were scheduled to sing at the ninety-fifty birthday party of Armand Hammer, the billionaire philanthropist. Ann-Margret's name came up, and she said, "Let's call her." Ann-Margret was playing at Caesars Palace. She dialed the number. "This is Phyllis McGuire," she said to the telephone operator. "I'd like to speak to Ann-Margret. She's still sleeping? At two o'clock in the afternoon? My God, she only had one show last night. OK, tell her I called."

"New York is like roots for me," she said. "It was the

first big city we saw after Ohio." For years she kept a Park Avenue apartment. Then she bought a town house on one of the most exclusive streets on the Upper East Side of Manhattan. "Do you know where Givenchy is? Two houses behind that." She bought the house, she said, "lock, stock, and barrel, including antiques, china, crystal, and silverware, from a son of King Fahd of Saudi Arabia," who was afraid of being assassinated, following the assassination of Anwar Sadat in Egypt, and took up residence instead in the Waldorf Towers, where many heads of state, and families of heads of state, stay for purposes of security. Phyllis loved the house dearly but spent only twenty-one days in it in 1987, so when her great friend Meshulam Riklis, the vastly rich ($440 million) financier husband of Pia Zadora, asked if he could buy it, she sold it to him. In order not to be without a nest in New York, she borrowed the Pierre Hotel apartment of another great friend, the vastly rich ($950 million) financier Kirk Kerkorian, and liked it so much that she talked Kerkorian into selling it to her, completely furnished.

"I'm a good businesswoman," she said, a fact that is borne out by most of her acquaintances. "If I weren't performing, I would have to constantly be working at something. I love business."

I didn't have to mention Sam Giancana. She brought him up. "I've had four serious involvements in my life, and one was a marriage. That was only for about ten minutes. Two of the men are still my friends, Simon Srybnik and Dr. Stanley Behrman, the head of oral surgery at New York Hospital. Even after Simon married Judy, and Stanley married Nancy, we stayed friends." She paused before continuing. "And then there was Sam." When she said Sam, she whispered his name. There is no doubt she loved him.

Even William Roemer, the former FBI agent who dogged Sam's life for a decade, says, "Phyllis really loved Sam, and Sam loved her." Phyllis's great friend the Broadway producer Dasha Epstein says, "She disappeared out of our lives when she was going with Sam. She said, 'I know it's difficult for my friends, and I understand.' That was so like Phyllis."

"My life is so much more than that—with Sam," Phyllis said. "That was only a chapter. I'm not ashamed of my past. I was doing what I honestly felt." She sat back in her rose damask Bergère chair and continued. "Sam was the greatest teacher I ever could have had. He was so wise about so many things. Sam is always depicted as unattractive. He wasn't. He was a very nice-looking man. He wasn't flashy. He didn't drive a pink Cadillac, like they used to say. He was a beautiful dresser. Dorothy Kilgallen thought he was my attorney when she met him. The two great losses of my life were my father and Sam."

She is now working on her autobiography to set the record straight. "I've got to get this out. I've got to get on with my life. It's holding me up. I have things to say that haven't been said," she told me. "Like about the late Mayor Daley of Chicago, even if his son is the new mayor." "It's a heavy-duty story," she was quoted in Marilyn Beck's column as saying. "I've been in thirty-four books in the last twelve to fifteen years, and it's time my story was finally told correctly. I don't need a Kitty Kelley doing to me what she did to Sinatra and [what she's doing to] Nancy Reagan."

She denies, for example, the story about the $100,000 marker that Giancana told Moe Dalitz to eat. "I never lost more than $16,000 gambling at any one time," she said.

She also discounts many of the stories about her in the book *Mafia Princess,* written by Sam Giancana's daughter Antoinette. "I tried to stop that book," she said. "It wasn't accurate. Toni got all her information through the Freedom of Information Act. She didn't know any firsthand. She and her father hadn't been close. She used to come and stay here, in the guesthouse."

In 1961, at the height of Phyllis's fame, her affair with Giancana was still not known to the public. The FBI, which tracked Giancana's every move, had chosen not to expose the relationship, understanding that such publicity would be detrimental to McGuire's career. But in the spring of that year, agents bugged their motel room in Phoenix and learned they would be traveling on American Airlines to New York with a stopover at O'Hare Airport in Chicago. The FBI decided to subpoena Phyllis with the proviso that if she cooperated with them by answering their questions in a room within the terminal, they would withdraw the subpoena and she would not have to appear the next day. She knew that if she were to appear, it would become publicly known that she was the mistress of the Mob chief. What the FBI agents asked her to do was cooperate with them in the future by letting them know where Sam was at all times. Phyllis agreed to do what they asked, and they took the subpoena back, but, according to several reliable sources, she didn't keep her promise.

William Roemer's job that day was to keep Giancana occupied while Phyllis was being questioned, and he and Giancana got into a screaming match at the airport, climaxing when Sam said he was going to have his friend Butch Blasi machine-gun him down. Roemer, probably the greatest authority on Sam Giancana, remembers him very differently from the way Phyllis does. His book, *Roemer: Man Against the Mob,* will be published in October by Donald I. Fine. He told me on the phone from his home in Tucson, "Sam was ugly, balding—wore a wig at the end of his life. Little, slight, dumpy, a deese-dem-dose guy, scum of the earth, killer, the dregs of society, the worst kind of person. We hated each other. I hated him, and he hated me."

Roemer said that the Mob was extremely upset with Giancana when he was going with Phyllis. They thought he wasn't minding the store. "He fell in love with her and traveled all over the world with her," Roemer said. He agrees that Phyllis, in the tradition of wives, daughters, and lovers of Mob members, knew little of Sam's life away from her. He told me that when Phyllis first thought about writing her book, she called him—Sam's nemesis—to say that she had met a lot of people during her years with Sam but that she didn't actually know who they were or what they had done. Some of them, she said, she knew only by their nicknames, like "Chuckie" (English), "Butch" (Blasi), and "Skinny" (D'Amato)—all figures in the racketeering life of Sam Giancana.

"Did Sam leave any money to Phyllis?"

"Nobody could ever prove that he left her money," answered Roemer. Although Giancana left an estate valued at only $132,583.16 when he died, that meant nothing. The kind of money that people like Sam Giancana have is not banked or left in the ordinary ways of money management. Roemer said it is possible that Giancana had a hundred million dollars.

"It very definitely hurt our careers for about a year," Phyllis McGuire said about her affair with Giancana. "We were blacklisted on TV, but that ended."

"In your interview with Dorothy Kilgallen, you said you were going to give him up," I said.

"Yes, I know. I said in that interview that I'd never see him again. Well, I did." She shrugged, and then threw out one of the amazing bits of information that flow freely from her tongue. "Kilgallen was murdered," she said. "She didn't commit suicide." Dorothy Kilgallen, who supposedly died of a sleeping-pill overdose in 1964, had in that same year interviewed Jack Ruby, the assassin of Lee Harvey Oswald, the man who assassinated President Kennedy. "I saw her three days before, dancing at El Morocco with Johnnie Ray. She was murdered. I didn't believe the suicide story then. I don't believe it now. Dorothy was the most beautiful corpse I ever saw."

Although Phyllis McGuire did not mention him in her list of suitors, there has been another romantic involvement since Sam, a bigger-than-life character named Mike Davis, and they are still close friends. The owner of Tiger Oil, Davis is based in Houston, but he is always on the move. Phrases like "my jet" pop up in his conversation, as do such names as Bunker Hunt, of the Texas Hunts, and Adnan Khashoggi, the international arms dealer, currently in hot water, with whom Davis has been a sometime partner. "Tiger Mike," as some people call him, is of Lebanese extraction. He was once the chauffeur of Phyllis's great friend Helen Bonfils, and married Bonfils upon the death of her husband in 1956. Helen Bonfils was reportedly in her late sixties at the time, and Davis was in his late twenties. Bonfils, who took over the running of the *Denver Post* when her father died, was also involved in producing Broadway shows. She helped finance Davis's start-up in Tiger Oil. Davis's interest in Phyllis began while she was still involved with Giancana. McGuire told me she once pulled him behind a slot machine and warned him, "You better stay away from me. Do you want to end up on the bottom of Lake Mead?"

On several occasions, Frank Sinatra's name came up in our conversation, and I sensed a certain amount of animosity. "We are cautiously friends," she said slowly. "He is the most talented but most contradictory person. He has surrounded himself with an entourage who yes him to death. How can you expand yourself surrounded by yes-men? I've stayed in his house, and he has bored me to death. He tells the *sa-a-ame* stories he's been telling for years, and all I ever heard were his records, which he played *over and over* again." She covered her ears as she told this. "I thought to myself, I'll never do that in my house with my records. You *never* hear my own music played on my system."

She recounted to me a story that I had read in Kitty Kelley's unauthorized biography of Sinatra, *His Way.* Sinatra, who was making $100,000 a week in Las Vegas, agreed, along with Sammy Davis, Jr., Dean Martin, and Eddie Fisher, to appear for nothing in a club called Villa Venice, which was a front for Giancana. Afterward, Giancana wanted to send a gift to each of them, and Phyllis picked out Sinatra's gift. She suggested sending Steuben crystal, having seen stemware in Sinatra's house that he told her was Steuben. "I say Steuben. Frank said Steu*banne.* He thought what he had was Steuben, but it wasn't. Steuben always says Steuben on the bottom, but his didn't. I called Gloria, who was Frank's secretary, to see if they should be monogrammed, but she said no to the monogram, because people tended to walk off with anything that had Sinatra's monogram on it. I sent him a service for thirty—martini glasses, white-wine glasses, red-wine glasses, champagne glasses, and water tumblers. I spent over $7,000 on that gift, and the S.O.B. never sent a thank-you note."

"Did you get any flak from Sinatra from telling Kitty Kelley the story about the Steuben glasses?"

"None whatever," she said, shaking her head emphatically. "He knows better. Let me tell you about Frank. He doesn't know how to say, 'I'm sorry,' and he doesn't know how to say, 'Thank you.' He could never admit he made a mistake. I sent my Lear to Houston to pick up Dr. DeBakey when Frank's mother was killed, because they were friends, but he never said thank you for that either."

"Didn't you make a movie with Sinatra?"

"Hmmm," she answered, nodding her head. *"Come Blow Your Horn.* Everyone said Sam got that movie for me with Frank, which was *not* true. I played a buyer from Neiman-Marcus, a part that was not in the stage play. He was supposed to kiss me in one scene, and I was wearing my diamond drop earrings." She held up her fingers to indicate a good three inches of diamonds, from the lobes to the shoulders. "When he kissed me, he put his hands over my ears like this." She covered her ears with her hands. "That was the last important picture Frank did."

"Why did you ever stop singing?"

"Oh, we lost our confidence at different times—me less than Dorothy and Christine," said Phyllis. "Dorothy got married. Christine got married. They had guilt trips thinking they should be home with their children."

When she sings, she said, she feels tidal waves of love coming from the audience, "like a full moon when the ocean is active." On the night I flew to Chicago to watch the McGuire Sisters perform at the Moulin Rouge in the new Fairmont Hotel, the room was packed. The crowd was an older crowd, but then, the cover charge was twenty-five dollars per person, on top of drinks and dinner. "People feel they know us," said Phyllis. "They love us. They watched us grow up on TV." Sitting at a front-row table was Irv Kupcinet, the dean of Chicago columnists, and his wife, Essie. "Ladies and gentlemen," came the announcement over the loudspeaker, *"the McGuire Sisters!"*

And there they were, Dorothy, Christine, and Phyllis, with Phyllis, as always, in the middle. Fake eyelashes, glitter on their blue eyeshadow, honey-colored falls on their honey-colored hair, and peach dresses covered with crystals. When they sang their familiar hits, like "The Naughty Lady of Shady Lane," "Melody of Love," and "Sugartime," which put them on the cover of *Life* magazine in 1958, they got excited applause of recognition. Phyllis gave the audience their cover charge's worth. She did vocal impersonations of Judy Garland, Louis Armstrong, Ethel Merman, Pearl Bailey, and other stars of her era. And she was right: the audience loved them.

"Where do you sing next?"

"We might make a deal with Steve Wynn for the Mirage," said Phyllis. The Mirage, due to open before the end of the year, is the newest of the hotels on the Vegas Strip. We were sitting at a table in a corner of the bar of the Fairmont, late, after her second show. Her sisters had gone upstairs. She was in a long red dress and wore dark glasses because she was still wearing her stage makeup.

"I don't fear living, and I don't fear dying," she said. "You only live once, and I'm going to live it to the fullest, until away I go. And I'm going to continue singing as long as somebody wants me."

June 1989

Social Death
in
Venice

Aᴛ ꜰɪʀsᴛ it seemed like a re-enactment of the sort of turn-of-the-century match Henry James or Edith Wharton might have written about, the marriage of a New World heiress and an Old World prince, a swap of money and title beneficial to both sides. Indeed, as we approach the turn of another century, the allure of grand titles for socially ambitious mothers with marriageable daughters seems not to have diminished, judging by the remarkable events in Venice during Easter weekend this year. No story by Henry James or Edith Wharton, however, would have ended with headlines such as this: ʜᴇɪʀᴇss ᴊɪʟᴛᴇᴅ ᴀs ʙʀɪᴅᴇɢʀᴏᴏᴍ ʀᴜɴs ᴏꜰꜰ ᴡɪᴛʜ ʙᴇsᴛ ᴍᴀɴ.

In this version of the tale, the heiress is an Australian named Primrose Dunlop, and the nobleman is the awesomely titled Prince Lorenzo Giustiniani Montesini, count of the Phanaar, Knight of Saint Sophia, Baron Alexandroff. A poor prince who claims to be "a small link in a chain that goes back to Constantine," Prince Giustiniani, known to his friends as Laurie, is employed as a steward on Qantas Airlines. Lorenzo Montesini, as he was then called, appeared on the social scene of Sydney in 1983, at a charity party at Fairwater, the mansion of Lady Fairfax, the widow of the Australian press lord. Affable, charming, socially adept, Lorenzo soon was in demand as an extra man. "He charmed his way into everyone's house here," one Sydney social figure told me. "He was asked to all the parties, between flights."

When the Egyptian-born Montesini, who is forty-four, chubby, bouncy, elfin, and very short, arrived in Sydney from Melbourne, he came with his longtime companion, Robert Straub, with whom he had served in Vietnam. In Woolloomooloo, a middle-class suburb of Sydney, the men converted two rose pink cottages into their home, which they filled with gilded mirrors, Persian carpets, rococo furnishings, and tables covered with framed photographs of well-known people. Montesini described the princely possessions as "family things."

Primrose Dunlop, the woman in question, was not a blushing debutante in her first bloom. Nor was she really an heiress, but merely the stepdaughter of a rich man who has two daughters of his own, who do not care much for their stepsister. Primrose is thirty-six, had been married before, briefly and unhappily, and is called Pitty Pat to distinguish her from her mother, Lady Potter, who is also named Primrose. Pitty Pat has had a variety of jobs over the years: she sold pots and pans in a department store, wrote social columns for two Sydney tabloids, did public-relations work for the British mogul Lord McAlpine, and, most recently, clerked as an eight-dollar-an-hour assistant to a haberdasher named John Lane, a great friend of her mother's, who sometimes escorted Lady Potter on the endless round of parties and boutique openings that her much older husband did not wish to attend.

Lady Potter, who once raised French poodles and is

most often described by her friends as vivacious, became the fourth wife of Sir Ian Potter in 1975. Sleek, stylish, and very well dressed, she speaks in the grand vocal tones of a society lady. Her previous marriage, to Dr. Roger Dunlop, a surgeon, who is the father of Primrose, ended in divorce. Lady Potter, a tireless fund-raiser for charity, with a hardy appetite for publicity and social recognition, had set her sights far beyond Sydney and Melbourne. Described by an English acquaintance who has sat next to her at dinner on several occasions as "an expert dropper of key names meant to establish her credentials," Lady Potter is referred to in the Australian social columns as "the Empress" and is said to revel in her nickname. She is considered by many to be the queen bee of the Sydney-Melbourne social axis, and her public-relations consultant, Barry Everingham, has gone so far as to describe Sir Ian and Lady Potter as the closest thing that Australia has to royalty.

Sir Ian, eighty-eight, is one of Australia's most respected businessmen, but age has caught up with the old man. A number of people I spoke with described him as slightly "gaga." Others said he was amazingly sharp for a man of his age. He played an integral, albeit passive, part in the Venetian nuptials, however, because his money was paying for everything. His fortune, which has been estimated at $48 million by some, less by others, was to finance the splendid wedding for the bride, and it was thought by many to be the lure for the groom. Sir Ian has a daughter named Robin from his first marriage, and a daughter named Carolyn Parker Bowles from his second marriage. Mrs. Parker Bowles, who lives in London, is the mother of Sir Ian's two grandsons. "Sir Ian is a self-made man of enormous ability who, until all this, has been very quiet. He is a great Australian," one Australian businessman told me. "The poor man has been dragged into a situation which will appear in his obituary." .

Last year Lorenzo Montesini brought out a novel about Sydney society called *Cardboard Cantata*, which he dedicated to Lady Potter. Since no publisher picked up on it, the book was printed privately. It has been rumored that Lady Potter financed the publication of the four thousand copies, and she gave a launch party for the book, in an art gallery, which attracted three hundred of the city's smartest citizens. It was on the occasion of that party that Lorenzo first aired his previously unsuspected titles of prince, count, knight, and baron.

The sheer awfulness of Lorenzo Montesini's book was conveyed to me by the editor of an Australian magazine, who said, "I defy you to read it." In an earlier, snobbier time, it would have been called a shopgirl's book. The three leading characters, who vie with one another for leadership of Sydney society, are named Babylonia Grushman, Cooii Rundle, and Lady Millicent Bosenquet. Another character is described as coming from a "well-to-do but poor family." Despite its social send-off, the book was, predictably, a colossal flop. Stacks of unsold copies gathered dust until the recent publicity created a belated demand and elevated them to the status of collector's items. But the point was not the book, and the literary life was not the prince's ambition. It seemed that it was the book *party* that led to the plans for a wedding. That night Lady Potter told the press, "I've known Lorenzo for years. He's a dear sweet boy. Ian and I look upon him as family." The steward-author-prince smiled and said, "I have arrived."

From there, things moved quickly. The rose pink cottages became the setting for a round of parties, at which Pitty Pat and Lady Potter were always present. "Unless you entertain, you're dead," said Lorenzo in an early television interview, speaking in his chatty manner, seated on a thronelike chair. "Montesini brought a manservant down from Thailand and dressed him in a *King and I* costume with the Giustiniani coronet on it," said a friend who attended his parties. Surprisingly, it was Robert Straub, Lorenzo's great friend, who inadvertently brought about the engagement when he jokingly remarked one evening after dinner, "Think about it, Primrose. If you were to marry Lorenzo, you would become a princess." Although the remark was greeted with hoots of laughter, it set the idea in motion.

Soon after that, Lady Potter confirmed in a magazine interview that Lorenzo "telephoned and formally asked for my daughter's hand in marriage. . . . I said that as long as he makes her happy, the answer's yes." He gave her an engagement ring of aquamarine and diamonds, modernized from a piece handed down to him by his grandmother.

No one loves a party more than Lady Potter, and she saw fit to celebrate the joyous news of her daughter's engagement with two, one in Melbourne and a second in New York, at fashionable Mortimer's, to which she invited some of the most promotable of New York's social names, including Leonard Lauder and Nan Kempner.

The romantic city of Venice was decided on as the location for the wedding. Not only was Giustiniani one of the great titles of Venice, but Lady Potter had been renting palazzi there for several years and had come to know the small and exclusive English-speaking colony. In preparation, Pitty Pat became a Catholic; she received instruction from Father Vincent Kiss, and she was sponsored by John Lane, her boss and her mother's walker. The Sydney and Melbourne newspapers followed every detail of the arrangements. The date was set for April 16, the day after Easter. The wedding would take place in the Basilica di San Pietro, to which the bride would be oared in one of a flotilla of gondolas, followed by a grand reception and candlelit dinner in the marble hall of the Palazzetto Pisani on the Grand Canal, which the bride's mother had leased for the occasion. Seventy Australian guests were invited to the lavish event.

Despite encouragement from Lady Potter, the affianced couple appeared in public infrequently, giving rise to rumors that theirs was a nonromantic liaison reeking of ulterior motives on both sides. When Montesini and Robert Straub, whose relationship was causing titters in Lady Potter's circle, showed up at a party to celebrate the opening of a Chanel boutique in Sydney, John Lane, acting for Lady Potter, said to Lorenzo, "Don't be seen in public with that man again." The bride's family was less than enthusiastic when Lorenzo announced that Straub would be his best man. Dissension arose. There were rumors, all unconfirmed, that lurid photographs existed.

Stories persisted in Sydney society that the prince was in it for the money. He himself reported to Pitty Pat that John Laws, one of the highest-paid radio announcers in the world, had told him, while he was pouring champagne for him in the first-class cabin on a Qantas flight, that his title should be worth at least $2 million to the Potters. Lorenzo was shocked. "People suggest that there is money in this for me. That's utter rubbish," he protested.

Before their departure for Venice, the prince and his princess-to-be posed for pictures and gave an interview for a long article in *Good Weekend* magazine in the *Sydney Morning Herald,* and it was that article, with the royal-looking photographs, that began the unraveling of their plans. Previously unknown relations of the prince came out of the woodwork and mocked his pretensions, disputing both the title and his right to use it. One cousin, Nelson Trapani, a forty-nine-year-old retired Queensland builder, told the press, "Really, all this speculation about a title is a load of bulldust. I'd sooner sit down with a pie and watch the telly."

Nonetheless, the group, which included Father Kiss, who was to perform the ceremony, took off amid whispers that all was not as it was supposed to be, with either the title or the romance, or anything else. Dr. Roger Dunlop, Pitty Pat's real father, was so opposed to his daughter's choice of husband that he boycotted the wedding ceremony.

If Lorenzo was having second thoughts, he nonetheless went along with the plans, flying to Venice with Robert Straub and John Lane, Lady Potter's great friend, who had been assigned the paternal function of giving the bride away, owing to the refusal of her real father and the inability of her stepfather because of his age. The groom-to-be was the only member of the wedding party without a confirmed seat on the plane. He traveled standby economy-class at his own expense. A curious twist of alliances occurred during the trip. Lane, who had previously been unfriendly to Montesini and Straub and had warned them at the Chanel opening not to appear together in public, discovered, Lorenzo later said, that "we were really quite nice guys after all and not as bad as we had been painted."

On Good Friday, as Leo Schofield, an Australian journalist, and other guests were boarding their plane in Sydney for the long flight to Venice, they heard that the wedding had been called off.

What had up to then been merely a Sydney-Melbourne gossip-column story quickly turned into international headlines, and Pitty Pat and Lorenzo became, however briefly, household names, more famous in their disaster than they would ever have been in their marriage. "If it was publicity they all wanted," said one friend, "they have succeeded beyond their wildest dreams."

Although it was widely touted in the Australian press that the guest list had been made up of a glittering gaggle of international socialites, there wasn't a recognizable name in the group. "Not a single man, woman, or dog in Venice ever heard of any of these people," said one longtime resident of the city.

There was a problem with accommodations from the beginning. Lord and Lady Potter and Pitty Pat were housed on an upper floor of the Palazzetto Pisani, and the prince, his best man, and John Lane were housed in a small flat on the ground floor, or water floor, consisting of two tiny rooms. The space was crowded and uncomfortable, and the bathroom facilities were not to the trio's liking. At a cocktail party held at the Palazzetto, which is owned by the Countess Maria Pia Ferri, another Venetian countess is said to have exclaimed to the bridegroom when he was introduced to her as Prince Giustiniani, "Oh, you must be related to my friend Cecy Giustiniani." Cecy Giustiniani is the venerable Dowager Countess Giustiniani, and soon telephones were jingling up and down the Grand Canal. People ran to their *Libro d'Oro,* the Italian book of nobility, but no one could find a Prince Giustiniani. Every Venetian with whom I spoke drew attention, often huffily, to the fact that "Prince" is not a Venetian title. "Count" is the title that counts in Venice, as any countess will tell you.

The Dowager Countess Giustiniani vehemently refuted the claim of Lorenzo Montesini that he was Prince Giustiniani, stating that her name had been violated. "The male line of the Venetian Giustinianis ended thirty years ago with the death of my dear husband, the Count Alvise

Giustiniani," she said. "A Prince Giustiniani does not exist. To claim this is the most monstrous rubbish. This alleged title is false, false, false." So began the wedding week.

The Palazzetto Pisani soon became a battleground, with a butler carrying notes back and forth between floors. According to reports, the Potter family asked Lorenzo to substantiate his claim to the title before the wedding took place. The relationship with Robert Straub was also in dispute. The family was concerned about a projected newspaper story on Straub which would provide details of his life in Melbourne before he and Lorenzo moved to Sydney. Straub believed that someone considered more suitable was waiting in the wings to replace him as his best man. Lady Potter had reckoned that, once in Venice, Lorenzo would capitulate and Robert would go away, but this was not to be. Lorenzo and Straub and Lane left the Pisani and moved to a pension on the Giudecca Canal, which Lorenzo later described as "a hotel for middle-class English traveling elcheapo." In the course of the move, Lorenzo claimed to have lost their passports, and he reported this to Pitty Pat.

The next morning, on the advice of John Lane, Lorenzo got on the telephone and told Lady Potter, not his wife-to-be, that the wedding was off. It then became the sad duty of Lady Potter to inform her daughter, the bride, that the groom was jilting her.

One of the Australian guests told me, "I thought they'd go through with it. After all, it seemed very much a marriage of convenience, all because of the title. It was really a larky thing to do, a combination of an ambitious mother wanting to feel well placed and a financially ambitious groom." The same guest described running into Lorenzo in the bar of the Hotel Cipriani after the breakup but before he bolted from Venice with his best man. "He seemed totally devastated by the whole thing. He said, about himself and Pitty Pat, 'We'd been old friends. It was to have been a marriage of style.' "

Evelyn Lambert, the Texas chatelaine of the Villa Lambert in the Veneto outside of Venice, who rented her house to Lady Potter one year, told me, "I called her after the cancellation and she said she was not angry with Lorenzo. Venice thinks the whole thing was a publicity stunt, but I don't think so. The three men decided this was not going to work. I read in the *Sydney Morning Herald* that I was giving a bridal lunch on Good Friday. Honey, I'm a Catholic by conversion. I don't give lunch parties on Good Friday. I don't even *eat* on Good Friday."

One of Pitty Pat's cousins acted as family spokesman and made calls to all the guests to inform them that the wedding was off. "The families of both the bride and groom have searched high and low for an answer to an inexplicable riddle and a way to redeem the damage— spiritual, psychological, and material," he said. "To say the bride and her mother are distraught is understatement. They are utterly devastated. It is as though a bomb had exploded. The groom's decision and what made him take this step came out of the blue. His family had already handed over generations of jewels and heirlooms to Primrose.

"We had no inkling. No one fully understands the emotional bond between those two men who ran away together. We are trying to trace them. They might be in Timbuktu as far as we know.

"We would love a dialogue with Lorenzo to see exactly why it happened and to put things in perspective. Nothing is irredeemable. If only he had spoken openly with the bride, we would have understood. If at this late stage he were to come forward with regrets, we feel the bride would

still accept him. Primrose is a tough girl, and she is fighting against distress, shame, and a feeling of ridicule. Fortunes have been spent by scores of people on this stylish
wedding—return airfares from Melbourne, not to mention
presents. But this matters least of all. It is the wounded
bride we first have to deal with."

Many of the people who spoke with both mother and
daughter were amazed by their composure. But, after all, in
their world appearance is everything. A few days after the
fiasco, the Potters and Pitty Pat left Venice and proceeded
to Paris, where Lady Potter celebrated her birthday at
Maxim's just as she had planned to right along.

A few days later in Melbourne, the premier of the state of
Victoria, in a televised speech from the floor of Parliament
House, accused the opposition party of being a mismatched
marriage—worse than that of Pitty Pat Dunlop and the
prince. The Melbourne newspapers carried the remark on
their front pages.

In Sydney the called-off marriage was the most exciting
event in years. "We fell about laughing here," said a friend
of both parties. "It was all a publicity stunt to turn them
into international figures, and it backfired on them."

People talked of nothing else. And when they finished
talking to one another, they talked to the press, if asked. In
an article by Daphne Guinness, Caroline Simpson, a member of the powerful Fairfax family, spoke her mind. "Hasn't
this whole thing been a joke from the beginning?" she
asked. "None of us thought it would get to the wedding
stage and the church, did we? Dr. Dunlop came to see my
mother [Betty Fairfax] this afternoon. They talked for
hours. I think he had a lot to do with stopping it. It is
really an extraordinary thing for a mother to push a child

in that way." There was a certain amount of glee in social circles that Lady Potter "had egg all over her face." "The person I feel sorry for is Ian Potter," said Sheila Scotter, another social leader, "and his absolutely darling daughter Carolyn Parker Bowles, who *does* move in society circles in London with certain royals, including the monarch."

On her way back to Sydney via Paris and New York, Primrose Dunlop arranged to go public with her story on Australia's "60 Minutes" when she returned. The rumor was that she was paid $38,000 by the network, and that she would drop a bombshell on the show.

If the producers of "60 Minutes" really *did* pay Pitty Pat $38,000, they were rooked, for there was no bombshell. Or perhaps, as has been suggested, libel laws being what they are, the bomb was considered inadvisable, and was defused. The interview was benign, even boring. "Everyone here feels cheated by it," said a friend of Montesini's. "Such a pathetic amount was produced. Anyway, I heard they only paid her $23,000."

Pitty Pat was interviewed in the apartment of her mother and stepfather, and viewers had no sense of watching a sad and sympathetic jilted woman. She seemed arch and superior, holding her eyebrows high and looking down her nose at Jeff McMullen, the Morley Safer of Australia's "60 Minutes," as if she were granting an audience to a troublesome commoner.

"That's Mummy and H.M. the Queen," she said, showing a photograph of Lady Potter in a deep curtsy before Queen Elizabeth.

The only surprise in the program came when McMullen asked, "Were you sexually compatible with the prince?"

"Yes, we were. Wouldn't you be with someone you were going to marry?"

"Would you take him back?"

"Yeah. He's a decent guy."

She said she did not believe that Lorenzo was gay. If something had happened in his past, it was of no concern to either of them. She mentioned the possibility of lurid photographs—that was probably the predicted bombshell —but said she didn't believe they existed.

"Do you think Lorenzo's a prince?" asked Jeff McMullen, pointing out that Montesini's relatives had mocked the title.

"I don't know," replied Pitty Pat. "I would like to see his grandmother's will. She wanted him to take up the title. That's where it all started." She added that titles did not matter to her.

She said that she didn't think Lorenzo had been in it for the money. "Besides," she said, "my stepfather does not give away his money lightly." She said that the story had been started by John Laws, the radio announcer, who suggested to Lorenzo while airborne that his title was worth a fortune to the Potters. For that, she said, she felt a great deal of resentment for John Laws.

When asked how she felt about the premier's mentioning her name in Parliament, she became imperious in her dismissal of him. "How tacky. What a common remark," she snapped.

She then allowed herself to be talked into telephoning her almost-husband on national television in order to ask him why he had never consulted her about calling off the marriage. The prince-steward was out, on a flight presumably, and she got his answering machine.

"It's me," she said, and asked him to call her when he returned. In closing, she told McMullen that the heartache she felt was worse than the embarrassment.

• • •

Montesini, in an intimate moment with his friend the Australian journalist Daphne Guinness, gave his account of the fiasco. He claimed that Lady Potter had announced his engagement without his knowledge when he was in Tokyo for Qantas. "I felt trapped by it," he said, "pushed on by Pitty Pat's mother into something that got out of hand." However, he went along with it, "swept into the euphoria of such a grand occasion as a wedding in Venice."

"I could not see past April 16. I could not think beyond getting to Venice and going to the church. I could not begin to think of the night of the sixteenth, and where I would sleep after the wedding. I even rehearsed going up the aisle and standing in front of father Vincent Kiss and when it came to the bit about 'Do you take Primrose to be your lawful wedded wife?' shouting 'NO!' and turning round and running out of the church."

However, he did not mention these inner torments, at least not to his fiancée and her family. According to him, the real reason for the breakup was the Potters' desire to terminate his friendship with Straub. When asked about the rumor that there had been a wedding settlement of some $2 million, Lorenzo said, "Take a naught off and you'd be nearer the mark, but I haven't been given a penny." In Venice, he said, John Lane told him that Lady Potter had changed her will so that he couldn't get his hands on the fortune that will eventually be Pitty Pat's. That, Lorenzo claimed, coupled with the information that Pitty Pat had said that after the sixteenth she would be a princess traveling first-class, made him feel used.

One week later, however, he also went public, in the Australian magazine *Women's Day*. Whether, like Pitty Pat, he was getting paid for his revelations is not known. But his statement, like hers, was a party-line exercise in face-saving. "I did not have the money to give her the life-style she would have expected," he said. "I loved her—and I always will—but as the rumors, all of which are untrue, began to circulate, I realized I was out of my depth and that it would be best to call off the marriage." He said that he had had a close and satisfying sexual relationship with Primrose, and he described her as sensual. "Every time I looked at her, I was reminded of a Byzantine empress." He denied that he was gay, and he downplayed the importance of his title. "It must be understood that Prince Giustiniani is a courtesy title only, and there is no way Primrose could use it on her passport, or use it in real life. She understood that completely. We often talked about it and laughed about it."

He was most grieved, he said, by her appearance on "60 Minutes." "It was horrendous when, on the program, she tried to ring me and I heard my own voice on my telephone answering machine."

SPECIAL REPORTING FROM SYDNEY BY DAPHNE GUINNESS

August 1990

KHASHOGGI'S FALL
A Crash in the Limo Lane

ADNAN KHASHOGGI was never the richest man in the world, ever, but he flaunted the myth that he was with such relentless perseverance and public-relations know-how that most of the world believed him. The power of great wealth is awesome. If you have enough money, you can bamboozle anyone. Even if you can create the *illusion* that you have enough money you can bamboozle anyone, as Adnan Khashoggi did over and over again. He understood high visibility better than the most shameless Hollywood press agent, and he made himself one of the most famous names of our time. Who doesn't know about his yachts, his planes, his dozen houses, his wives, his hookers, his gifts, his parties, his friendships with movie stars and jet-set members, and his companionship with kings and world leaders? His dazzling existence outshone even that of his prime benefactors in the royal family of Saudi Arabia—a bedazzlement that led to their eventual disaffection for him.

Now, reportedly broke, or broke by the standards of people with great wealth—his yacht gone, his planes gone, his dozen houses gone, or going, and his reputation in smithereens—he has recently spent three months pacing restlessly in a six-by-eight-foot prison cell in Bern, Switzerland, where the majority of his fellow prisoners were in on drug charges. True, he dined there on gourmet food from the Schweizerhof Hotel, but he also had to clean his own cell and toilet as a small army of international lawyers fought to prevent his extradition to the United States to face charges of racketeering and obstruction of justice. Finally, Khashoggi dropped his efforts to avoid extradition when the Swiss ruled that he would face prosecution only for obstruction of justice and mail fraud, not for the more serious charges of racketeering and conspiracy. On July 19, accompanied by Swiss law-enforcement agents, he arrived in New York from Geneva first-class on a Swissair flight, handcuffed like a common criminal but dressed in an olive-drab safari suit with gold buttons and epaulets. He was immediately whisked to the federal courthouse on Foley Square, a tiny figure surrounded by a cadre of lawyers and federal marshals, where Judge John F. Keenan refused to grant him bail. He spent his first night in three years in America not in his Olympic Tower aerie but in the Metropolitan Correctional Center. No member of his immediate family was present to witness his humiliation.

Allegedly, he helped his friends Ferdinand and Imelda Marcos plunder the Philippines of some $160 million by fronting for them in illegal real-estate deals. When United States authorities attempted to return some of the Marcos booty to the new Philippine government, they discovered that the ownership of four large commercial buildings in New York City—the Crown Building at 730 Fifth Avenue, the Herald Center at 1 Herald Square, 40 Wall Street, and 200 Madison Avenue—had passed to Adnan Khashoggi. On paper it seemed that the sale of the buildings had taken place in 1985, before the fall of the Marcos regime, but authorities later charged that the documents had been fraudulently backdated. In addition, more than thirty paintings, valued at $200 million, that Imelda Marcos had allegedly purloined from the Metropolitan Museum of Manila, including works by Rubens, El Greco, Picasso, and Degas, were being stored by Khashoggi for the Marcoses, but it turned out that the pictures had been sold to Khashoggi as part of a cover-up. The art treasures were first hidden on his yacht and then moved to his penthouse in Cannes. The penthouse was raided by the French police in search of the pictures in April 1987, but it is believed that Khashoggi had been tipped off. He turned over nine of the paintings to the police, claiming to have sold the others to a Panamanian company, but investigators believe that he sold the pictures back to himself. The rest of the loot is thought to be in Athens. If he is found guilty, such charges could get him up to ten years in an American slammer.

In a vain delay tactic meant to forestall the extradition process as long as possible, he had at first refused to accept the hundreds of pages of English-language legal documentation in any language but Arabic, although he has spoken English nearly all his life and was educated partially in the United States.

People wonder why he went to Switzerland in the first place, when he was aware that arrest on an American warrant was a certainty there and that Switzerland could and probably would extradite him if the United States requested it. The answer is not known, although there is the possibility that Khashoggi, like others in that rarefied existence of power and great wealth, thought he was above the law and nothing would happen to him. Alternatively, there is the possibility, which has been suggested by some of his friends, that he was tired of the waiting game and went to

Bern to face the situation, because he was convinced that he had done nothing wrong and was innocent of the charges against him. There was neither furtiveness nor stealth, certainly no lessening of his usual mode of magnificence, in his arrival in Switzerland on April 17. He flew to Zurich by private plane. A private helicopter took him from the airport to Bern, where he had three Mercedeses at his disposal and registered in a very grand suite at the exclusive Schweizerhof Hotel. Ostensibly, his reason for visiting the city was to be treated by the eminent cellular therapist Dr. Augusto Gianoli with revitalization shots, whereby live cells taken from the embryo of an unborn lamb are injected into the patient to ward off the aging process. Dr. Gianoli's well-to-do patients often rest in the Schweizerhof after receiving the shots.

But apparently the revitalization of vital organs wasn't the only reason Adnan Khashoggi was in Bern on the day of his bust. He was killing two birds with one stone, and the other bit of business was an arms deal. Those closest to him are highly sensitive about the fact that he is always described in the media as a Middle Eastern arms dealer. True, he started out like that, they say, but they object to the fact that the arms-dealer label has stuck, and cite, instead, his other achievements. As one former partner told me, "Adnan brought billions and billions of dollars' worth of business to Lockheed and Boeing." Be that as it may, Khashoggi will always be best remembered in this country for his anything-for-a-buck participation in the Iran-contra affair, one of the most pathetic episodes in the history of American foreign policy, as well as a blight forever on the Reagan administration. True to form, the business he was conducting in his suite at the Schweizerhof that day was a sale of armored weapons.

When the Swiss police arrived at the suite, the other

two arms dealers mistakenly thought they were after them, and a slight panic ensued. The arms dealers left immediately by another door in the suite and were out of the country by private plane within an hour of Khashoggi's arrest. Khashoggi, remaining totally calm, asked the police if they would place him under house arrest in his suite in the Schweizerhof Hotel instead of putting him in jail, but the request was denied. Then he asked them not to handcuff him, and the request was granted. The prison in Bern where he was taken, booked, fingerprinted, and photographed is barely a five-minute walk from the Schweizerhof, but the group traveled by police car. The friends of Adnan Khashoggi deeply resent that the Swiss government released his mug shots to the media as if he were an ordinary criminal. "I went immediately to Bern after the arrest," said Prince Alfonso Hohenlohe, one of Khashoggi's very close friends in international society and a neighbor in Marbella, Spain, "but they wouldn't let me in to see him. I sent him a bottle of very good French red wine and a message to the jail. I hear he is the best prisoner they have ever had. I would cut off my arm to get him out of this situation."

For years now, misfortune has plagued Khashoggi. In 1987, Triad America Corporation, his American company, which was involved in a $400 million, twenty-five-acre complex of offices shops, and a hotel in Salt Lake City, filed for bankruptcy after its creditors, including architects, contractors, and banks, demanded payment. Khashoggi blamed the failure on "cash-flow problems." His most recent woe, reported by Reuters after his imprisonment in Bern, is that the privately owned National Commercial Bank of Saudi Arabia is suing him for $22 million, plus interest. The process of falling from a great height is subtle in the beginning, but there are those who have an instinctive ability to sniff out the first signs of failure and fading fortune. Long before the public disclosures of seized planes and impounded houses and bankruptcies, word went out among some of the fashionable jewelers of the world, from Rome to Beverly Hills, that no more credit was to be given to Adnan Khashoggi, because he had ceased to pay his bills. Then came the whispered stories of how he was draining money from his own projects to maintain his life-style; of unpaid servants in the houses and unpaid crew members on the yacht; of unpaid maintenance on his two-floor, 7,200-square-foot condominium with indoor swimming pool at the Olympic Tower on Fifth Avenue in New York; of unpaid helicopter lessons for his daughter, Nabila, even while the extravagant parties proclaiming denial of the truth continued. In fact, the more persistent the rumors of Khashoggi's financial collapse grew, the more extravagant his parties became. Nico Minardos, a former associate of Khashoggi's who was arrested during Iranscam for his involvement in a $2.5 billion deal with Iran for forty-six Skyhawk aircraft and later cleared, said, "Adnan is a lovely man. I like him. He is the greatest P.R. man in the world. When he gave his fiftieth-birthday party, our company was overdrawn at the bank in Madrid by $6 million. And that's about what his party cost. Last year he sold an apartment to pay for his birthday party."

Probably the most telling story in Khashoggi's downfall was repeated to me in London by a witness to the scene, who wished not to be identified. The King of Morocco was staying in the royal suite of Claridge's. The King of Jordan, also visiting London at the time, came to call on the King of Morocco. There is a marble stairway in the main hall of Claridge's which leads up to the royal suite. Shortly after the doors of the suite closed, Adnan Khashoggi, having heard of the meeting, arrived breathlessly at the hotel by taxi. Used to keeping company with kings, he sent a message up to the royal suite that he was downstairs. He was told that he would not be received.

Shortly after I was asked to write about Adnan Khashoggi, following his arrest, his executive assistant, Robert Shaheen, contacted this magazine, aware of my assignment. He said that I should call him, and I did.

"I understand," I said, "that you are the number-two man to Mr. Khashoggi."

"I am Mr. Khashoggi's number-one man," he corrected me. Then he said, "What is it you want? What will your angle be in your story?" I told him that at that point I didn't know. Shaheen's reverence for his boss was evident in every sentence, and his descriptions of him were sometimes florid. "He dared to dream dreams that no one else dared to dream," he said with a bit of a catch to his voice. He proceeded to list some of the accomplishments of his boss, whom he always referred to as the Chief. "The Chief was responsible for opening the West to Saudi Arabia. The Chief saved the Cairo telephone system. The Chief saved Lockheed from going bankrupt." He then told me, "You must talk with Max Helzel. He is a representative of Lockheed. Get him before he dies. He is getting old. Mention my name to him."

An American of Syrian descent, Shaheen went to Saudi Arabia to teach English in the late fifties, and there he met Khashoggi. He has described his job with Khashoggi in their long association as being similar to that of the chief of staff at the White House. Anyone wishing to meet with Khashoggi for a business proposition had to go through him first. He carried the Chief's money. He scheduled the air fleet's flights. He traveled with him. He became his apologist when things started to go wrong. After the debacle in Salt Lake City, he said, "People in Salt Lake City can't hold Adnan responsible. He delegated all responsibility to American executives, and it was up to them to make a success. Adnan still believes in Salt Lake City." And he became, like his boss, a very rich man himself through the contacts he made. At the close of our conversation, Shaheen told me that it was very unlikely that I would get into the prison in Bern, although he would do what he could to help me.

The night before I left New York, I was at a dinner party in a beautiful Fifth Avenue apartment overlooking Central Park. There were sixteen people, among them the high-flying Donald and Ivana Trump, one of New York's richest and most discussed couples, and a major topic of conversation was Khashoggi's imprisonment. "I read every word about Adnan Khashoggi," Donald Trump said to me.

A story that Trump frequently tells is about his purchase of Khashoggi's yacht, the 282-foot, $70 million *Nabila,* thought to be the most opulent private vessel afloat. In addition to the inevitable discotheque, with laser beams that projected Khashoggi's face, the floating palace also had an operating room and a morgue, with coffins. Forced to sell it for a mere $30 million, Khashoggi did not want Trump to keep the name *Nabila,* because it was his daughter's name. Trump had no intention, ever, of keeping the name. He had already decided to rename it the *Trump Princess.* But for some reason Khashoggi thought Trump meant to retain the name, and he knocked a million dollars off the asking price to ensure the name change. Trump accepted the deduction.

"Khashoggi was a great broker and a lousy businessman," Trump said to me that night. "He understood the art of bringing people together and putting together a better deal than almost anyone—all the bullshitting part, of talk and entertainment—but he never knew how to invest his money. If he had put his commissions into a bank in Switzerland, he'd be a rich man today, but he invested it, and he made lousy choices."

In London, on my way to Bern, I contacted Viviane Ventura, an English public-relations woman who is a great friend of Khashoggi's. She attended Richard Nixon's second inauguration in January 1973 with him. Ventura told me more or less the same thing Shaheen had told me. "The lawyers won't let anyone near him. They don't want any statements. There's a lot more to it than we know. This is a terrible thing that your government is doing. Adnan is one of the most generous, most caring men."

The five-foot-four-inch, two-hundred-pound, financially troubled megastar was born in Saudi Arabia in 1935, the oldest of six children. His father, who was an enormous influence in his life, was a highly respected doctor, remembered for bringing the first X-ray machine to Saudi Arabia. He became the personal physician to King Ibn Saud, a position that brought him and his family into close proximity with court circles. Adnan was sent to Victoria College in Alexandria, Egypt, an exclusive boys' academy where King Hussein was a classmate and where the students were caned if they did not speak English. Later he went to California State University in Chico, and was overwhelmed by the freedom of the life-style of American girls. There he began to entertain as a way of establishing himself, and to broker his first few deals. Early on he won favor with many of the Saudi royal princes, particularly Prince Sultan, the eighteenth son, and Prince Talal, the twenty-third son, who became his champions. In the 1970s, when the price of Arab oil soared to new heights, he began operating in high gear. Although Northrop was his best-known client, he also represented Lockheed, Teledyne National, Chrysler, and Raytheon in the Middle East. By the mid-1970s, his commissions from Lockheed alone totaled more than $100 million. In addition, his firm, Triad, had holdings that included thirteen banks and a chain of steak houses on the West Coast of the United States, cattle ranches in North and South America, resort developments in Fiji and Egypt, a chain of hotels in Australia, and various real-estate, insurance, and shipping concerns. The first Arab to develop land in the United States, he organized and invested many millions in Triad America Corporation in Salt Lake City. He became an intimate of kings and heads of state, a great gift giver, a provider of women, a perfect host, and the creator of a life-style that would become world-renowned for its extravagance. Even now, in the overlapping murkiness of deposed dictators, the baby Doc Duvaliers, those other Third World escapees with their nation's pillage, are living in the South of France in a house found for them by Adnan Khashoggi, belonging to his son.

Perhaps not surprisingly, having presented myself as a journalist from the United States, I was not allowed to visit Khashoggi in the prison at 22 Genfergasse in Bern. It is a modern jail, six stories high, located in the center of the city. The windows are vertically barred, and the prisoners take their exercise on the roof. At night the exterior walls are floodlit. For a city prison there is an amazing silence about the place. No prisoners were screaming out the windows at passersby. There were no guards in sight on the elevated catwalk. Much has been made of the fact that

Khashoggi got his meals from the dining room of the nearby Schweizerhof Hotel, but that and a rented television set and access to a fax machine were in fact his only privileges. In the beginning, waiters in uniform from the hotel would carry the trays over, but they were photographed too much and asked too many questions by reporters. The waiters and the maître d' that I spoke with in the restaurant of the Schweizerhof were reluctant to talk about the meals being sent to the jail, as if they were under orders not to speak. The evening I waited to see Khashoggi's meal arrive, a young girl brought it on a tray. She was not in uniform. She got to the jail at precisely six, and the gourmet meal was wrapped in silver foil to keep it hot.

Everywhere, people speak admiringly of Nabila Khashoggi, the first child and only daughter of Adnan, by his first wife, Soraya, the mother also of his first four sons. Nabila is the only family member who remained in Bern throughout her father's ordeal, although one of the sons, Mohammed, is said to have visited once. A handsome woman in her late twenties, Nabila at one time had aspirations to movie stardom. In 1981, she became so distraught over the notoriety and sensationalism of her mother's divorce action against her father that she attempted suicide by taking an overdose of sleeping pills. Between father and daughter there is enormous affection and mutual respect. It was after her that Khashoggi named his spectacular yacht.

Nabila visited the prison on an almost daily basis, providing comfort and news and relaying messages to her father. The rest of the time she remained in total seclusion in her suite at the Schweizerhof. On occasion she dined at off hours in the dining room, but she did not loiter in the public rooms of the hotel, and reporters, however long they sat in the lobby hoping to get a look at her, waited in vain. I wrote her a note introducing myself and left it at the desk. I mentioned the names of several mutual friends, among them George Hamilton, the Hollywood actor, who had sold Nabila his house in Beverly Hills for $7 million three years ago, during the period when Nabila was trying to launch a career as a film actress. The house was allegedly a gift to Hamilton from Imelda Marcos when she was still the First Lady of the Philippines. I also mentioned in my note that I had been in touch with Robert Shaheen, Khashoggi's aide and friend, and that he was aware that I would contact her.

From there, I walked back to my hotel, the Bellevue Palace, and as I entered my room the telephone was ringing. It was Nabila Khashoggi. Polite, courteous, she also sounded weary and wept out; there was incredible sadness in her voice. She said that the lawyers had forbidden her or any member of her family to speak to anyone from the press, and that it would therefore not be possible for me to interview her. She thanked me, when I asked her how she was holding up, and said that she was well. In closing, she said in a very strong voice, "I think you should know that Robert Shaheen has not worked for my father for several years, and that we do not speak to him." This information shocked me, after Shaheen's passionate representation of himself to me as Khashoggi's closest associate, but it was only the first of many surprises and contradictions I would encounter in the people who have surrounded Adnan Khashoggi during his extraordinary life. Intimates of Khashoggi told me that he often had fallings-out with those close to him, and that sometimes they would be reinstated in his good graces, and sometimes not.

Later that day Nabila Khashoggi called again to ask if I spoke German. I said no. She said there was an article in that day's *Der Bund*, the Swiss-German newspaper, that I should get and have translated. The article was positive in tone, and said that perhaps the Americans did not have sufficient evidence to cause the Swiss to extradite Khashoggi. John Marshall, a British newspaperman based in Bern, said about the article, "The supposition is that the Americans have jumped the gun. The charges presented so far will not stand up in the Swiss court." Everywhere, I heard people say, "If Khashoggi tells what he knows, there will be enormous embarrassment in Washington." The reference was not to the charges pending against Khashoggi in the matter of Imelda and Ferdinand Marcos. It had to do with Iranscam. Roy Boston, a wealthy developer in Marbella and a great friend of Khashoggi's, said, "I can't imagine that the Americans really want him back in the United States. It would be a mistake. The president and the former president would be smeared. And the same with the King of Saudi Arabia. Adnan would never say one word against the king. But the Americans? Why should he keep quiet? If he really starts talking, good gracious me, there will be red faces around the world."

One of the unknown factors in the Khashoggi predicament is whether the King of Saudi Arabia will come to his aid, and on that point opinions differ. "I don't know how the king feels about Adnan now," said Roy Boston. "He did a lot of handling of Saudi affairs, with the king and without the king. There is always the possibility that he is still doing things for the king."

John Marshall said, "If the King of Saudi Arabia stands behind him, he will never let Khashoggi go to jail in the United States."

"Do you think the king will come to Khashoggi's rescue?" I asked Nico Minardos.

"No way!" he said. "The king doesn't like him. Only Prince Sultan likes him now."

. . .

The most mystifying family matter, during Khashoggi's imprisonment, was the nonappearance of Lamia Khashoggi, the beautiful second wife of Adnan, who never visited her husband in Bern. Several people close to the Khashoggis feel that their marriage has for some time been more ceremonial than conjugal. Lamia sat out her husband's jail time at their penthouse in Cannes with their son, Ali. I listened in on a telephone call placed by a mutual European friend who asked if she would talk with me. Like Nabila, she declined, under lawyers' orders. When the friend persisted, she acted as if she had been disconnected, saying, "I can't hear you. I can't hear you. Hello . . . hello?" and then hung up.

Until recently, Lamia, who was born Laura Biancolini in Italy, was a highly visible member of the jet set, palling around with such luminous figures as the flamboyant Princess Gloria von Thurn und Taxis, the young wife of the billionaire aristocrat Prince Johannes von Thurn und Taxis. At the Thurn und Taxises' eighteenth-century costume ball in their five-hundred-room palace in Regensburg, Germany, in 1986, Lamia Khashoggi made an entrance that people still talk about. Dressed as Mme. de Pompadour, she came down the palace stairway flanked by two Nubians —"real Nubians, from the Sudan"—carrying long-handled feathered fans. Her wig was twice as high as the wig of her hostess, who was dressed as Marie Antoinette, and her gold-and-white gown was so wide that she could not navigate a turn in the stairway and had to descend sideways, assisted by her Nubians. It was felt that she had attempted to upstage her hostess, a no-no in high society, and since then, though not necessarily related to the incident, their friendship has cooled. In the midst of the Thurn und Taxises' million-dollar revel, attendees at the ball tell me, there was much behind-the-fan talk that the Khashoggi fortune was in peril. Khashoggi had secured oil and mining rights in the Republic of the Sudan and had used those rights as collateral to borrow money. When his friend Gaafar Nimeiry, the president of the Sudan, was overthrown in 1985, the succeeding administration canceled the contracts he had negotiated, and one Sudanese broadcaster protested that Nimeiry had sold the Sudan to Adnan Khashoggi.

Laura Biancolini began traveling on Khashoggi's yacht, along with what is known in some circles as a bevy of lovelies, at the age of seventeen. She converted to Islam, changed her name to Lamia, and became Khashoggi's second wife before giving birth to her only child and Adnan's fifth son, Ali, now nine, in West Palm Beach, Florida. Marriage to a man like Adnan Khashoggi cannot have been easy for either of his wives. Women for hire were part and parcel of his everyday life, and he often sent girls as gifts to men with whom he was attempting to do business. "They lend beauty and fragrance to the surroundings," he has been quoted as saying.

His previous wife, who was born Sandra Patricia Jarvis-Daly, the daughter of a London waitress, married him when she was nineteen, long before he was internationally famous. She also converted to Islam and took the name Soraya. They first lived in Beirut and later in London. A great beauty, she is the mother of Nabila and the first four Khashoggi sons: Mohammed, twenty-five, Khalid, twenty-three, Hussein, twenty-one, and Omar, nineteen. Although their marriage was an open one, the end came when he heard that she was having an affair with his pal President Gaafar Nimeiry of the Sudan. He was already involved with the seventeen-year-old Laura Biancolini. In Islamic tradition, a divorce may be executed by the male's reciting "I divorce thee" three times. Subsequently, Soraya experienced financial discontent with her lot and complained that the usually generous Khashoggi, whose life-style cost him a quarter of a million dollars a day to maintain, was being tight with his alimony payments to the mother of his first five children. With the aid of the celebrated divorce lawyer Marvin Mitchelson, she sued her former husband for $2.5 billion, which she figured to be half his fortune. She had, in the meantime, married and divorced a young man who had been the beau of a daughter she had had out of wedlock before marrying Khashoggi and bearing Nabila. She had also engaged in a highly publicized love affair with Winston Churchill, the grandson of the late British prime minister and the son of the socially unimpeachable Mrs. Averell Harriman of Washington, D.C. Concurrently with that romance, she bore another child, her seventh, generally thought to be Churchill's child but never publicly acknowledged as such. As choreographed by Marvin Mitchelson, the alimony case received notorious worldwide coverage, which caused great embarrassment to all members of the family, as well as an increased disenchantment with Khashoggi on the part of the Saudi royal family. Ultimately, Soraya received a measly $2 million divorce settlement, but, more important, she was also reinstated in the family. Right up to the bust and confinement in Bern, she attended all the major Khashoggi parties and even posed with Adnan and Lamia and their combined children for a 1988 Christmas family photograph.

Khashoggi's private life has always been a public mess. "I haven't spoken to my ex-uncle since 1983, after the Cap d'Ail scandal, when one of his aides went to jail for prosti-

tution and drugs," said Dodi Fayed, executive producer of
the film *Chariots of Fire* and the son of the controversial
international businessman Mohammed Al Fayed, the
owner of the Ritz Hotel in Paris and Harrods department
store in London, over which there was one of the bitterest
takeover battles of the decade. Dodi Fayed's mother,
Samira, who died two years ago, was Adnan Khashoggi's
sister. Khashoggi and Mohammed Al Fayed were once
business partners. Since the business partnership and the
marriage of Samira and Fayed both broke up bitterly, the
relationship between the two families has been poisonous.
Dodi Fayed's use of the term "ex-uncle" indicates that he
no longer even considers Khashoggi a relation.

The Cap d'Ail affair had to do with a French woman
named Mireille Griffon, who became known on the Côte
d'Azur as Madame Mimi, a serious though brief rival to the
famous Madame Claude, the Parisian madam who serviced
the upper classes and business elite of Europe for three
decades with some of the most beautiful women in the
world, many of whom have gone on to marry into the
upper strata. Partnered with Madame Mimi was Khashoggi's employee Abdo Khawagi, a onetime masseur. Madame Mimi's operation boasted a roster of three hundred
girls between the ages of eighteen and twenty-five. A per-
fectionist in her trade, Madame Mimi groomed and dressed
her girls so that they would be presentable escorts for the
important men they were servicing. The girls, who were
sent to Khashoggi in groups of twos and threes, called him
papa gâteau, or sugar daddy, because he was extremely generous with them. In addition to their fee, 40 percent of
which went to Madame Mimi, the girls received furs and
jewels and tips that sometimes equaled or surpassed the
fee. One of the greatest whoremongers in the world, Khashoggi was generous to a fault and provided the same girls

to members of the Saudi royal family as well as to business associates and party friends. His role as a provider of women for business purposes was not unlike the role his uncle Yussuf Yassin had performed for King Ibn Saud. After the French police on the Riviera were alerted, a watch was put on the operations and the madam's telephone lines were tapped. In time an arrest was made, and the case went to trial in Nice in February 1984, amid nasty publicity. Madame Mimi, who is believed to have personally grossed $1.2 million in ten months, got a year and a half in jail. Khawagi, the procurer, got a year in prison. And Khashoggi sailed away on the *Nabila*.

Of more recent vintage is the story of the beautiful Indian prostitute Pamella Bordes, who was discovered working as a researcher in the House of Commons after having bedded some of the most distinguished men in England. In a three-part interview in the London *Daily Mail,* she made her sexual revelations about Khashoggi shortly after he was imprisoned in Bern, a bit of bad timing for the beleaguered arms dealer. Pamella was introduced into the great world by Sri Chandra Swamiji Maharaj, a Hindu teacher with worldly aspirations known simply as the Swami or Swamiji, although sometimes he is addressed by his worshipers with the papal-sounding title of Your Holiness. The Swami, who is said to possess miraculous powers, has served as a spiritual and financial adviser to, among others, Ferdinand Marcos, who credited him with once saving his life, Adnan Khashoggi, Mohammed Al Fayed, and both the Sultan of Brunei and the second of his two wives, Princess Mariam, a half-Japanese former airline stewardess. (Princess Mariam is less popular with the royal family of Brunei than the sultan's first wife, Queen Saleha, his cousin, who bore him six children, but Princess Mariam is clearly the sultan's favorite.) The Swami played a key role in the Mohammed Al Fayed–Tiny Rowland battle for the ownership of Harrods in London when he secretly taped a conversation with Fayed which vaguely indicated that the money Fayed had used to purchase Harrods was really the Sultan of Brunei's. The Swami sold the tape to Rowland for $2 million. Subsequently, he was arrested in India on charges of breaking India's foreign-exchange regulations.

The Swami introduced Pamella Bordes to Khashoggi after she failed to be entered as Miss India in the Miss Universe contest of 1982. Pamella, a young woman of immense ambition, was invited to Khashoggi's Marbella estate, La Baraka, shortly after meeting him. In her *Daily Mail* account of her five-day stay, she said, "I had a room to myself. I used to get up very late. They have the most fabulous room service. You can order up the most sensational food and drink anytime you want." She despised the other girls who were sent along on the junket with her, referring to them as "cheapo" girls who "ordered chips with everything. They smothered their food with tomato ketchup and slopped it all over the bed. It was disgusting." The girls were taken shopping in the boutiques of Marbella and told to buy anything they wanted, all at Khashoggi's expense. In the evening, they dressed for dinner. She described Khashoggi as always having a male secretary by his side with a cordless telephone. "Non-stop calls were coming in. . . . It was business, business non-stop." She slept with him in what she described as the largest bed she had ever seen. "I was very happy to have sex with him, and he did not want me to do anything kinky or sleazy."

After their liaison, she became part of the Khashoggi bank of women ready and willing to be used in his business deals. In the article, she described in detail a flight she was sent on from Geneva to Riyadh to service a Prince Mohammed, a senior member of the royal family, "who would be a key man in buying arms and vital technology." The prince came in, looked her over, and said something to his secretary in Arabic. The secretary then took Pamella into a bathroom, where she was told to bathe and to wash her hair and blow-dry it straight. The prince, it seemed, wanted her with straight hair. Then she went to the prince's room and had sex with him. The next day she was shipped back to Geneva. "He was somebody very, very important to Khashoggi. Khashoggi was keeping him supplied with girls. Khashoggi has all these deals going, and he needs a lot of girls for sexual bribes. I was just part of an enormous group. I was used as sexual bait."

In an astonishing book called *By Hook or by Crook,* written by the Washington lawyer Steven Martindale, who traveled for several years with Khashoggi and the Swami, the author catalogs Khashoggi's use of women in business deals. The book, which was published in England, was then banned there by a court order sought not by Khashoggi but by Mohammed Al Fayed.

In Marbella, Adnan Khashoggi is a ranking social figure and a very popular man. He has a magnificent villa on a huge estate that he bought from the father of Thierry Roussel, the last husband of the tragic heiress Christina Onassis. After Khashoggi bought his house in Marbella in the late seventies, he said to Alain Cavro, an architect who for twenty years has worked exclusively for him and who refers to him as A. K., "I want to add ten bedrooms, salons, and a big kitchen, and I want it right away. I need to have it finished in time for my party." Cavro told me that he had ninety-three days, after the plans were approved. Workers worked twenty-four hours a day, in shifts, and the house was completed in time for the party. "A. K. has a way of convincing you of almost anything," Cavro told me. "He can persuade you with his charm to change your mind after you have made it up. He builds people up. He introduces people in such a flattering way as to make them blush. He finds very quickly the point to touch them the most. Afterwards, people say, 'You saw how nice he was to me?' People feel flattered, almost in love with him."

Khashoggi was responsible for bringing Prince Fahd, now King Fahd, of Saudi Arabia to Marbella for the first time. That visit, which resulted in Fahd's building a mosque and a palace-type residence in Marbella, designed by Cavro, changed the economy of the fashionable resort.

In the summer of 1988, a Texas multimillionairess named Nancy Hamon chartered the ship *Sea Goddess* and invited eighty friends, mostly other Texas millionaires, on a four-day cruise, starting in Málaga, Spain. The high point of the trip was an elaborate and expensive lunch party at the Khashoggi villa in Marbella. Khashoggi, already in severe financial distress, put on the dog in the hope of lining up some of these rich Texas backers to shore up his failing empire.

"Oh, darling, it was an experience," said one of the guests. "There were guardhouses with guards with machine guns, and closed-circuit television everywhere. The whole house is gaudy Saudi, if you know what I mean. They have Liberace's piano, with rhinestones in it, and the chairs are all trimmed with gilt, and a disco, naturally, with a floor that lights up. Do you get the picture? You can see Africa and Gibraltar from the terrace—that was nice. They had flamenco music pounding away at lunch. Some of the guests got into the flamenco act after a few drinks. I'll say this for Mr. Khashoggi, he was a tremendously gracious host. And so was the wife, Lamia. She had on a pink dress trimmed with gold—Saint Laurent, I think—and rubies, lots of rubies, with a décolletage to set off the rubies, and ruby earrings, great big drop earrings. This is lunch, remember. He has built a gazebo that could hold hundreds of people, with silver and gold tinsel decorations, like on a Christmas tree. The food was wonderful. Tons of staff, as well as a lot of men in black suits—his assistants, I suppose. After lunch we were taken on a tour of the stables. The stables are in better taste than the house. Everything pristine. And Arabian horses. It was marvelous. It was amazing he could continue living on that scale. Everyone knew he was on his uppies."

These days, Khashoggi is constantly discussed in the bar of the exclusive Marbella Club. Very few people who know him do not speak highly of his charm, his generosity, and the beauty of his parties. The cunning streak that flaws his character is less apparent to his society and party friends than it is to his business associates. "When Adnan comes back here, I told Nabila that I'll give the first dinner for him," said Roy Boston. "He has been a considerable friend to some people here in Marbella. He is always faithful to his friends. He remembers birthdays. He does very personal things. That's why we like him. Now that he's in trouble, no one here is saying 'I don't like him' or 'I saw it coming.' "

"He is a fantastic host," said Prince Alfonso Hohenlohe. "He takes care of his guests the whole night—heads of state, noble princes, archdukes. He has a genius for seating people in the correct place. He always knows everyone's name, and he can seat 150 people *exactly* right without using place cards. All these problems he is in are because of his great heart and his goodness. I was at a private dinner party in New York when Marcos asked him to help save them. For A. K., there were no laws, no skies, no limits. With all the money he had, he should have bought the *New*

York Times, or the *Los Angeles Times,* and NBC. He should have bought the media. The media can destroy a president, and it can destroy Khashoggi."

One grand lady in Marbella reminisced, "Which party was it? I don't remember. Khashoggi's birthday, I think. There were balloons everywhere that said I AM THE GREATEST on them, and he crowned himself king that night and walked through the party wearing an ermine robe. It was so amusing. But odd now, under the circumstances." Another said, "He's the only host I've ever seen who walks each guest to the front door at the end of the party. Even when we left at 8:30 in the morning, he walked us out to our cars. He's marvelous, really." Another, an English peeress, said, "Alfonso Hohenlohe's sister, Beatriz, the Duchess of Arion, invited us to dinner at Khashoggi's. I said I wouldn't *dream* of going to Mr. Khashoggi's on a second-hand invitation, and the next thing I knew, the wife, what's-her-name, Lamia, called and invited us, and then they sent around a car, and so, of course, we went. There were eighty, seated. It was for that Swami, what's-his-name, with a vegetarian dinner, because of the Swami— delicious, as a matter of fact. I said to my husband, or he said to me, I don't remember which, 'That Swami's a big phony.' But Mr. Khashoggi was very nice, and he entertains beautifully. Most of the people down here just feel sorry for him. For God's sake, don't use my name in your article."

An American writer who spends time in the resort said to me, "That gang you were with last night at the Marbella Club, they're all going to like him, but I know a lot of people here in Marbella who don't like him, the kind of people he owes money to. He gives big parties and owes money to the help. I'll give you the number of the guy who fixes his lawn mowers. He owes the lawn-mower fixer $2,000."

Whether Khashoggi is really broke or not is anybody's guess. Roy Boston said, "Is he broke? I can't answer that. Four weeks before he was arrested, he gave a party here that must have cost a fortune. It was a big show, so he can't be that broke, but he might be officially broke. If you were once worth $5 billion, you must have a little nest egg somewhere. He's not stupid, you know." A former American associate, wishing anonymity, said, "Adnan is not broke. I don't care what anyone says. He's still got $40 million coming in from Lockheed. That's a commission alone." Steven Martindale thinks he really is broke. "He owes every friend he ever borrowed money from." When Khashoggi's bail was set in New York at $10 million one week after his extradition, however, his brothers paid it immediately.

In his business dealings with the Sultan of Brunei, Khashoggi never rushed things. "Khashoggi had a personal approach: he was willing to show the Sultan a good time, willing and eager to take the Sultan around London or bring a party to the Sultan's palace in Brunei. He gave every appearance of not needing the Sultan, but rather of being another rich man like the Sultan himself who just wanted to enjoy the Sultan's company," writes James Bartholomew in his biography of the Sultan of Brunei, *The Richest Man in the World.* Business, of course, followed.

Alain Cavro, who supervised all the building and reconstruction projects undertaken by any of the companies within the Khashoggi empire, was a close observer of the business life of Adnan Khashoggi. In 1975, Cavro became president of Triad Condas International, a contemporary design firm that built both palaces and military bases, mostly in the Middle East and Saudi Arabia. When Khashoggi met with kings and heads of state, he would usually take Cavro with him. Khashoggi would say to his hosts, "Give me the honor to demonstrate what we can do, either something personal for you or for the country." He meant a new wing for the palace, a pavilion for the swimming pool, a new country club, or, possibly, but not usually, even something for the public good. Whatever it was that was desired, Cavro would do the drawings overnight and then Khashoggi would present the architectural renderings and follow that up with the immediate building of whatever it was, as his personal gift to the king or head of state. In the inner circle this process was called Mission Impossible; it was designed to show what A. K. could do. "In Africa, heads of state are impressed with magic," said Cavro. Business followed. Cavro, totally loyal to A. K., said, "But these gifts must not be construed as bribes, but rather as a demonstration of how he could do things fast and well. A. K. felt that the heads of state were doing him a favor to allow him to demonstrate how he did things."

Cavro described to me Khashoggi's total concentration when he was involved in a business deal. When the pilot of one of his three planes would announce that they were landing in twenty minutes and that the chief of state was waiting on the tarmac, Khashoggi would go right on with what he was doing until the last possible second. Then he would change into either Western or Eastern garb, depending on where he was landing. In each of his private jets were two wardrobes: one contained his beautifully tailored three-piece bespoke suits from London's Savile Row, in all sizes to deal with his constantly fluctuating weight; in the other were white cotton *thobes,* headdresses, and black ribbed headbands, the traditional Saudi dress. As he deplaned, he would go immediately into the next deal and give that affair his full attention. He was also able to conduct several meetings at the same time, going from room to room, always zeroing in on the exact point under discussion. He constantly emphasized how important it is to understand what the other party to a deal needs and wants.

But long before Adnan Khashoggi's arrest in Bern and his extradition to the United States, his time had passed. His position as the star broker of the Arab world was no longer unique. He had set the example, but now the sons of other wealthy Saudi families were being educated in the United States and England, in far better colleges and universities than Chico State, and were being trained to perform the same role as Khashoggi, with less flash and flamboyance. Khashoggi had, in fact, become an embarrassment. A Jordanian princess described him in May of this year as a disgrace to the Arab world.

With sadness, Cavro told me, "Salt Lake City was the beginning of the end for him. And he lost so much money. A. K. began to change. The parties were too extravagant. And his personal life." He shook his head. "Everything was too frantic. Even his brother wanted him to lower his lifestyle. That kind of publicity is a disease."

September 1989

MEMENTO MORI

I have never murdered any one, for I was carefully brought-up, and brought-up to be careful. I have, however, known some murderers—pleasant enough fellows—and I have sometimes wanted to commit a murder.

From Valentine's Days, *London, 1934,*
by Valentine, Viscount Castlerosse,
later the Earl of Kenmare, fourth husband of
Enid Lindeman Cameron Cavendish Furness Kenmare.

THERE ARE people in fashionable society who, throughout their lives, carry with them the burden of their scandals, as ineradicable from their personality as a tattoo on their forearm. Ann Woodward, the beautiful widow of the handsome and very rich William Woodward, never again after her husband's death walked into a drawing room, or anywhere else, without someone whispering, "She's the woman who shot and killed her husband." Perhaps it was by accident, as she claimed. Perhaps not. It didn't matter. It was what people said about her, and she knew they said it. The same is true of Claus von Bülow, the husband of the beautiful and very rich Sunny von Bülow. Even acquitted, as he was, he will never enter a room, or a restaurant, or a theater, without someone whispering, "He's the man who was accused of trying to kill his wife."

Another such person, forever notorious, was the beautiful Enid Kenmare, or Lady Kenmare, or, to be perfectly correct, the Countess of Kenmare, a mythic figure of the French Riviera and chatelaine of a great house, the villa La Fiorentina, who lost four husbands, all by death. W. Somerset Maugham, at a lunch party on the Côte d'Azur shortly after he moved permanently to the Riviera, said, "Apparently there is a lady who lives on Cap Ferrat who has killed all her husbands." Unknown to him, the lady about whom he was speaking, Enid Kenmare, was at the lunch party and heard the remark. She took no offense, and in time she and Maugham became the greatest of friends and played bridge together constantly; she even hid his Impressionist-art collection from the Nazis for him. But people came to say about her, wherever she went, "She's the lady who killed all her husbands," a legend that persisted for thirty years, into her old age, and that still is repeated eighteen years after her death.

The beauty of the much-married and much-widowed Enid Kenmare was so renowned in the years before and after the Second World War that it was said people stood on chairs in the lobby of the Hôtel de Paris in Monte Carlo to catch a glimpse of her as she passed through. She was reported to be fabulously rich, owing to the various inheritances from her deceased husbands, who included an American millionaire, Roderick Cameron, and three English aristocrats: Brigadier General Frederick Cavendish, Viscount Furness, and the Earl of Kenmare. She was also a constant and successful gambler, who frequented the casinos of Monte Carlo and Beaulieu nightly, playing mostly trente-et-quarante. Her friends of that period claim that people would drop their cards or chips to look at her when she swept past the entrance without bothering to show the required passport, so well known was she. There were always great stacks of chips in front of her, and she never showed any emotion, whether she lost or won. According to one popular story, she purchased her magnificent estate at Cap Ferrat with her winnings from a single big gambling night at the casino, but, like every story about her, it may or may not be true. "Enid became such a character that people began to invent stories about her, and she told stories about herself that contributed to that sort of talk," Anthony Pawson, a septuagenarian bon vivant, told me in London shortly before his death in December. "Enid was a mythomaniac," said an old bridge partner of Lady Kenmare's on the Riviera. "She'd invent stories, and that could be dangerous. You don't know why those people lie, but they do."

"She had fantastic posture, wore cabochon emeralds or rubies, and dressed for the evening in diaphanous and flowing gowns," remembered one of her friends. "It wasn't so much that she was superior as that she was in another sphere almost. She sort of floated, and she had the most amazing eyes."

Enid Kenmare's "other sphere" was, from all accounts, dope. "She kept her beauty because she didn't drink, but she was a heroin addict. Legally a heroin addict. She was on the drug list, you know, registered. Marvelous skin, never went in the sun," said a gentleman in New York. Another gentleman, in London, said, "She smoked opium certainly, and took heroin." A lady friend, more cautious, said, "I never noticed when people took dope." But another lady friend said, "She lived in a haze of drugs." Everyone commented on the fact that she drank Coca-Cola morning, noon, and night.

"If Enid were alive today, she would be, let me see, ninety-eight or ninety-nine, I suppose," said the Honorable David Herbert of Tangier, the son of, brother of, and uncle of various Earls of Pembroke, who knew Enid Kenmare for years and attended her fourth wedding, to Valentine Kenmare. "She walked down the aisle like a first-time bride," he told me, remembering the occasion. "She was very very wicked. Once, she said to me, 'Do I look like a murderess? Tell me, do I?'"

The other great beauties of her era, to whom she was often compared—Diana Cooper, Daisy Fellowes, and Violet Trefusis—are all dead. So, too, are most of the men she knew. But there are a number still, deep in their eighties now, or nineties, who remember her. Some are in rest homes. Some have come on hard times and live in greatly reduced circumstances from the period in which they flourished. Some are on walkers or canes. One died a week after I spoke with him in his modest bed-sitting-room in London. Another had a stroke. Still another had become so deaf that it was impossible to communicate with her. Different people remembered Lady Kenmare differently. One old gentleman said, "We used to call Enid the cement Venus. Actually, I think Emerald Cunard made up that name." Another said impatiently, "No, no, not *cement* Venus. It was the *stucco* Venus. That's what we called her. Stucco. Not cement." Some remembered her quite erroneously. A grand old dowager marchioness, wearing a fox fur around her shoulders, walked slowly across the lobby of Claridge's in London, leaning on her stick. "I remember Enid," she said.

"She pushed Lord Furness out the porthole." And there are also the friends of her children, who are now in their sixties and seventies, who were, in those days, the younger crowd. "I don't think Enid killed anybody, but she might have given them drugs and helped them along," said one friend of her son Rory, who died in 1985 at the age of seventy.

She was born Enid Lindeman in Australia, one of five children. Her father, Charles Lindeman, raised horses and introduced vines to New South Wales, thereby pioneering the wine industry in that country. In later years, when she bred racehorses in Kenya, she would talk about riding bareback as a child. Her rise to international social status began at the age of sixteen, when she allegedly became the mistress of Bernard Baruch, the American financier and presidential adviser, who was then in his forties. During their liaison, Enid, an accomplished artist, had a brief stint in Hollywood as a scenery painter. Their friendship lasted until the end of Baruch's life, when Enid returned to New York to say good-bye to him before he died. A skeptic remarked to me that the trip was to ensure that she would be "remembered financially by Mr. Baruch."

Baruch felt that his beautiful young mistress should be married properly, and it was he who introduced her to her first husband, the American Roderick Cameron, who, like Baruch, was much older than she. They were married in 1913, and he died the following year, leaving her with a son, also called Roderick Cameron, known as Rory, who would himself in time become a known figure in social, literary, and decorating circles.

In 1917 she married for the second time, in England, where she had moved, to Brigadier General Frederick Cavendish, known as Caviar Cavendish. "At that time, it was the thing to do, to marry soldiers," said Tony Pawson. Peter Quennell, the octogenarian writer, described Enid then as "a very autocratic beauty, greatly admired by her husband's junior officers." At White's Club in London, an elderly gentleman listening to this description guffawed and winked, to indicate that the admiration of the young officers was romantic in nature. Enid was presented at court to King George and Queen Mary when she became Mrs. Cavendish, and was said to be the most beautiful Australian ever presented. The marriage to General Cavendish, who, had he lived longer, would have become Lord Waterpark, produced two children, Caryll, a son, who is the present Lord Waterpark, and Patricia, a daughter, who is now Mrs. Frank O'Neill, and lives in Cape Town, South Africa, where she continues to manage a stud farm that her mother purchased before her death. That marriage also produced a considerable inheritance.

In 1933, Enid Cavendish married the very rich Lord Furness, known as Duke, short for Marmaduke, heir to the Furness shipping fortune. He had a private railroad car, two yachts, and an airplane. They were each other's third spouse. Lord Furness was himself no stranger to homicidal rumor and controversy. His first wife, Daisy, had died aboard his yacht the *Sapphire,* on a pleasure cruise from England to the South of France, and he had buried her at sea. "They say she was pushed off the yacht, but no one could ever prove it," said Tony Pawson. Thelma Furness, his second wife, in her memoir, *Double Exposure,* glides over the event of her predecessor's death. "They were forced to bury her at sea. There were no embalming facilities on the yacht, and they were too far out to turn back to England and not near enough to Cannes to make port." Had he been tried and convicted, it is said that, as an English lord, he would have been hanged with a silk rope, but there was never an arrest or a trial. Thelma, during her marriage to Furness, had become the mistress of the then Prince of Wales, and it was she who, inadvertently, brought her friend Wallis Warfield Simpson into the orbit of the prince, thereby losing her lover, her friend, and her husband. After Furness's subsequent marriage to Enid, he several times sought out his former wife, with whom he remained on friendly terms, for solace. His marriage to Enid was never happy. Thelma Furness was of the opinion that Enid got Furness on drugs. In her book, she tells of an occasion when Furness was nervously biting his knuckles. "We went up to Duke's suite. . . . Duke took off his coat and asked me to give him an injection—a *piqûre.* I couldn't do this because I did not know how; I had never handled a hypodermic needle. Finally, he asked me simply to pinch his arm, and he gave himself the injection." Of the last time she saw him on the Riviera, she wrote, "I've never seen a man look so frail, so mixed-up, so ill. I cried, 'Oh, Duke, if I could only put you in my pocket and take you away.' "

Elvira de la Fuente, a longtime Riviera resident who was a great friend of both Enid and her son Rory and a fourth at bridge with Somerset Maugham, sat on the quay at Beaulieu recently and talked about Furness's death in 1940. "Furness died at La Fiorentina," she said. "He used to get drunk every night. He was carried out of there when he died. There was a rumor that Enid killed him. I don't think she did, but she was quite capable of letting him die." The most persistent story of Furness's death was that it took place in the little pavilion at La Fiorentina, which Enid had constructed overlooking the sea, and where she and her friends played cards every day. On the night Furness became ill, she went back to the house to get his pills, locking the door behind her. The next morning he was found dead in the pavilion. Furness's death left Enid a very rich woman, and Thelma Furness tried to have her charged with murder, but Walter Monckton, the pre-eminent lawyer of the day, refused to take the case, and it never went to trial.

Enid's last marriage, to the sixth Earl of Kenmare, took place in 1943. He was an enormously fat man, 255 pounds, who once accidentally sat on a dog and killed it. Known as Valentine Castlerosse until he became an earl, he had a reputation for lechery and avid gambling that made him disliked in certain segments of society. He was the first English aristocrat to write a gossip column. Hopelessly in debt, he was rescued by Lord Beaverbrook, who paid him £3,000 a year plus expenses to write a column for the *Sunday Express.* Kenmare's family estates in Ireland were massive, 118,600 acres, but yielded only a modest annual income by the standards of the day, £34,000. He once said of his life, "I dissipated my patrimony; I committed many sins; I wasn't important." Elvira de la Fuente remembers that Enid sent her son Rory a telegram saying, "Do you mind if I marry Valentine Castlerosse?" "Valentine used to be married to Doris Castlerosse, who was a great friend of Vita Sackville-West and Virginia Woolf. She'd be about a hundred now," said de la Fuente. Doris Castlerosse died of an overdose of sleeping pills mixed with drink in 1943. Three weeks after the inquest into her death, Enid and Kenmare were married in a Catholic ceremony in the Brompton Oratory. One guest described the event as "taking place in a nightclub setting, for all the titled crooks and rogues in London were there." When Kenmare died less than a year after the marriage, Chips Channon, the English diarist, wrote of him, "An immense, kindly, jovial witty creature, Falstaffian, funny and boisterous, and always grossly overdressed; yet with a kindly heart and was not quite the fraud he pretended to be." "Enid was supposed to have given him an injection, but I never believed that," said Tony Pawson. As Kenmare had no direct heir, the inheritance was to go to his bachelor brother, Gerald. Eventually it went to Beatrice Grosvenor, the daughter of his sister, but Enid, in one of her boldest ventures, claimed to be pregnant, although she was approaching fifty at the time. She was thus able to hold on to the income from the Irish lands for an additional thirteen months. Said Tony Pawson about the pregnancy, "I never heard that, but Enid was up to that sort of thing."

David Hicks, the English decorator married to the daughter of Earl Mountbatten, was a frequent visitor at La Fiorentina. "They used to say about Enid, she married first for love: Cameron. And then to Cavendish, for position—it was a very good name. Then Furness for the money. And Kenmare for the title," he said. But there were lovers too. "The Duke of Westminster was in love with her," said Tom Parr, the chairman of Colefax and Fowler, the London decorating firm. The Duke of Westminster, Britain's richest man, had been a friend of two of Enid's husbands, Furness and Kenmare, and the third of his four wives, Loelia, Duchess of Westminster, was sometimes a visitor at La Fiorentina. "There was one of the Selfridges too, of the store," said Elvira de la Fuente. "A rich man. He gave her money. He was very unattractive too. Some women can only go to bed with handsome men. With Enid, it didn't seem to matter."

"Before the war, the international upper classes were doping a great deal, but none of them showed it," said Tony Pawson. "They weren't like those drug addicts today."

"There was a terrible scandal in New York, but I wouldn't want to talk about that," said an ancient lady in

London. In Paris, an ancient gentleman said, lowering his voice, "Have you heard what happened in New York? Such a scandal!"

The New York scandal they were referring to was what has become known in social lore as the Bloomingdale scandal. Donald Bloomingdale, a sometime diplomat, was forty-two, handsome, a rich man who enjoyed an international social life, maintaining apartments in Paris and New York. "Donald had very chic French friends," said Elvira de la Fuente. "He spoke French well. He was quite a snob. He married one of the Rothschild heiresses, the sister of one of them, but the marriage didn't last." Donald Bloomingdale was also a particular friend of Enid's son Rory. "Rory was very much in love with Donald Bloomingdale, but at the time Donald was in love with an Egyptian, called Jean-Louis Toriel, who was very drugged," Elvira de la Fuente told me. Toriel was an unpopular figure among the fashionable friends of Donald Bloomingdale. Tony Pawson remembered that Toriel had a dachshund that he turned into a drug addict. "A horrid little skeletal thing. Too awful. He was really evil." On several occasions, Bloomingdale went away for drug cures, but, because of Toriel, he always went right back on drugs, once while driving to Paris immediately after his release from a clinic in Switzerland.

In the winter of 1954, Enid Kenmare and Donald Bloomingdale were in New York at the same time. People remember things differently. Some told me it happened at the Pierre. Some said it happened at the Sherry-Netherland. And some said it happened at the since-razed Savoy-Plaza Hotel, which used to stand where the General Motors Building now stands on Fifth Avenue. At any rate, Donald Bloomingdale wanted some heroin, and Lady Kenmare gave it to him. One New York friend of Donald Bloomingdale's told me the heroin was delivered in a lace handkerchief with a coronet and Lady Kenmare's initials on it. Another New York friend said the heroin was in the back of a silver picture frame containing a photograph of Lady Kenmare. However it was delivered, the dosage proved fatal. "It was apparently a bad mixture," said Tony Pawson. The rich Mr. Bloomingdale, who would have been far richer if he had outlived his very rich mother, Rosalie Bloomingdale, was found dead of an overdose the next morning by a faithful servant. Good servant that he was, he knew how to handle the situation. It was not his first experience in such matters. He called the family lawyer immediately. The lace handkerchief with the coronet, or the picture frame with Enid's picture, or whatever receptacle the heroin had come in, was removed, as were the implements of injection. The family lawyer called the family doctor, and the police were notified. Meanwhile, Lady Kenmare was put on an afternoon plane with the assistance of her good friends Norman and Rosita Winston, the international socialites, who for years had leased the Clos, a house on the grounds of La Fiorentina. "She was out of the country before any mention of Donald's death was ever made," said Bert Whitley of New York, who leased another house on the grounds. The servant, who had been through previous scrapes with his employer, was left money in Bloomingdale's will, as were Rory Cameron and Jean-Louis Toriel, the Egyptian, who later also died of a heroin overdose. The newspapers reported that Bloomingdale's death had been caused by an overdose of barbiturates. No connection between the countess and the death of Donald Bloomingdale was ever made publicly. "But everybody knew," I was told over and over. "Everybody knew."

Probably nobody knew better what happened that night than Walter Beardshall, who was Lady Kenmare's butler and valet at the time and who remains her fervent supporter to this day. Now crippled by post-polio syndrome, Mr. Beardshall lives in Brooklyn, New York, where he is mostly confined to a motorized wheelchair. "I traveled around the world with Her Ladyship," he told me. "Elsa Maxwell spread the rumor that I was her gigolo, and everyone gossiped about us, but I wasn't. I was twenty-four at the time, and Lady Kenmare was sixty-two." According to Beardshall, the incident happened at the Sherry-Netherland. "Mr. Bloomingdale had a permanent suite at the Sherry-Netherland, and we were his guests there. He filled Lady Kenmare's room with flowers and everything. The next morning the telephone rang very early, and Her Ladyship asked me to come to her room as quickly as possible. 'How fast can you pack?' she asked. 'We're leaving for London.' We had only just arrived in New York. She said, 'I had dinner last night with Mr. Bloomingdale. He told me I could borrow his typewriter so that I could write Rory a letter. When I called him this morning, his servant told me that he was dead. I was the last person to see him alive. We have to leave. You know how the American police are.' "

After the Bloomingdale incident, Somerset Maugham dubbed his great friend Lady Kenmare Lady Killmore, although some people attribute the name to Noel Coward. At any rate the name stuck.

"Did Enid ever talk about Donald Bloomingdale?" I asked Anthony Pawson.

"It was always a tricky subject," he said. "She didn't talk too much about it, because of all the rumors going round."

"Did Rory talk about it?" I asked a lady friend of his in London.

"Those stories about Enid were never discussed. I mean, you can't ask if someone's mother murdered someone. Rory told me, though, that once, when she arrived on the *Queen Mary,* the tabloids said, 'Society Murderess Arrives,' " she replied.

"When Donald died in New York that time, we all expected to know more about it, but nothing came out," said Elvira de la Fuente. "She ran from New York after that."

Daisy Fellowes, another of the stunning women of the period and a famed society wit, maintained a sort of chilly friendship with Enid. The daughter of a French duke and an heiress to the Singer sewing-machine fortune, she didn't think Enid was sufficiently wellborn, describing her as "an Australian with a vague pedigree." Once, in conversation, Enid began a sentence with the phrase "people of our class." Mrs. Fellowes raised her hand and stopped the conversation. "Just a moment, Enid," she said. "Your class or mine?" After the Bloomingdale affair, Daisy Fellowes announced she was going to give a dinner party for twelve people. "I'm going to have all murderers," she said. "Very convenient. There are six men and six women. And Enid Kenmare will have the place of honor, because she killed the most people of anyone coming."

Lady Kenmare was aware of the stories told about her, and she was sometimes hurt by them. Roderick Coupe, an American who lives in Paris, told me of an occasion when the social figure Jimmy Donahue, a Woolworth heir, cousin of Enid's friend Barbara Hutton, and often rumored to have been the lover of the Duchess of Windsor, asked Enid to his house on Long Island. After a pleasant dinner, he began to ask her why she was known as Lady Killmore. She explained to him that it was a name that caused her a great deal of heartache. Donahue, who had a cruel streak, persisted. "But why do people say it?" he asked several more times. Enid Kenmare finally announced she was leaving. Donahue told her he had sent her car back to New York. Undeterred, she made her way to the highway and hitchhiked to the city.

"She was one of the most accomplished women. She rode. She shot. She fished. She painted very well. She sculpted. She did beautiful needlework. She cooked marvelously. There was nothing she couldn't do," said Tony Pawson. Looking through album after album of photographs of life at La Fiorentina, with its unending parties, one doesn't see an angry or worried face among the people pictured. Any age, any generation, eighteen to eighty, in and out of the house, and dogs everywhere. Although Lady Kenmare was thought of as a famous hostess, a word she greatly disliked, her lunch parties at La Fiorentina were often haphazard affairs, with unmatched guests. Celebrities such as Greta Garbo, Barbara Hutton, Claudette Colbert, Elsa Maxwell, and the Duke of Vedura came, but so did people no one had ever heard of. Guests would be thrown together —friends of Rory's, friends of hers, the well known and the unknown, the young and the old, the inexperienced and the accomplished—with no care as to a balance of the sexes at her table. Enid was diligently unpunctual, arriving, vaguely, long after her guests had been seated, once prompting Daisy Fellowes to remark on her hostess's absence, "Busy with her needle, no doubt." Another guest remembered, "She had no sense of time whatsoever. She'd arrive when the meals were over, or be dressed for the casino, in evening dress and jewels, in the afternoon." Tom Parr said, "She was an ethereal character, nice to us who were Rory's friends, adorable even, but then she'd float off." On one occasion, she was struck by the handsomeness of a young man sunning himself by her swimming pool.

"Do please stay on for dinner," she said. "But, Lady Kenmare, I've been staying with you for a week," the young man replied.

"Enid was completely original. Very elegant. Very distinguished. She always made an entrance, like an actress, carrying a flower," said Jacqueline Delubac, a retired French actress who was once married to Sacha Guitry. She was always surrounded by dogs, "a mangy pack," according to John Galliher of New York. Walter Beardshall remembers her entrances more vividly. "All her guests would already be seated. First you would hear the dogs barking. And then you would hear her voice saying, 'Be quiet. Be quiet.' Then you would hear her high heels clicking on the marble floor. And then the dogs would enter, sometimes twenty of them, miniature poodles, gray and black. And then she would come in, with a parrot on one shoulder and her hyrax on the other." She fed her hyrax from her own fork; although at the cinema she would sometimes pull lettuce leaves from her bosom to feed it. Many people mistook the hyrax for a rat. It is a small ungulate mammal characterized by a thickset body with short legs and ears and rudimentary tail, feet with soft pads and broad nails, and teeth of which the molars resemble those of a rhinoceros and the incisors those of rodents. She taught the hyrax to pee in the toilet, standing straight up on the seat, and sometimes she let her guests peek at it through the bathroom window, keeping out of sight, since the hyrax was very shy. She trained her parrot to speak exactly like her. When the telephone rang, the parrot would call out, "Pat, the telephone," so that Enid's daughter, Pat, would answer it.

The fashion arbiter Eleanor Lambert often stayed with Rosita and Norman Winston in the Clos on Enid's property. She said that Lady Kenmare never seemed to sleep.

She remembered looking out of her window during the night and seeing her walking through her garden dressed in flowing white garments, with the hyrax on her shoulder. "She looked like the woman in white from Wilkie Collins's book," Eleanor Lambert said.

"Enid was never social, really," said Elvira de la Fuente. "You could ask her to sit next to a prince or a waiter, and it never mattered to her." Indeed, the girl from Australia never went grand in the grand life she espoused and kept marrying into. She remained fiercely loyal to her Australian family back home, at one time investing money in the failing wine business even though her lawyers advised her not to. "They are my family," she said to them, according to Beardshall, who traveled to Australia with her. Along the way in her rise, she lost her Australian accent. Tony Pawson said she had "an accent you couldn't quite define, Americanized but not really American." James Douglas, who used to escort Barbara Hutton to La Fiorentina, said, "There was no trace of Australian at all, but sometimes her sister came from Australia to visit her, and then you could hear the way she once had talked." However, she did acquire irregularities of speech that were unique for a woman in her position at that time. According to Walter Beardshall, she used certain four-letter words before people started printing those words in books. He remembered a time when the Countess of Drogheda asked her, "What was Kenmare's first name, Enid?" Enid replied, "Fucked if I know. I was only married to him nine months before he died."

Some people say that Enid thought she would marry Somerset Maugham after Lord Kenmare's death, but more people scoff at this. "Nonsense!" said David Herbert. Tony Pawson agreed. "I don't believe she ever wanted to marry Willie Maugham. Unless it was for the money. Willie wasn't interested in ladies, you know." Jimmy Douglas said, "It's too ridiculous. What about Alan Searle [Maugham's longtime companion], for God's sake?" And Elvira de la Fuente said, "Enid had no friends, really, except Willie Maugham. She adored him. She and Maugham were a funny couple. They were intimate because of bridge. They played all the time. He was already old and grumpy at the time. It was companionship and affection, but there was no thought of romance."

At one time, friends say, Enid, who kept a residence in Monte Carlo and was a citizen of Monaco, harbored a desire for her daughter to marry Prince Rainier and become Her Serene Highness, the Princess of Monaco, but the prince showed no romantic inclinations toward Pat, nor did Pat toward the prince. Pat preferred dogs and horses, and was not cut out for princess life, or even society life on the Riviera, and soon decamped to Kenya and Cape Town to breed horses. Bearing no grudge toward the prince, Enid happily attended his wedding to Grace Kelly. As the tall, statuesque Lady Kenmare emerged from the cathedral at the end of the service, she was cheered by the crowds, who mistook her for a visiting monarch.

"Before anything else, Enid was a mother," said Yves Vidal of Paris and Tangier, who was a frequent visitor at the villa. "Most of the things she did, marrying all those men, were for the children more than herself." "She never *never* did what family people do—criticize and mumble about her children," said Elvira de la Fuente. Walter Beardshall said she tried to keep her drug taking from her children. "Once, Pat found one of her syringes. 'What's this, Mummy?' she asked. 'Oh, it's Walter's,' Lady Kenmare replied. 'He leaves his stuff all over the place. Get it out of here, Walter. Take it to your own room.' "

But it was with Rory, her older son, that she was the closest. "I always thought Rory was in love with Enid," said a London lady. "At Emerald Cunard's parties, they used to come in together, covered in rings and not speaking." Certainly they had an extremely close mother-son relationship. "It was really Rory's life that Enid came to lead, after all the marriages," said Elvira de la Fuente. "He used to say to her as a joke, 'Now you'll never find a fifth husband after you've killed four of them.' They lived as a couple, but it wasn't incestuous. Rory told Enid he was a homosexual when he was forty. She had never suspected. It was a terrible shock to her, but a shock she overcame in a day or two." Yves Vidal said, "She didn't really like social life. She was actually miscast in the grand life of a chatelaine and hostess of the Riviera." Another guest said, "She was in a way a passenger at La Fiorentina. As she got older, people began to think of it as Rory's house. This famous lady was always in the background. Sometimes she'd go for days without coming out of her bedroom."

The magnificent house, located on the finest property on the Riviera, commands the entrance to Beaulieu Bay. It was considered a strategic position during the war, and the Germans, who occupied the house, built extensive fortifications on their property against an Allied invasion. Near the end of the war they blew up the fortifications, destroying half of the house and most of the gardens. When the house was returned to the family, Rory redesigned it in the Palladian style, and the interiors were decorated by him. As Enid Kenmare grew older, she developed curvature of the spine, and her once-perfect posture gave way to a bent-over condition. She began leasing the house. Elizabeth Taylor and Mike Todd occupied it for a time, and for years the

American philanthropist Mary Lasker rented it during the peak months. The house is now owned by Harding and Mary Wells Lawrence, the former chairman of Braniff Airways and the founder of the advertising agency Wells, Rich, Greene. Mary Lawrence said, "When we bought La Fiorentina, there were no lights in the bathrooms. Lady Kenmare couldn't bear to look at herself in the mirror anymore."

She moved to Cape Town, South Africa, where she bought a stud farm and raised racehorses. Her daughter, Pat, had preceded her there. For a while Enid employed Beryl Markham, the author of *West with the Night,* to train her horses, but the two women, who had known each other since Enid's marriage to Lord Furness, were such strong personalities that their partnership did not work out. Pat had two lions she had brought up from the time they were cubs that had the run of the house. A New York friend of Pat's who used to visit La Fiorentina every summer also visited the two women in Cape Town. She remembers seeing one of the lions drag an unperturbed Enid through the living room and out the French doors. "She was not remotely frightened, and later Pat told me, 'It happens all the time.'"

"Enid was mysterious," said Yves Vidal. "I remember once watching her run down the steps of La Fiorentina followed by her dogs. She was so beautiful, and she knew she was very beautiful. Until the end, she kept a wonderful allure. What made her life and ruined her life at the same time was her beauty."

March 1991

THE PASSION
OF
BARON THYSSEN

IT WAS a late-fall twilight on Lake Lugano. We were standing in the open window of an art-filled sitting room in the Villa Favorita, one of the loveliest houses in the world, looking out over the lake, listening to waves lap against the private dock below. Across the water the lights of Lugano, a city of 30,000 people and fifty banks in the Italian-speaking corner of Switzerland, were coming on. My companion in reverie, the Baron Hans Heinrich Thyssen-Bornemisza, has been looking out at the same view for over fifty years, since his father, Baron Heinrich Thyssen-Bornemisza, bought the seventeenth-century villa from Prince Friedrich Leopold of Prussia in 1932. For those who need an introduction, Baron Hans Heinrich Thyssen-Bornemisza is generally conceded to be one of the richest men in the world ("in the billions," say some people, "in the high hundred millions," according to others), as well as the possessor of one of the world's largest private art collections, which is rivaled in size and magnificence only by that of the Queen of England. It was the art collection I was there to discuss, for the baron, now in his sixty-seventh year, has begun to have thoughts about mortality, and for the last five years the disposition of his collection has been uppermost in his mind.

He is called Heini by those close to him, and that evening he was dressed in a dinner jacket and black tie, awaiting the arrival of guests for dinner. The Thyssen fortune, he was telling me, had been made originally in iron and steel in Germany. "My mother irons and my father steals," he said, in the manner of a man who has told the same joke over and over. Early in life, his father had left Germany and moved to Hungary, where he had married into the nobility; thus the title baron and the addition of the hyphen and the name Bornemisza. The current baron's older brother and two sisters were born in Hungary, but the Thyssen-Bornemisza family fled to Holland when the Communist leader of Hungary, Béla Kun, sentenced the children's father to death for being a landowner. Heini Thyssen was born in Holland and spent the first nineteen years of his life there.

The baron's attention was distracted from his story by the arrival at the dock below of a flag-bedecked lake boat bringing his guests, thirty-one formally attired members of the Board of Trustees and the Trustees' Council of the National Gallery of Art in Washington, D.C., who were on a two-week tour of Swiss and Italian churches, museums, and private collections, headed by the gallery's director, J. Carter Brown. Among the members of this art-loving group were the Perry Basses of Fort Worth, the Alexander Mellon Laughlins and the Thomas Mellon Evanses of New York, and the Robert Erburus of Los Angeles.

"But it's too early," said the baron, looking down. "They've come too early. The baroness is not ready to receive them." And then he added, to no one in particular, "Send them away." He had his gun-toting American bodyguard tell the driver of the boat to spin the distinguished guests around the lake for half an hour and then come back. As we watched the drama from upstairs, we could hear Carter Brown call out, "Ladies and gentlemen," and then explain to his group that they were not to get off the boat yet but would instead take another short ride. This announcement apparently created some discord, because people began to get off anyway. The baron shrugged, sighed, smiled, and went down to greet them. Drinks were served on an outdoor loggia overlooking the lake. A night chill had set in, and the ladies hugged fur jackets and cashmere shawls over their short black dinner dresses and pearls. For some time the Baroness Thyssen-Bornemisza did not appear.

Tita Thyssen, a former Miss Barcelona and later Miss Spain, picked by a jury that included the American-born Countess of Romanoes and the great bullfighter Luis Dominguín, is the baron's fifth and presumably last baroness and, if all goes according to plan, his first and last duchess, for the *on-dit* in swell circles is that the King of Spain is prepared to confer on her the title of duchess when the Thyssen collection, or at least 700 of the A and B pictures in the 1,400-picture collection, goes to Spain permanently. That "permanently" is the catch.

"Where is she?" one wife asked, meaning their hostess.

"We heard she's not coming at all," said the lady to whom she spoke.

"I heard that too," said the first lady, and they exchanged "Miss Barcelona" looks.

But then the baroness did appear, the last arrival at her own party, although she was only coming from upstairs. She was stunning, blond, tanned from the sun, dressed in a long black strapless evening gown. "Balmain," I heard her say to someone. She has the persona of a film star and understands perfectly the technique of making an entrance. In an instant she was the center of attention, and earlier opinions of her were soon favorably revised. Like all the baron's wives, his fifth baroness is the possessor of some very serious jewelry. On her engagement-ring finger was a large marquise diamond that had once belonged to the baron's second wife, the ill-fated Nina Dyer, who married the baron at the age of seventeen and divorced him at the age of twenty-five to marry Prince Sadruddin Aga Khan, the half-brother of the late Aly Khan and the uncle of the current Aga Khan. Indifferent to gender when it came to love partners, Nina also dallied with a succession of ladies, who called her Oliver and vied with her husbands when it came to showering her with jewels. One of her most ardent admirers, an international film actress, gave her a panther bracelet designed by Cartier with an inscription in French which read, "To my panther, untamed by man." Before she was forty, Nina committed suicide. "She'd just had it," was the explanation someone who knew her gave me. Her jewelry, according to the baron, was stolen by her friends at the time of her death. Years later, he saw a picture of the marquise-diamond ring in an auction catalog. Although it had no listed provenance, he recognized it as the diamond he had given Nina years before, and bought it back for his fifth wife for $1.5 million.

The baroness was wearing diamond-and-ruby earrings, and around her neck, hanging on a diamond necklace designed to accommodate it, was the Star of Peace, which she had told me earlier in the day was the "biggest flawless diamond in the world." I explained to one of the guests who gasped at its size that it was 167 carats. The baroness heard me say it. "One hundred and sixty-*nine*," she corrected me, and then, hearing herself, she roared with laughter.

Tita Thyssen speaks in a husky, international voice, often changing languages from sentence to sentence. She is fun, funny, and flirtatious, with a nature that is best described as vivacious. She is refreshingly outspoken, and makes no bones, for example, about her dislike of her immediate predecessor, the former Denise Shorto of Brazil, whose divorce from the baron was extremely acrimonious, resulting in a settlement rumored to be in the neighborhood of $50 million, in addition to jewels worth $80 million. At one point in the proceedings Denise Thyssen was briefly jailed in Liechtenstein for leaving Switzerland with unpaid bills in excess of $1.5 million, and the baron accused her of failing to return certain jewelry and other items belonging to his family. Ultimately, Denise was allowed to keep all the jewels, on the ground that they were gifts made to her during her marriage, not Thyssen heirlooms. "A gift is a gift," she was quoted as saying. We are talking here about very, very, very rich people. Now in her late forties, Denise Thyssen lives in Rome with Prince Mariano Hugo zu Windisch-Graetz, who is in his midthirties, and their liaison is not smiled upon by the Prince's family. She refused to be interviewed for this article with the pointed comment that "Heini's present wife is very publicity-minded. This article belongs to her. I don't see my place in it."

"I believe in destiny," Tita Thyssen said, discussing the Star of Peace. "This stone proves to me that destiny is always there. I first saw it in the rough, before it was cut, in the Geneva office of Harry Winston, before I met Heini. They left me alone with it and let me play with it. They told me they were thinking of doing an adventure with somebody and cutting it. The person involved turned out to be Heini, but I did not know him yet. I talked with the store from time to time, and three times it was almost sold. Then Heini gave it to me."

Among the guests that evening was her friend and jeweler, Fred Horowitz, who used to be with Harry Winston and is now an independent jeweler with offices in Geneva and Monte Carlo. It was through Horowitz that the baroness met Heini Thyssen. She was staying with him and his then wife, Donatella, who is now married to the Mercedes-Benz heir Mick Flick, on their boat in Sardinia. "It was time for me to go back to my house on the Costa Brava, but my friends begged me to stay one more day, and I did," said the baroness. The next day Horowitz took her to a party on Heini Thyssen's yacht. "The look he gave me when we met, now that I know him better, is the look he gets when he sees a painting that he knows he is going to buy. He knew he was going to get it." Then she added, "Only I'm more expensive than a painting, and you don't have to change the frame with me." Her husband listened to her story, amused.

According to one guest on the Thyssen yacht that day, Tita and Heini remained aloof from the party and played backgammon for hours. Also on board was Thyssen's fourth wife, Denise, though their marriage was already in its last stages. Seeing her husband and Tita together for so long, she made a slighting remark of the "upstart" variety about Tita, and with that the two women's mutual dislike began.

"We have never been apart more than a day since we met," Tita said, taking her husband's hand. "We have been married three and a half years now, but we have been together seven. We discuss everything."

Spotting Fred Horowitz, she turned her attention from the National Gallery group to him. "It doesn't hang right," she said about the enormous stone she was wearing. Horowitz had made her the two-row necklace of matched diamonds from which the Star of Peace hung as a pendant. The diamond was too heavy for the necklace and tipped upward. For several minutes she and Horowitz and his new wife, Jasmine, also jewel-laden, discussed in French what was wrong with the diamond necklace. Then realizing that she was neglecting her guests, she turned back to them and said, in a playful, self-deprecating manner, "These are very nice problems to have."

At dinner we sat at five place-carded tables of eight, and she held her table in thrall, all the while chain-smoking cigarettes. The fifth baroness is steeped in the lore of her husband's family and, like him, is an expert storyteller. She told one story about Heini's stepmother, the beautiful Baroness Maud von Thyssen, who during her marriage to Baron Heinrich Thyssen, fell madly in love with twenty-six-year-old Prince Alexis Mdivani, "one of the marrying Mdivani brothers," as they were called. Alexis had just negotiated a lucrative divorce from the American heiress Barbara Hutton. The lovers rendezvoused in a remote village in Spain. After the tryst, Maud had to return to Paris, and the prince drove her to her train at breakneck speed in the Rolls-Royce that Hutton had given him. "There was a terrible crash," the baroness said. "Mdivani was killed. Maud's beautiful face was half-destroyed. Heini's father divorced her." At that point a waiter accidentally dropped a dozen dinner plates on the stone floor, with a crash that brought the room to silence. The baroness looked over, shrugged, and returned to her conversation with the same aplomb that her husband demonstrated at his table across the room. Why let a few broken plates ruin a good party?

A stranger to art before her marriage, the baroness has become deeply involved in her husband's collection, and if she is not as conversant as he on the subject of old masters, she has made herself more conversant than you or I— knowledgeable enough to be the main force behind her husband's selection of Spain, over England, West Germany, the United States, Japan, and France, as the resting place for his treasure. Many people consider the choice odd, since the baron himself has no real connection with Spain and no long-standing friendships there. It is the baroness's dream, however, according to one Spanish Tita watcher, to live in Spain and to be accepted by people who once neglected and even snubbed her.

There are pictures everywhere in the villa. Up a second-ary stairway, outside the men's lavatory, hangs an Edvard Munch, and in every corridor is a profusion of pictures, around any one of which the average millionaire might build an entire room. The bar in the family sitting room is a seven-part coromandel screen, broken up to conceal a refrigerator, an icemaker, glasses, and liquor bottles. Walk-ing through a drawing room that the baron and baroness almost never go into, we passed a Bonnard portrait of Misia Sert, and in a formal dining room so infrequently entered that the light switch didn't work—a room too large for intimate groups but not large enough for big groups from museums—hung a pair of Canalettos.

"Would you like to see our bedroom?" the baroness asked her guests.

Is the pope Catholic? Of course we wanted to see the bedroom, which contains three Pissarros, a Renoir, a Tou-louse-Lautrec, a Winslow Homer, a Manet, and more that I don't remember. The pictures in the villa are quite differ-ent from the pictures that hang in the galleries of the museum next door—the Titians, the Tintorettos, the Carpaccio, the Goyas, and the El Grecos, which the baron would show the group the next day.

"Do you move these pictures with you to your other houses?" someone asked her.

"No, we have others."

Their bedroom, in contrast to most of the Mongiardino-decorated rooms, is soft and feminine, done in pale colors. It opens into Heini's enormous bathroom, which has a tub the size of a small pool, and into Tita's sitting room, which has an early Gauguin over the daybed and a Corot. Although it was October, the perpetual calendar on a side table still indicated June. The Thyssen-Bornemisza family crest is embossed on the message pad next to every telephone in the villa; the motto reads, *"Vertu surpasse richesse"*—Virtue surpasses riches.

The baroness opened the doors of closet after closet full of clothes. "Most of my clothes are still in Marbella," she said. She is dressed mostly by the Paris couturiers Balmain and Scherrer. When her schedule makes it impossible for her to attend the couture showings in Paris, the designers send her videotapes of their collections and she chooses from them.

"What's it like to live this way?" she was asked.

"It took me some time to get used to all this beauty," said the baroness quite modestly. "At first I was in shock."

"How long did it take before you got used to this kind of life?" I asked her.

"About two days," she answered, and burst out laughing at her joke.

Her native language is Spanish, which the baron does not speak well. His native languages are Dutch, Hungarian, and German, which the baroness does not speak well. When they are alone together, they speak sometimes in French and sometimes in English, heavily accented English, his Teutonic-sounding, hers with a very Latin inflection. "But," said the baroness, "if we have been with French friends, we continue in French for a day or so."

Their life is planned months in advance, mostly around art openings, for loans from their collection are constantly traveling from country to country and exhibition to exhibition. In their family sitting room, there are the inevitable silver-framed photographs of them, together or alone, with the Reagans, the Gorbachevs, the pope, and the president and matronly First Lady of Portugal, with whom Tita posed in a miniskirt six inches above the knee. They entertain at lunch. They entertain at dinner. They are forever on the move. The baroness knew as we talked in Lugano that seven weeks from that day she would be giving a party at L'Orangerie in Los Angeles ("Liza Minnelli can't come," she said to her husband. "Betsy Bloomingdale can"), and that the night before they would be dining in Palm Springs with Sir James Hanson, the British financier, and that they would be lunching the day after their party with Niki Bautzer, the widow of the Hollywood show-biz lawyer Greg Bautzer, at the Bistro Garden in Beverly Hills.

The baron is considered a prime kidnapping target. In all the houses there is closed-circuit surveillance with electrically operated doors. And bodyguards. And dogs. The bodyguards are American, part of a security force that handles only three international clients. The bodyguard I became acquainted with was a cross between Charles Bronson and Clint Eastwood. He packed two weapons beneath his suit, a pistol in a holster and what appeared to be a sawed-off machine gun tucked into the back of his trousers. He is with the baron all the time. "We never stay anywhere for longer than a week," he told me.

There are people who knew Tita before her marriage to Baron Thyssen who will tell you that she's changed, but, in all fairness, to enter the life she has entered and *not* change would be difficult for almost anyone. In addition to the Villa Favorita in Lugano, they have a new house on the outskirts of Madrid that rivals in movie-star luxe and size the Aaron Spelling mansion in California, as well as houses in Barcelona and Marbella and a house on the Costa Brava that was hers before they married; a town house on Chester Square in London; a house in St. Moritz and what she called a "small palace—tiny, really," in Paris, which they just purchased from the late Christina Onassis's last husband; a house in Jamaica; a suite at the Pierre Hotel in New York; and probably more that I did not hear about. Of course, there is a private plane for their constant peregrinations from house to house and art opening to art opening, and somewhere a yacht, which they occasionally use, and there are the servants who travel and the servants who stay put, plus the ever-present security guards.

The people who say that Tita Cervera has changed are the same people who say, with a roll of the eyes, "Have you met Mama yet?" By Mama, they mean Carmen Fernández de la Guerra, Tita's mother, whom I did not meet. She is, from all reports, not unlike the mother of Robin Givens, a strong and determined woman who plays a major part in her daughter's life. The Cerveras were originally a family of extremely modest means from Valladolid, a small city several hours from Madrid. Tita has always been, and continues to be, a devoted daughter. In the period before she met Thyssen, she was at an extremely low ebb in her life, with a child to support and no money. At her mother's insistence, she went to Sardinia in the hopes of meeting a rich man. That she connected with one of the richest men in the world, and then married him, must have surpassed even Carmen's wildest dreams. The baron, who was at first amused by his mother-in-law, is said now to want to spend less and less time with her. Although Carmen is headquartered mostly in Barcelona and Marbella, where she is frequently photographed for the Spanish magazines, her influence is such that recently she tried to keep her son-in-law from bringing Alexander, his fourteen-year-old son by Denise, into the Thyssens' house in London for fear that the boy, through his mother, would put an evil spell on the house. In fact, Tita and her mother are both worried about having evil spells put on them, and they have been known to ask Brazilian friends to bring them sandalwood twigs to ward off hexes.

Tita's own son, Borja, born out of wedlock by an unnamed father, was adopted by Baron Thyssen even before their marriage. The child was given the name Bornemisza and baptized with great style in the Lady Chapel of St. Patrick's Cathedral in New York, with the American billionairess Ann Getty for his godmother and the Duke de Badajoz, the King of Spain's brother-in-law, for his godfather. Since his mother's marriage to the baron, he has been given the full last name, Thyssen-Bornemisza. The eight-year-old Borja was nowhere in sight during my visit. The baroness said, "He used to live in Lugano. He is now going to live in Madrid."

The Duke de Badajoz has been the most influential figure in Spain in working with the Thyssens to bring their art collection to his country. Along with the Duchess of Marlborough and the late automobile tycoon Henry Ford, the duke was a witness when the Thyssens were married three and a half years ago at Daylesford, a magnificent English estate that the baron had purchased sixteen years earlier from the late press lord Viscount Rothermere. Although Daylesford was Thyssen's favorite house after the Villa Favorita, the estate has since been sold, for a reputed $16 million. The new baroness felt they spent too little time there to justify keeping such a large establishment, and preferred a house in Madrid, where they would be spending more and more of their time. According to one Spanish lady, Tita is also pushing her husband to sell the Villa Favorita.

The baroness was happily married for eight years to the late Lex Barker, who gained international fame as one of the successors to Johnny Weissmuller in the Tarzan films. She was Barker's fifth wife, too. "He dropped dead on Fifty-ninth and Lex on his way to lunch at Gino's," the baroness said. "Greg Bautzer phoned me in Geneva with the news." Barker had formerly been married to the fifties film star Lana Turner, and in the last year he has been accused by Turner's daughter, Cheryl Crane, in her memoir, *Detour,* of having repeatedly abused her sexually when she was ten years old. Crane gained her own measure of international fame several years after the alleged child abuse by stabbing to death her mother's lover, gangster Johnny Stompanato. Baroness Thyssen is fiercely loyal to the memory of her late husband, and she decried Crane's book. "I was so mad at that book," she said. "I was furious. I wanted to sue, but my lawyers told me you cannot sue over someone who's dead. If you're married to a man, you know very well if he likes little girls or not. Women fell down in front of Lex. He liked me. He liked women, not little girls, believe me. That woman is destroying the memory of Lex. I am trying to restore Lex's image."

The baroness is more reticent about discussing her second husband, Espartaco Santoni, a Spanish-Venezuelan movie producer and nightclub owner who now lives in Los Angeles. "We were only married a year," she said. During that marriage she acted in two films, one with Curt Jurgens and Peter Graves and the other with Lee Van Cleef. "In both those films I was killed for being unfaithful," she told me, laughing.

She said that the time she spent acting was the happiest period of her life, but she ended her acting career when that marriage ended. Now she paints, and she feels the same inner satisfaction doing it that she once felt acting. An acquaintance described her paintings to me as "colorful, light, and tropical, the kind you see on guest-room walls." But painting is only an occasional occupation, for her peripatetic life does not allow for a commitment to it. It is what she does in Jamaica. They spend two weeks a year at the house in Jamaica, called Alligator Head, which Baron Thyssen has owned since the fifties. There they relax completely, and the baroness paints. "I always say to my guests, 'If you have any problems, go talk to the butler or the maid, not me. I came here to relax and paint.' "

"That's a Van Gogh behind you," said the baroness.

"An early one," said the baron.

There was also a Van Gogh to the right of me and another one to the left. We were at lunch in the small family dining alcove of the Villa Favorita with the photographer Helmut Newton.

In the center of the table were pink and yellow flowers from the Thyssen-Bornemisza gardens and greenhouse. The flowers are changed for each meal, and arranged by the head gardener of the "six or eight, I can't remember" gardeners on the grounds. Lunch was served by the butler and a footman, both in dark coats and white gloves. The butler, Giorgio Pusiol, is one of the servants who travel. "Don't you think he's chic?" asked the baroness when he left the room. The footman went from place to place shaving white truffles onto the saffron rice that accompanied our osso buco.

The baron and baroness were both most agreeable to all of Helmut Newton's suggestions for photographing them, even when he asked them to change into evening clothes in the middle of the day and pretend lunch was dinner. The baroness began the meal wearing a strand of perfect pearls, the size of large grapes, later changed to her sapphires, both blue and yellow, the baron's latest gift to her, and then to her rubies, and with each set came a different dress from Balmain or Scherrer. "Change of colors, I see," said the baron as he leaned over to examine one necklace.

Suddenly, surprisingly, from out of nowhere, as coffee was being served, the baroness turned to me and said, "Have you ever heard of Franco Rappetti?"

"Yes," I replied. I had heard of Franco Rappetti, but having come to Lugano to discuss the transfer of a great art collection from Switzerland to Spain, I had hardly expected to get into the darkest shadow in the life of the baron, yet here it was, offered up with the demitasse by the baron's fifth wife. Anyone who has ever dipped into the Thyssen saga has heard of Franco Rappetti, a tall, blond, handsome Roman who was at one time the baron's European art dealer. He was also—and this is no secret, at least in the social and art worlds in which the Thyssens moved—the lover of Denise, the fourth baroness, during her marriage to the baron. A onetime playboy, compulsive gambler, and drug user, Rappetti has been described to me by a woman who knew him well as a man who shared women with many powerful men. On June 8, 1978, while on a visit to New York, Rappetti, thirty-eight, went out a window at the Meurice, a building on West Fifty-eighth Street favored by artistic Europeans who keep apartments in New

York. His mysterious death has fascinated society and the art world ever since.

"Did you hear how he died?" she asked.

"I heard he either jumped or was thrown out the window," I answered.

"Thrown," said the baroness, and then named the person who she believed had had it done. Only days before, a friend of mine had attended a lunch party in London following a memorial service for the Marquess of Dufferin and Ava; there the conversation had also turned to Franco Rappetti, for some reason, and one of the guests had named a well-known figure in the New York art world as the one who threw him out the window. The person the baroness named as having had Rappetti thrown and the person named at the London lunch party as having actually thrown him were not the same.

"He was thrown out the window," the baroness repeated. The baron was sitting with us but read a letter during the exchange. "He was going to have his face changed so he could not be recognized. He wanted to get away from someone."

"His faced changed?"

"Surgery." She named the person Franco Rappetti had wanted to get away from. "He was going to move somewhere and start a new life." She said that Rappetti had been acting in a hyper manner before the defenestration, and had been injected with a tranquilizer to calm him down. It was in that state that he was thrown.

Residents of the building who knew Rappetti disagree violently with the theory that he was pushed or thrown. "He was not murdered," said one emphatically. "He jumped. It's as simple as that. He was depressed. He had money problems."

Franco Rossellini, the Italian film producer and nephew

of the great director Roberto Rossellini, lives in apartment 10-J of the building. He said that police came rushing into his apartment before he knew what had happened and asked him if he knew who had jumped out the window and he saw the body, clad only in undershorts and an elaborate gold chain with charms and medals, lying ten floors below on the roof of a Volkswagen bus. "My God, for a moment I thought it was my butler," he told me. The body had come from the apartment above his, 11-J, where Rappetti had just arrived as a guest. One article written about the case stated that he had arrived "with a small suitcase and some very pure cocaine."

When the police left, Rossellini contacted Diane Von Furstenberg, the dress designer and perfume manufacturer, who was an acquaintance of Denise Thyssen's and who had, coincidentally, spoken with her on the telephone only a short time before. Although Denise Thyssen and Rappetti were in the city at the same time, supposedly neither knew the other was there. Von Furstenberg called the baroness at the Waldorf, realized she had not yet heard about Rappetti's death, put her mother on the telephone in order to keep Denise's line busy, and raced to the Waldorf Towers to break the news before she heard it from the police or news media. "Denise was hysterical," remembered Rossellini. Von Furstenberg then called Heini Thyssen in Europe to tell him what had happened, and contacted Rappetti's sister, who absolutely refused to believe that her brother had jumped. Later, Von Furstenberg accompanied Denise to the city morgue. Since Denise could not bear to go in and see her dead lover, Von Furstenberg identified the body. Only then was she able to relinquish the grieving baroness into the care of closer friends—Princess Yasmin Aga Khan, the daughter of Rita Hayworth; Nona Gordon Summers, then the wife of a London art dealer; and Cleo

Goldsmith, the niece of international financier James Goldsmith.

"Nobody pushed him out," Rossellini asserted. "That is a fact. He was running away all the time. He was paranoid. He thought someone was after him. He was not eating anything anymore. He was afraid someone was trying to poison him."

Just as authoritatively, a woman who knew Rappetti well insists that he was not a suicide. "Oh, no, I don't believe Franco jumped. He was so vain about his looks, he would never have gone out the window in undershorts."

"It would be almost impossible to throw a six-foot-three-inch, well-developed man out the window," said Mariarosa Sclauzero, the person most likely to know the exact circumstances of the death. Sclauzero, a writer, still lives in Apartment 11-J, along with her husband, Enrico Tucci. They were both close to Rappetti, and Mariarosa was in the apartment at the time of the death, though in a different room. According to Sclauzero and Tucci, Rappetti had arrived in New York two days before and had registered at the Summit Hotel, after stopping to see Tucci at his office, where he told him, "There is no way out. I have nobody in the world I can trust anymore, not even my butler." Alerted by Tucci that Rappetti was in a highly excitable state, Sclauzero went to the Summit and brought him back to the apartment. He was indeed carrying a suitcase, but, Sclauzero maintains, it contained no cocaine, just clothes and a picture of his small son.

Rappetti kept saying over and over, "They're after me. They want me dead. If anyone asks for me, say I am not here." In the next hour, he tried several times to telephone someone in Switzerland, but he could not get through. There were also several calls for him, supposedly from Paris, but Sclauzero sensed that they were local calls and said that he was not there. Rappetti had left his watch in Paris, and asked to borrow one of Tucci's watches and a T-shirt. He used the bathroom and went into one of the two bedrooms of the apartment to rest. Mariarosa remained in the living room, reading. When the police knocked on her door, after leaving Rossellini's apartment, and asked if she had a guest, she followed Rappetti's instructions and said no. Realizing, however, that something was wrong, she went into the bedroom and found the window wide open. Franco Rappetti was not there. On a table by the window were the watch he had borrowed and the T-shirt, folded. She admits it was a mistake to lie to the police. Later she was grilled for six hours.

"Franco Rappetti was pushed, but not physically," Sclauzero told me as we sat in Apartment 11-J of the Meurice. "Other people brought him to this despair. What he never said was who or why." She said that Rappetti was convinced that he was being poisoned by a servant in Rome, who was being paid by "other people," and that he was being pursued. She denied reports that he had money problems, arguing that he was worth about $5 million in art at the time of his death. She also said that after his death all the paintings in his apartment in Rome disappeared overnight.

The death was declared a suicide. Several well-heeled friends who were approached to lend their private planes to fly Rappetti's body back to Italy refused, on the ground that it would be unlucky to fly the body of a suicide. The day following the death, Heini Thyssen arrived at the Waldorf Towers. An oft-repeated story in these circles is that, on his arrival, Heini asked, "Does Denise blame me?" It is generally acknowledged that he arranged for the broken corpse to be shipped back to Genoa, Rappetti's birthplace, in a chartered plane. The body was accompanied by the grief-stricken Denise Thyssen and her sister Penny, who is married to Jamie Granger, the son of film star Stewart Granger. There are those who say the body was shipped before an autopsy could be performed. There are others who believe that Rappetti was already dead when he was thrown from the window. The man who made the arrangements to ship the body for Thyssen was another art dealer he did business with. His name was Andrew Crispo.

Many people who once moved in the orbit of this charismatic art dealer now seek to distance themselves as widely as possible from him. To the baron's great distress, his name has frequently been associated in recent times with that of Crispo, who figured prominently and salaciously in the 1985 sadomasochistic murder of a Norwegian fashion student named Eigil Vesti. Crispo was a prime suspect in the murder, but his young assistant Bernard LeGeros was tried and sentenced for the crime. This past October, Crispo, who is currently in prison for tax evasion, was tried on a forcible-sodomy charge and acquitted.

Thyssen and Crispo originally met at Crispo's gallery during an exhibition called "Pioneers of American Abstraction." Thyssen had lent one of his pictures, a watercolor by Charles Demuth, for the show. He complained that on the loan card beneath the picture the name Thyssen-Bornemisza had been misspelled. "How do you know?" asked Crispo. "Because I am Baron Thyssen," was the reply. Thereafter, Thyssen began buying pictures from Crispo.

Franco Rappetti, trying to hold on to his business relationship with Thyssen at the same time that he was conducting an affair with Thyssen's wife, had once told Crispo that he would have to pay him a commission on any pictures he sold to the baron. Crispo had refused. After Rappetti's death, Crispo became firmly entrenched as Baron

Thyssen's New York art dealer. In one month Thyssen spent $3 million on paintings, and the two men developed a close bond that has been the subject of endless speculation. Some people believe that the immensely rich baron financed Andrew Crispo's Fifty-seventh Street gallery. Others believe that there was a deep friendship between Crispo and the baron's oldest son, Georg-Heinrich, now thirty-seven. Georg-Heinrich, also called Heini, is the baron's child by his first wife, a German Princess of Lippe, who is now the Princess Teresa von Fürstenberg. "Teresa and Heini should have stayed married," said a grand European lady recently while lunching at Le Cirque. "She wouldn't have cared about his peccadilloes. Ridiculous, all those divorces." Young Heini lives in Monte Carlo and runs the vast family empire so that his father can devote himself entirely to the art collection. The Thyssen fortune, no longer connected with the original iron-and-steel business in Germany, is now derived from shipbuilding in Holland, sheep farms in Australia, glass, plastics, and automobile parts in America, and assorted interests in Canada and Japan. Whatever relationship or relationships once existed among father, son, and Andrew Crispo no longer do.

Tita Thyssen told a curious story about an American magazine which sent a crew to photograph her and her husband at their house in Jamaica and then used only a small picture of them, "Like a snapshot." "There was something funny about it," she said, shaking her head at the memory. "They stayed too long for a photography shoot—five days. I felt they were after something. Then we found out that the photographer was the boyfriend of Crispo's boyfriend."

The baron now joined the conversation. "Crispo sold pictures to other people and then declared on the books that I had bought them so his buyers could avoid paying the New York City tax. Two-thirds of the pictures he said that I bought he actually sold to other people."

The baroness nodded her head in agreement.

"What do you call those films where people are killed?" he asked.

"Snuff?" I said. A snuff film is one in which a person is murdered, usually ritualistically, on-camera.

"Snuff, yes. One of the newspapers in New York tried to say that I financed snuff films for Andrew Crispo." He shuddered in disgust.

"Why didn't you sue?" I asked.

He waved my question away with a dismissive gesture. "This is such bad coffee," he said, putting his cup on the table and standing. "These people do not know how to make coffee. You can get better coffee in an airplane." The conversation was over. Neither Rappetti nor Crispo was mentioned again. Back to art.

"The baron is a man in love with his collection. Everything for him is his collection. He loves it. He is *in* love with it," said the Duke de Badajoz, who is not only the great good friend of both the baron and baroness but also the man who has been, after Tita, the prime influence in guiding the baron's decision to allow the collection to go to Spain. "After all the effort of his father and him to collect and amass 1,400 pictures, half of which are quite unique, it was more than natural that he was worried for a long time as to what would happen to the collection when he dies. He did not want it dispersed and auctioned. He has been looking around for some years for what could be a solution for the principal part of his collection, the A pictures."

Clearly, the pictures are the focus of the baron's life. "I'm a lucky fellow. These pictures of my father's I have known for fifty years, and I've been collecting for thirty-five years so I know them all." Walking through the graceful galleries that his father built to house the early part of the collection and that he opened to the public after his father's death in 1947, Thyssen was drawing more interest from the browsing tourists and art lovers than the paintings themselves. He moved with the assurance of a celebrity, knowing he was being looked at and talked about. When people came up to ask him to autograph their Thyssen-Bornemisza catalogs, he was completely charming. As he signed the books, he would say a few words or make a joke. He was dressed, as he almost always is, in a blue blazer with double vents, which his London tailor makes for him a dozen at a time, gray flannels, and a striped tie. In his hand he carried a large, old-fashioned key ring, unlocking certain rooms as we entered them and then locking them again as we left.

"I bought this yesterday," the baron said, looking at a Brueghel painting of animals. "I bought it from my sister. It's not in the catalog. It belonged to my father, and my sister inherited it." He moved on. "Now, this picture I bought from my other sister." Although the baron inherited the major part of the collection when his father died, he has spent years buying back the pictures that his two sisters inherited. It is for this reason that he is determined that his collection be kept intact when he dies. Thyssen also had an older brother, whose story remains somewhat vague. "He lived in Cuba," said the baron. "Then he moved to New York and lived at the Plaza Hotel. He lived completely on vitamins. He ODed on vitamins."

"ODed?"

"Hmm, dead," he said. He walked into another room.

"This is my favorite picture," he said, peering as if for the first time at a Ghirlandaio portrait of Giovanna

Tornabuoni, a Florentine noblewoman, painted in 1488. "She died very young, in childbirth. We have never known if the picture was painted before or after her death. It was in the Morgan Library in New York. They had to buy some books, so they sold it." He continued to make comments as he passed from one painting to the next: "A Titian, very late. He was almost ninety when he painted that . . . Who was that man who gave the big ball in Venice after the war? Beistegui, wasn't it? That pair of Tintorettos comes from him . . . Everything in this room was bought by me and not by my father. I call it the Rothschild room. All the pictures in this room I bought from different members of the Rothschild family . . . My father bought this Hans Holbein of Henry VIII from the grandfather of Princess Di, the Earl of Spencer. The Earl bought a Bugatti with the money. When the picture was shown in England, Princess Margaret said to me, 'Harry is one up on you.' She was talking about his six wives, and my five. I said, 'He didn't have to go through all these tedious legal proceedings I do.' "

Of course, only a fraction of the baron's pictures were on view. Several of his Degas were in New York at the Metropolitan Museum of Art. Some of his old masters had been lent to the U.S.S.R. and were at that moment in Siberia. Still others were on loan to exhibitions around the world. He shook his head at the complexity of owning such a large collection.

The baron unlocked a door, and we entered a part of his private museum called the Reserve. It is here that pictures for which there is no room in the galleries hang on both sides of movable floor-to-ceiling racks twenty to twenty-five feet high. In one room a restorer with a broken arm, on loan from the J. Paul Getty Museum in California, was cleaning a fifteenth-century Italian portrait. "We have no room for this Edward Hopper," the baron said of a picture of a naked woman sitting on a bed, "and there's no place for that Monet." He rolled the racks back. There was also no place for a Georgia O'Keeffe and an Andrew Wyeth and what seemed like several hundred others.

"That's a fake Mondrian there," he said, approaching it and squinting at it. "I bought it by mistake. An expert told me he saw Mondrian paint it, and I believed him."

"Why do you keep it?"

"I prefer to keep a small fake to a big fake," he said, smiling.

Behind a door, almost out of sight, hung a picture of the baron himself. He made no comment about the portrait until I mentioned it. "That's me by Lucian Freud," he said. The picture, which I had seen at the Lucian Freud exhibition at the National Gallery in Washington, is chilling; it suggests that there is a dark side to this billionaire. "I was getting a divorce at the time," he said, as if explaining Freud's unflattering rendition. People who know the baron well say that it is an extraordinarily accurate portrait. "That is Heini totally," said an American woman who had apparently known the baron extremely well for a short time between marriages and asked not to be identified. "He went into unbelievable mood swings."

Helmut Newton asked the baron to pose next to the Lucian Freud portrait. He did. "Your chin up a bit," said Newton. The baron raised his chin. "Maybe that's how I will look someday, but it's not how I look now." As we were leaving the room, he said, "There's another Greco."

Once the Spanish government agreed to put up the necessary capital to house the paintings, and figured out what compensation should be made to the heirs of Baron Thyssen for renouncing their claim to his pictures, the deal was more or less in order. The baron has five children, starting with Georg-Heinrich from his first marriage. He has two children by his third wife, the former Fiona Campbell-Walter: Francesca, known as Chessy, who is an actress, and Lorne, an aspiring actor. After their divorce, Fiona, a beautiful English model, fell madly in love with Alexander Onassis, Aristotle's son by his first wife, Tina Livanos. Although Fiona was acknowledged to be a positive influence on Alexander, who was younger than she, Aristotle Onassis despised her. In 1973, Alexander Onassis was killed in a plane crash. Thyssen also has a child, Alexander, by his fourth wife, Denise, as well as his adopted son, Borja, brought by Tita to the fifth marriage.

"All the paintings legally belong to a Bermuda foundation, a trust, made by Baron Thyssen," the Duke de Badajoz explained to me in his office in Madrid. "After all the proposals from all the countries were together, the Bermuda foundation met and decided the ideal solution would be to make a temporary arrangement and, if it worked out, to make the final solution."

The Spanish government will provide a palace known as the Villahermosa to house the Thyssen-Bornemisza collection. When the old Duchess of Villahermosa died almost sixteen years ago, the time of block-long palaces for private living was at an end, and her daughters, two duchesses and a *marquesa,* sought to sell it. The enormous pink brick palace was first offered to the Spanish government for a relatively modest amount of money. For whatever reasons, the government turned down the offer, and a bank purchased the palace. In order to make the building work as a commercial institution, the inside was stripped, so all architectural details of the once-elegant structure have been obliterated, including what many people told me was one of the most beautiful staircases in Madrid. Then the bank went bankrupt, and the palace was bought by the Ministry of Culture, for more than five times what the government would originally have had to pay.

The palace is huge. There are two floors below ground level which will be made over for restaurants, an auditorium for lectures, and parking space. There will be three complete floors of galleries, and the top floor will be used for offices. Several hundred of the A and B pictures from the Thyssen collection will hang in the Villahermosa Palace. A convent in Barcelona is being refitted to hang seventy-five of the religious paintings in the collection. The rest will continue to hang in the private galleries of the Villa Favorita in Lugano.

The estimated time for the reconstruction of the palace is between eighteen months and two years. The ten-year loan period for the collection will not begin until the pictures are actually hung in the Villahermosa. In bottom-line terms, the loan of the pictures is in reality a rental for a ten-year period. "There is an annual fee of $5 million paid as a rent to the Bermuda foundation," said the Duke de Badajoz. Spain also has to provide insurance and security.

Critics of what has come to be known as the baron's Spanish decision say that he coyly received proposals from a host of suitors, playing one off against the other, when all the time he knew he was going to defer to his wife's wishes and send the collection to Spain, at least for a decade. Prince Charles flew to Lugano to lunch at the Villa Favorita in an effort to get the collection for England, and Helmut Kohl, the chancellor of West Germany, made a similar foray, offering a Baroque palace or a brand-new museum to house the collection. It is not out of the question that one or the other of these countries will be so favored when the baron's permanent decision is made. A London newspaper stated at the time of his last divorce that he had a tendency to ask for his gifts back, although the journalist was referring to jewels and not paintings. An interesting observation made to me by a prominent woman in Madrid was that, whatever decision is made, the Spanish pictures in the collection—the Velázquezes, the Goyas, the El Grecos—will never be allowed to leave the country. All the reports over the last year about the agreement have included the added attraction of Tita Thyssen getting the title of duchess. "It has never been part of the negotiation," said the Duke de Badajoz. "It is the king's privilege to grant such a thing." In fact, Baron Thyssen will be offered a dukedom, which would elevate the baroness to duchess. "Of course, you cannot make a duke for ten years," said the Duke de Badajoz, which means, in practical terms, that the baron and baroness would not be elevated to duke and duchess if at the end of the ten-year loan period they decided to remove the pictures to England, or France, or West Germany, or Japan, or the United States. In the meantime, the Spanish government has already decorated Baron Thyssen with the Grand Cross of Carlos III, one of Spain's highest honors, for outstanding service to the Spanish government, and has decorated the baroness with an Isabel la Católica medal, for outstanding civil merit.

For the present, Baron and Baroness Thyssen will be spending more and more time in Madrid to be near the Villahermosa during the reconstruction period and to take part in deciding how the collection will be hung. Their new house on the outskirts of Madrid, in an area that is reminiscent of the Bel-Air section of Los Angeles, is the kind of house that Californians talk about in terms of square feet. It is immense, with an indoor swimming pool next to the gymnasium, and an outdoor pool which may be one of the largest private swimming pools in the world.

The décor is pure movie star: beige marble, beige terrazzo, beige travertine, indoor waterfalls, plate glass in all directions, and a security system that defies unwanted entry. "I want to get rid of all this," said the baroness after her first night there, waving her hands with a sweeping gesture at the custom-made beige leather sofa and chairs. "And all that in there," she continued, waving at the furniture in another of the many rooms, shaking her head at its lack of beauty. They bought the almost new house furnished. She said that she would give all this "modern furniture" to a benefit for the poor that the aristocratic ladies of Madrid were putting on and that she would furnish the new house with the antique furniture from Daylesford, which has been in storage since that estate was sold.

The Thyssens were scheduled to leave the following morning in their private plane for Barcelona, where the baroness and the Spanish opera singer José Carreras were to receive awards from the city of Barcelona. "It will be nice to settle down and decorate this new house. We are having the gardens all done over too. We've also bought the lot next door so there will be privacy. And there's the new house in Paris that I have to do over. All this traveling. It gets so tiring."

As we walked through her new gardens, she said, "When I die, I am going to leave all my jewelry to a museum. I hate auctions, when it says that the jewelry belonged to the late Mrs. So-and-so."

January 1989

JANE'S
TURN

❧

REMEMBER, I've been in this business fifty-four years. I made eighty-six pictures and 350 television shows. I have not been idle." As she spoke, she leaned forward and her forefinger tapped the table to emphasize her accomplishment. The speaker was Jane Wyman, a no-nonsense star in her mid-seventies, who is one of the highest-paid ladies in show business. Her immensely successful television series for Lorimar, "Falcon Crest," is in its ninth year, and it is she, everyone agrees, in the centerpiece role of Angela Channing, that the public tunes in to see. She got an Academy Award in 1948 for *Johnny Belinda,* in which she played a deaf-mute who gets raped. She was nominated for Oscars on four other occasions, and she has also been nominated twice for Emmys. She has behind her what can well be called a distinguished career.

We met in a perfectly nice but certainly not fashionable restaurant called Bob Burns, at Second Street and Wilshire Boulevard in Santa Monica, California, not far from where she lives. Bob Burns is her favorite restaurant, where she has her regular table, a tufted-leather booth. It is one of those fifties-style California restaurants that are so dark inside that when you step in from the blazing sunlight you are momentarily blinded and pause in the entrance, not sure which way to go. When she arrived, I was already at the table. My eyes had become accustomed to the dark, and I was able to watch her getting her bearings in the doorway. It was twelve noon on the dot, and we were the first two customers in the restaurant. Even to an empty house, though, she played it like a star. She is taller than I had expected. Her posture is superb. Her back is ramrod-straight. She is rail-thin, too thin, giving credence to the speculation that she is not in good health. She walks slowly and carefully. Some people say she is seventy-two, some say seventy-five, others say older. What's the difference? She looks great. Her hairdo, bangs over her forehead, is the trademark style she has worn for years. "Is that you?" she asked, peering.

"Yes." I rose and walked toward her.

She held out her hand, strong and positive. The darkness of the restaurant was flattering to a handsome woman of a certain age, but that is not her reason for liking the place. "The three people who own it went to school with my kids," she said. The words "my kids" were said in the easy manner any parent uses when talking about his or her children. She happens not to be close to either of hers, but we didn't talk about that.

She is private in the extreme, almost mysterious in her privacy, a rich recluse who chooses to live alone, without servants even, in an apartment in Santa Monica overlooking the Pacific Ocean. She is a woman in control at all times. There is not a moment off guard. What you see is the persona she wants you to see, and she reveals nothing further. Any aspect of her career is available for discussion, but don't tread beyond. And for God's sake, I was told, don't mention you-know-who or she'll get up and walk out. Simply put, it pains her that a marriage that ended forty-one years ago seems to interest the press and public more than her career.

"The reason I enjoy TV more than pictures now is that I like the pace better. You've got so many hours to do so much, and you have to get it done. I was on *The Yearling* for eleven and a half months! Sometimes we only did two pages of dialogue in four days," she said. She shook her head in wonderment at the difference in the two media. She was ready to order lunch. "Are the sand dabs breaded?" she asked the waitress. "Why don't we have a Caesar salad first?" she suggested.

For several years before "Falcon Crest" went on the air, she was in a state of semiretirement, spending most of her time painting. Although I have not seen any of her pictures, I have heard from her friends that she is an extremely talented landscape artist. In 1979 her work was exhibited in a gallery in Carmel, California, and so many of the pictures were sold that she now has none of her own work in her apartment. During those years, she said, she was always being sent film and television scripts, "like *Baby Jane,* or playing a lesbian, and I didn't want to do that. But when I was sent the pilot script for 'Falcon Crest,' I could see so many facets to the character of Angela Channing. I said, 'I'll give it two years.' It's now nine."

"People say that you control 'Falcon Crest'," I said.

"I am a creative consultant only. They run things by me, or I run things by them. I just want to keep up the quality of the show," she replied. "I usually have my chair at an odd place on the set where no one can bother me.

And I do help the young actors on the show. I hold a riding crop out, saying 'Don't do that!' "

"Is it true that actors on the show are told not to speak to you?"

"I hope not," she answered.

An actor who had appeared in a part that ran for three episodes told me that he had been informed by his agent, who in turn had heard it from the assistant director, that he was not to approach Miss Wyman on the set, as she did not like to be disturbed. He was also told never to go to her dressing room. He was also told that President Reagan was not to be discussed on the set, ever. The surprise to this particular actor was that Miss Wyman "could not have been more delightful, or friendly. She came right up and introduced herself. One time I did knock on the door of her dressing room. I told her that I didn't think that the scene that we were to do together worked, and she asked me in, and we went over it and made some changes.

Susan Sullivan, who played her daughter-in-law on the series for eight years, said, "Jane is the most professional person I have ever worked with. I have seen her battle through illnesses and fatigue and still keep working. She says, 'Let's get this done. We have a job to do,' and everyone gets behind her. She is always willing to help younger actors. She gives instructions nicely and with humor. She once told me, 'You can tell anybody anything if you do it with humor.' She ruled the set with a kind and intelligent hand."

Rod Taylor, who plays her current husband in the series, agreed. "Sure, she rules the set, but everybody expects that. I adore her."

David Selby, who plays her son and has developed the closest friendship of any of the cast members with her, said, "Never once has she asked to be excused from standing in while the other actors in the scene are having their close-ups. She would be upset if you did your close-up without her. She has never once been late. If we go out to dinner, we go to her favorite little spot. I've never been to her apartment."

Another cast member said, "I've spent years working with her, and I still don't know her. She does not let herself be known."

An insider on the show had told me that an attempt would be made on Angela Channing's life in the new season of the series. "Is it true that you are going to be smothered with a pillow in the third episode and that the audience won't know whether you're dead or alive?"

Her eyes became very large. She was surprised that I knew that. She thought for a moment how to answer. "I *am* going into a coma for a while," she said. She has a way of letting you know when she is finished with a topic, without actually telling you that she is.

"Do you have a social life?" I asked.

"Not really. When you're on a series, it, the series, becomes your life. I don't go out." She gets up at 4:30 each morning the series is in production. "I can't drive in the dark, so I'm picked up by a studio driver. I leave my apartment at exactly 5:50. It's a long drive to the studio. I do my own makeup when I get there.

"I'm a great reader. And I have some close friends. We do a lot of telephoning. My friends understand me when I say, 'Everything is on hold until the series is finished.'" Among her closest friends are the two great film and television stars Loretta Young and Barbara Stanwyck, both of whom have had careers and led lives similar to Jane Wyman's. "Jane is a good girl. She's also a very determined woman," Barbara Stanwyck told me. "She has worked very hard for her successful career. I do mean hard, and she deserves all her success because she earned it." She then added, "I know this is a story about Jane, so be very good and very kind. She would be to you."

In an interview with Jane Wyman from the forties, published in a movie magazine of the period and discovered in the Warner Brothers archives at the University of Southern California, the writer noted, "Talking to her, one gets the impression she's wound up like a tight spring." Approximately forty years later, the same line could still be written about her, except for when she is talking about her career. Then she relaxes. She is a virtual oral historian of the decades she spent at Warner Brothers. She was under contract to Warner's for years, beginning in 1936 at $166 a week. She had been at Fox and Paramount before that. Somewhere along the line, her name was changed from Sarah Jane Fulks to Jane Wyman. "I stayed at Warner's until I went into television," she said. She started out as a wisecracking comedienne and singer, with no interest whatever in dramatic roles. "Jane Wyman has no yen for drama," read one of her early press releases. "Leave that to other people," she was quoted as saying. Her studio biography described her as "pert, vivacious, with plenty of pep. Jane Wyman is a human tornado." Not all of her films were distinguished, but her memory is as astonishingly sharp for details of the making of middling and less-than-middling films as it is for those of such classics as Billy Wilder's *The Lost Weekend.* "We were in a three shot," she said, remembering one B-picture incident. "I was in the middle. Jack Carson was on one side, and Dennis Morgan on the other."

The star names flew from her lips. She calls James Cagney Cagney and Bob Hope Hope. "Cagney was my dream man," she said. "Hope wanted me to do this picture with him. You know Hope." Ann Sheridan. Humphrey

Bogart. Joan Blondell. Bette Davis. "Bette Davis's dressing room was right next to mine, but we were never friends." Olivia de Havilland. Errol Flynn. "Jack Warner would never put me into any of their costume epics. He said I had the wrong looks. I think Jack was probably right."

She had an early marriage to Myron Futterman, a New Orleans dress manufacturer, about whom almost nothing is known. In 1940 she married Ronald Reagan, a fellow contract player at Warner Brothers, with whom she made four films. Their wedding reception was held at the home of the most famous of all Hollywood gossip columnists, Louella Parsons, who was raised in Dixon, Illinois, where Reagan grew up. Every movie magazine of the period recorded the idyll of the young stars' marriage, in the approved, studio-orchestrated publicity jargon. When Jane became pregnant, the studio announced that she was expecting a bundle from heaven. The bundle from heaven was Maureen Reagan, now forty-eight, who was born in 1941. Four years later the young couple adopted a son, Michael. They were promoted by Warner's as the dream Hollywood couple, and every fan magazine monitored their lives. "Ronnie and I are perfect counterparts for each other. I blow up, and Ronnie just laughs at me. We've never had a quarrel, because he's just too good-natured," said Jane in one interview. Several years after that, the lovebirds became known in the press as "Those Fightin' Reagans," and rumors of a rift in the marriage were rampant. Louella Parsons, who thrived on such matters, told Jane in a column, "I want to write a story and settle all this talk once and for all." Jane was quoted by Louella as replying, "Believe me, I'm going to find out who has started all this talk. . . . Can't gossips let us keep our happiness?"

In 1947 the marriage did break up. "We're through," Jane said to a columnist during a trip to New York. "We're finished, and it's all my fault." Reagan found out about the termination of his marriage when he read it in the column. He gave long interviews to Louella and to her archrival, Hedda Hopper, both of whom took his side. "If this comes to a divorce, I'll name *Johnny Belinda* as co-respondent," Hedda Hopper quoted him as saying. Jane had become so immersed in her new career as a dramatic actress that she wore pellets wrapped in wax in her ears so that she would not be able to hear during the filming of the deaf-mute movie. Hedda Hopper had more to say on the subject: "I can't really believe it yet. I don't think Ronald Reagan does either. It caught him so flatfooted, so pathetically by surprise. I talked to Ronnie the day he read in the newspapers what Jane should have told her husband first."

They were divorced in 1948, the same year she won the Academy Award. Jane got custody of the two children, and Reagan got weekend visitation rights. Jane testified that her husband's overriding interest in filmland union and political activity had driven them apart. Friends speculated at the time that Jane's emergence as a bona fide star and Reagan's concurrent slide from box-office favor contributed to the breakup. Others felt that Jane was simply bored with him. Before the governorship and his truly remarkable rise as a recognized world leader, friends from that period remember, he did indeed engage in long, ponderous, yawn-producing discourses on a variety of subjects. An ongoing joke in Hollywood during his campaign for the governorship of California was a remark attributed to Jane Wyman about her former husband. When asked what he was like, she allegedly said, "If you asked Ronnie the time, he'd tell you how to make a watch."

In 1954 Reagan married the actress Nancy Davis, who had been a contract player at MGM. Not long afterward, Jane married the bandleader and musical arranger Freddie

Karger, a popular and handsome man-about-town in Hollywood. She divorced him a year later. Karger is often mentioned in Marilyn Monroe biographies as one of her lovers. Years later Wyman married Karger again, and then divorced him again. She has not married since.

In 1954 Jane was converted to Catholicism through the intervention of her great friend Loretta Young. Her Catholicism is a mainstay in her life. In fact, when asked her age, according to friends, she very often replies, "I'm thirty-five." She is counting from the year of her conversion to Catholicism. "She goes to Mass all the time," said a member of the cast of "Falcon Crest." "Sometimes she even has Mass said in her room." One of the ongoing characters in the series is a Catholic priest. "We need a lot of advice, because some of the characters are Catholic in the show," said Jane. The priest character is played by a real priest, Father Bob Curtis, a Paulist.

After *Johnny Belinda,* her career totally dominated her life. "She told me she could never even cook a hamburger. She taught her kids early that she wasn't going to be there," said an actor friend of hers. She had made the long and difficult transition from contract player to leading lady to star, and she hung on to that position through the forties and into the mid-fifties, playing what she has called four-handkerchief roles in such classic films of the genre as *Magnificent Obsession* and *The Blue Veil,* which remains her favorite. "I was in the middle of the woman's cycle in picture making," she said. She talked about her contemporaries. "Greer, Irene, Olivia, Joan, Bette, Loretta, Barbara, and don't forget Ginger . . . I never really knew Ava." She was talking about Greer Garson, Irene Dunne, Olivia de Havilland, Joan Fontaine, Bette Davis, Loretta Young, Barbara Stanwyck, Ginger Rogers, and Ava Gardner. "The thing was, we were all different," she said. The *New York*

Times film critic Bosley Crowther wrote about her in 1953, "Her acting of drudges has become a virtual standard on the screen." But then the cycle of women's films ended. She decided to retire in 1962.

Several seasons ago Lana Turner, who was one of the queens of MGM when Jane was one of the queens of Warner Brothers, came on "Falcon Crest" as a semiregular. From the beginning, there was a coolness between the two stars. Lana, according to one source, took five or six hours to get ready, and Jane, for whom promptness is a passion, could never tolerate that. Someone closely connected with the show told me that Jane watched Lana on a talk show one night and felt that she was taking credit for "Falcon Crest"'s coming in number two in the ratings. "Imagine her taking credit for the show's success," said Jane at the time. Lana did not appear on the show again.

In the old days of the studios and contract players, the young actors were taught how to conduct themselves in interviews. They never said anything negative about anyone, and that training is still evident today.

"Was there a difficulty between you and Lana Turner?" I asked.

"Enough said, right there," answered Jane Wyman. She looked at me in a way that said very clearly that Miss Turner was a topic she had finished discussing. Her praise for her fellow actors on the series is unqualified, however. "I love to work with David Selby." "Lorenzo Lamas can do almost anything. He's a wonderful dramatic actor." "I said, 'I want Rod Taylor in the show.' He was occupied doing something else. I said, 'We'll wait.'"

"I never asked anything about her children. I have never approached that relationship with her," said an actor on the series. "I think she was hurt by Michael's book, but she has never said one harsh word about them. The only time I ever heard her mention the name of the president, she said something kind."

Both of her children have written books in which they announced things to their parents that they had not told them before. Maureen wrote that she had been a severely battered wife in her first marriage, and Michael confessed that he had been sexually molested by a man when he was a child. Since Joan Crawford's daughter Christina wrote *Mommie Dearest*, it has become the vogue among the adult children of the famous to cash in on their privileged unhappiness by spilling the beans on their celebrity dad or mom. Maureen wrote that Jane had not come to her first wedding. Michael wrote that Jane had sent him away to boarding school when he was six. Even the siblings did not seem to get along. Michael, in his book, recounts an incident that happened when he was four years old. He told Maureen that he knew a secret. "What?" she asked. He told her that she was getting a new blue dress for Christmas. Infuriated that he had ruined her Christmas surprise, she snapped, "I know a secret too. You're adopted."

"Do you see your grandchildren?" I asked. Maureen has no children, but Michael has two, Cameron and Ashley.

"Once in a while," she replied slowly. The subject was approaching the danger area. "They're in school when I'm working. They're adorable kids, Cameron and Ashley. Cameron's always saying to me, 'Gramma, how old are you?' And I say, 'I'm as old as my little finger.' And he says, 'How old is that?' and I say, 'As old as I am.'"

"Have you always been so reluctant to be interviewed?" I asked.

"No," she said. "My life's an open book. Everyone knows everything about me. There are all those magazines with lies in them." She had ordered a Diet Coke, and she took a sip. "I used to be interviewed a lot. But the last time I was, I had what seemed to be a very nice interview with the reporter, and then the piece came out. The first line was something like 'This is the president's ex-wife.' That's when the guillotine fell. I don't have to be known as that. I've been in this business longer than he has. It's such bad taste. They wouldn't say it if I was Joe Blow's ex-wife. It wouldn't even be mentioned."

With that said—and it was the closest she got to the unmentionable subject, the former president of the United States—she shifted topics abruptly. "We're going to have fun this year on the series. We have such a good producer, and the writers are wonderful. I feel like I'm doing the first show. The enthusiasm is just wonderful. The 'Falcon Crest' that *I* want is going on this year."

However reluctant she may be to discuss it, how can her relationship with Ronald Reagan not be discussed? She is the only former wife of a United States president in the history of the country. It is certainly true that if she had been married to Joe Blow it would never be mentioned. Her marriages to Myron Futterman, who manufactured dresses, and to Freddie Karger, who led the dance band on the roof of the Beverly Hilton Hotel in Beverly Hills, are never mentioned. But between those two marriages was her longest marriage, to a movie star of the period, with whom she had two children and who later became the governor of the state of California and then the president of the United States. It is part of her history. It will be the lead in her obituary when she dies.

It is a curious coincidence of fate that the eight years of her emergence as the First Lady of television should almost exactly parallel the eight years of her former husband's second wife's emergence as the First Lady of the land. The relationship between the two women is, has always been, and ever will be poisonous, although Jane Wyman has never uttered a single word in public about or against Nancy Reagan. Apparently Mrs. Reagan has not returned the courtesy. There are publishing rumors that her forthcoming book, *My Turn,* contains several obliquely critical allusions to Jane Wyman in reference to the bringing up of the two children Jane had during her marriage to Ronald Reagan. "Jane was a star. Nancy never was," a Los Angeles socialite acquainted with both said to explain the bad blood between the two women. "For seventeen years, Jane has kept her mouth shut. Nancy hates Jane with such a passion because it's the only part of Ronnie that she doesn't control. If you had mentioned Ronnie to Jane, she would have gotten up and walked out." A person friendly with Nancy Reagan told me that in the scrapbooks she keeps of newspaper clippings about her romance and marriage to Ronald Reagan, all mentions of Jane Wyman have been blacked out. In turn, a person friendly with Jane Wyman told me in private Jane sometimes refers to Nancy Reagan as Nancyvita.

Until recently, Jane was a regular and favored patron of the famed Hollywood restaurant Chasen's, as well as a close personal friend of Maude Chasen, the widow of David Chasen, who founded the restaurant fifty-three years ago. Although her friendship with Maude continues, she is, by unstated mutual agreement, almost never seen there these days. Chasen's has become the more or less official restaurant of the recent president and his wife, and Jane Wyman's absence from the premises averts the possibility of a chance encounter.

A journalist friend told me about interviewing the former president in the private quarters of the White House. He had been warned in advance that the name Jane Wyman was never mentioned in the presence of the First Lady. But since Miss Wyman had been married to the president for eight years, the journalist ventured very cautiously, when they were deep into the conversation, to bring up her name. To his surprise, the president began to tell a friendly anecdote about his first wife. Midway through the story, Nancy Reagan walked into the room. Without a second's hesitation, the president shifted to another topic right in the middle of a sentence, and the subject of Miss Wyman did not come up again.

Every star of Jane Wyman's caliber pays a price for fame, and she has endured for over fifty years. Although she is husbandless and vaguely estranged from her children, her splendid isolation must not be confused with loneliness. Where she is is where she has always wanted to be from her early contract days.

Like all success-oriented people, she is not without her detractors. Robert Raison was Jane Wyman's agent for nearly thirty years, as well as her friend and sometime escort to social functions in the television industry. He was also the agent of Dennis Hopper, Michelle Phillips, and all of the Bottoms brothers. He had a reputation for developing close friendships with his clients. He negotiated the seven-year deal for Jane when she decided to play the role of Angela Channing on "Falcon Crest." At the end of the seventh year of the series, Raison heard from Jane's lawyer that he was through. "When she fired me, she never told me herself. I heard it from her lawyer," said Raison. When he asked why, the lawyer told him to call Jane and discuss it with her. "I did," said Raison. "I told her I wanted to hear it from her mouth. You know what she said?"

"No."

"She said, 'You and me, Bobby, we've run out of gas.' I was going to sue her, but the lawyers settled it for a given amount of money. I can't discuss that amount."

Raison is now writing a book about his years with Jane Wyman. It is tentatively titled *Jane Wyman, Less than a Legend: A Memoir in Close-Up.* Although angry and hurt, Raison still expresses residual tenderness for his former client. "Two days after the assassination attempt on the president, Jane sent him flowers to the hospital in Washington. Several days later, the president personally called to say thank you for the flowers," Raison recalled recently. He answered the telephone when the president called. "He said to me, 'Thank you for taking care of her, Bobby,'" said Raison.

The check came. In an interview situation like this one, the interviewer always picks up the check. As I reached for it, Jane Wyman tapped my hand and shook her head. "This is on Lorimar," she said.

We walked outside into the brilliant sunlight. Her red Jaguar was parked in the number-one space of the Bob Burns parking lot. We shook hands. "Where else can you meet such fascinating people and go to such places as people in our business do?" she said. "It's a fabulous life."

In an era of tell-all, Jane Wyman has made the decision to tell nothing. No confessions. No revelations. It's her life, and it's private. There are those who say it is her duty to inform historians of the eight years she shared with a man who later became the president of the United States, years that encompassed the peak of his minor movie stardom, his presidency of the Screen Actors Guild, and his role in the ignoble House Un-American Activities Committee hearings. But she sees it differently, and that's the way it is.

"She's one tough lady," said one of the cast members of "Falcon Crest." Yeah, but a lady.

November 1989

IT'S A
FAMILY AFFAIR

IT WAS a family affair. The father, the mother, the three sons, the two daughters, the estranged wife of one of the sons, a grandchild, boyfriends and girlfriends of all the children. And there were the father's half-sister and the mother's sisters and almost all their husbands, and a good many of their children. And cousins, lots of cousins, city cousins and country cousins, including, in the host's own words, "masses of Guinnesses." And friends, but only close friends, hardly a jet-setter in the whole bunch. This was, remember, a family affair.

But what a family and what an affair. Lord Glenconner, of England, Scotland, and the islands of Mustique and Saint Lucia in the British West Indies, who used to be called Colin Tennant before he inherited his father's title, was celebrating his sixtieth birthday in very grand style. For openers, he had chartered a brand-new 440-foot four-masted sailing vessel called the *Wind Star,* possibly the prettiest ship afloat, with a crew of eighty-seven, and had installed 130 of his nearest and dearest in its seventy-five staterooms, complete with VCRs and mini-bars, for a

week-long cruise from Saint Lucia to Martinique to Bequia
to Mustique, with parties all along the way, every noon and
every night, culminating in a costume ball called the Peacock Ball at the Glenconners' place, which some people call
a palace, on the beach in Mustique. And should there have
been any question of the financial burden imposed by such
an adventure, Lord Glenconner had taken care of that too,
by paying the fares of all his guests from London to Saint
Lucia, where he owns a second estate, called the Jalousie
Plantation, which he plans, in time, to turn into a hotel
and health spa. And should there have been any problem
about rounding up a suitable costume for the lavish India-
theme ball, Lord Glenconner had even anticipated that. In
his travels to India over the past year, while he was preparing for his birthday celebration, he had purchased a variety
of kurtas and Aligarh trousers and turbans and ghagra/
cholis and harem dresses in a whole range of sizes and styles
and had had them transported to the *Wind Star* so that his
guests could pick out what they liked. There were even two
seamstresses on board to make any necessary alterations.
The only thing you had to provide was your own jewelry.
He drew the line at that. But he did have a hairdresser for
the ladies, who doubled as a barber for the men, and a
masseuse and a masseur. And 360 movies to choose from
for the VCRs, including 58 pornographic ones. And all
taxi rides on the various islands were to be paid for by Lord
Glenconner. And there was to be absolutely no tipping.
Lord Glenconner had taken care of all that. It was, all the
way around, a class act.

  I arrived in Saint Lucia the day before the plane from
London arrived, and was met at Hewanorra airport by Lord
Glenconner and his estate manager, Lyton Lamontagne, at
whose house I spent the first night. Lyton Lamontagne, a
native of Saint Lucia in his late twenties, and his wife,

Eroline, went to school together in the town of Soufrière. He is handsome and she is beautiful. A trusted confidant of Lord Glenconner's, Lamontagne traveled to India with him last year and was instrumental in carrying out the far-sighted and sometimes seemingly impossible plans of the eccentric lord. Glenconner feels, as do others I saw in Saint Lucia, that in time Lyton Lamontagne could become the prime minister of the island. The Lamontagnes refer to Lord Glenconner as Papa, as do many of the natives on both Saint Lucia and Mustique, and there is a sense in their relationship of the nineteenth-century British Empire builder and his devoted overseer. In Soufrière, Glenconner lives in an old wooden house on the town square, so primitive that it has no electricity or running water, although it will have at some point in the future. He has to go to the nearby Texaco station to use the bathroom or wash, and this sort of inconvenience seems to appeal to him, although it is at variance with his elegance of manner, which is sometimes almost effete. He wears large straw hats, and for his birthday week he always dressed in white or black.

Lord Glenconner talked briefly about several last-minute drop-outs from the party. Mick Jagger could not take the time out to attend, although Jerry Hall would be joining the group when the boat docked in Mustique. David Bowie could not come. Lord Dufferin and Ava were ill. Carolina Herrera had to finalize a perfume deal in New York. Glenconner rolled his eyes in disappointment. He rolls his eyes a great deal, in exasperation, or wonder, or over lapses of taste. His own lapses, however, take on a sort of aristocratic whimsy, at least in his mind. He once allowed himself to be photographed defecating by the side of the road in India and sent the pictures to *Vanity Fair*.

We sailed in a small open boat to the Jalousie Plantation, where one of the main events of the week-long celebration was going to take place several days hence. His plantation lies between two peaks called the Pitons. The original house, on what was once a sugar plantation built by the French in the seventeenth or eighteenth century, is long gone, but stone walls from the original waterwheel are still standing. The principal house now is a small wooden bungalow, onto which had just been added a covered porch for the picnic party. The bungalow, which has gingerbread trimmings, was painted pink with yellow shutters, green floors, and blue interior walls, and looked like a set from the musical *House of Flowers*. Gamboling happily around the scene of preparations was a frisky young elephant called Bupa, which Glenconner had bought from the Dublin zoo and had sent out to his plantation. A native painter was finishing a mural on one side of the house, and Lord Glenconner examined the lavender leaves and red and orange flowers closely. "No, no, no, I don't like that color red at all," he said to the painter. "There's far too much brown in that red. I want a red red." They found a red red.

Then we went for the first of two trips to the airport, to meet Lady Glenconner, known as Lady Anne, who was arriving from Mustique with the eldest of her three sons, Charles, as well as her daughter-in-law, Tessa Tennant, the wife of her second son, Henry, and Viscount Linley, the son of Princess Margaret by the Earl of Snowdon. The contingent from London, which included the Glenconners' twin teenage daughters, Amy and May, was arriving on a second plane several hours later. Another son, Christopher, was arriving from Mexico. On the way to the airport Glenconner had the driver stop the car several times so that he could cut wild lilies growing by the side of the road to present to his wife. Lady Anne is a lady-in-waiting to Princess Margaret. Such close friends are the Glenconners of the princess that they have been living at Kensington Palace as her houseguests for nearly a year while their new London house has been undergoing extensive renovations and decoration. "I sleep in what was Tony Snowdon's dressing room, just this far from Princess Margaret," Lord Glenconner told me. He said when they were moving out of their old house, Princess Margaret came to help them pack; she donned a working smock borrowed from a maid and wrapped china in newspapers.

"I thought surely you'd have had a steel band on the tarmac when the plane arrived," Lady Anne said to her husband, patting her hair beneath a straw hat and supervising the transfer of all the luggage to the van that would take us to the boat. She is blond and calm and attractive.

"I hadn't thought of it," replied Glenconner, and I felt that in his mind he was trying to figure out if he could do just that before the plane from London arrived a few hours later. Although they are married and live together, or at least live under the same roof when the separate schedules of their lives overlap, they speak to each other with the friendly distance of a divorced couple meeting at their child's wedding.

Their oldest son, Charles, called Charlie, thirty, looked pale and disheveled. His father told him to wash his face and get a haircut as soon as we got on the ship. Although Lord Glenconner has publicly disinherited his eldest son, who is a registered heroin addict, with an announcement in the London *Daily Mail,* there seems to be no lessening of affection for him, nor is there any sort of middle-class covering up of a family embarrassment. "My son Charlie is a heroin addict and has been ever since he was fifteen," said Glenconner openly, not only to me but to several other people encountering the situation for the first time. Charlie remains a part of the family, disinherited but not cast out, and loved by all. In time he will become Lord Glenconner, for titles must go to the eldest son, but the estates, fortune, and castle in Scotland will pass to his brother Henry, who is estranged from Tessa, by whom he has a son, Euan, three.

When we got to the pier where the *Wind Star* was docked, the fence was padlocked, and two armed guards stared at us as if we were usurpers, making no attempt to open the gates for the van to enter. "I am the lessee of the boat," called out Lord Glenconner from the backseat of the van. The guards did not react. "Just say Lord Glenconner," said Charles from the front seat to his father. "I am Lord Glenconner," called out Lord Glenconner. The gates were opened.

Standing on deck, we watched the London crowd arrive, hot and tired and bedraggled, and trudge up the gangplank. A Mrs. Wills had lost her keys, and there was a great to-do. "Where's Mark Palmer?" someone called out. "I can't find my suitcases," someone else wailed. John Stefanidis, the famed London interior decorator, who helped the Glenconners with the Great House in Mustique and who is currently doing up their new London house, remarked to his deck companions, Lord and Lady Neidpath, with whom he had flown over from Mustique, "Rather elite, having arrived early."

In typical English fashion, no one was introduced. Those who already knew one another stayed together and looked at the others. There were no passenger lists in the staterooms, so it was impossible to put names to faces. Even during lifeboat drill, when we were separated into small groups, they did not introduce themselves. After a few days, people began to come into focus as one-line descriptions were repeated over and over: "He's Princess Margaret's son." "She's Rachel Ward's mother." "He was recently fired by Mrs. Thatcher." "She's the Duke of Rutland's sister-in-law."

One passenger of interest was Barbara Barnes, on holiday from Kensington Palace, where she is nanny to the royal princes, William and Henry. Nanny Barnes, a popular figure on the ship, used to be nanny to the children of Colin and Anne Glenconner, and the Princess of Wales had given her time off to attend the celebration and visit her former charges.

For a week we heard no news of the outside world. We were hermetically sealed in the elegant confines of the *Wind Star* when we were not ashore being picnicked. There was swimming off the ship and in the pool, and gambling in the casino, and a gym to work out in, and bars to drink at, and a disco to dance in, and all those videos, including the fifty-eight pornographic ones, with titles like *For Your Thighs Only* and *Lust on the Orient Express,* and even a library. John Nutting read the recent biography of Lord Esher. His wife read a biography of Francis Bacon. The Honorable Mrs. Marten read the new biography of Anthony Eden. Prince Rupert Löwenstein read the biography of Frank Sinatra by Kitty Kelley. Conversation, which never lagged, from breakfast to bedtime, was all about themselves. They never tired of discussing one another. One Englishman described the degree of friendship with another man on board as being not quite on farting terms.

"Tell me, how is young Lord Ivar Mountbatten, over there with the pretty Channon girl, related to Dickie?"

"He's through the Milford Haven branch."

"Claire tells me Tony Lambton's writing a biography of Dickie Mountbatten that's going to tell everything."

"Oh dear."

"The Guinnesses all stick together, have you noticed?"

"Lord Neidpath is very proud of his feet."

It is said that on all private boat trips the most unifying factor for harmony is a mutual dislike of one particular person aboard, and this trip was no exception. By the third day, all had agreed that they loathed the same certain person, and from that moment on, tales of that person's every move and statement were circulated.

"Don't believe any rumors unless you start them yourself," cautioned Lord Glenconner, in regard to all the rumors that were circulating about the trip. From passing yachts we heard that Michael Jackson was on board the *Wind Star,* but the person the passengers in the passing yachts mistook for Michael Jackson was called Kelvin Omard, a London actor and great friend of Henry Tennant, Lord Glenconner's second son. "Did you see *Water* with Michael Caine?" asked Tessa Tennant, Henry's wife. "Kelvin played the waiter."

"How much do you suppose this is all costing?" I inquired tentatively one day at lunch on Martinique, fully expecting to be put in my place with imperious stares for daring to ask such a vulgar question. I meant the whole week of it: the plane fares, the *Wind Star,* the parties, parties, parties, and the ball that was to come.

"That's what we're all wondering" was the immediate and unexpected answer, from one of my lunch companions, not a Tennant, at a table of Tennants. "We figure about a half-million." I didn't know if she meant pounds or dollars, but since she was English, I assumed pounds. As the week progressed, revealing constant new considerations on the part of our host for his guests, the cost question was brought up again and again, not only by me, an almost lone American on a boatload of Brits, but by a number of Brits as well.

"Colin is not limitlessly rich," said another passenger a few days later at dinner on board the *Wind Star,* pursuant to the same question. When I wrote down the phrase "not limitlessly rich," his wife said, "My God, you're not going to quote my husband, are you?"

"All I know is he sold some items at Sotheby's in order to charter the *Wind Star,* and paid for the charter in installments," offered someone else.

"Where is Lord Glenconner's money from?" I asked over and over.

"Sugar in the West Indies, nineteenth century, I would think" was one reply.

"Imperial Chemical" was another.

Lord Glenconner's explanation seemed to answer the question. "My great-grandfather invented the Industrial Revolution."

Like a mysterious shadow, a second ship was known to be looming in the distance, the *Maxim's des Mers,* the floating sister of the famed Parisian restaurant, carrying "the American crowd." At some point we would be rendezvousing with them. In speculation preceding the ball week, it had been rumored that Mick Jagger, David Bowie, Michael Caine, and others too famous for words would be among its passengers, supplying the magic mix of show biz with swells that guarantees fascination on both sides. At the helm of the *Maxim's des Mers,* at least as organizer of the famous, was André Weinfeld, the husband of Raquel Welch, and an invitation every bit as grand as the one to the Peacock Ball sent by Lady Glenconner and the one to a beach picnic on the morning following the ball sent by H.R.H. the Princess Margaret, Countess of Snowdon, had been dispatched by Miss Welch and Mr. Weinfeld bidding us, the passengers on the *Wind Star,* and other guests who would be joining our party in Mustique, to a dinner on board the *Maxim's des Mers* on the evening preceding the ball. Already, even before our rendezvous, rumors of defections from their guest list had circulated. We knew that such stalwarts of the international social scene as Carolina and Reinaldo Herrera and Ahmet and Mica Ertegün had dropped out, not to mention Mick and David, as they were referred to, meaning Jagger and Bowie, who had long since changed their plans.

The *Maxim's des Mers* came side by side with the *Wind Star* in the cove in front of Lord Glenconner's Jalousie Plantation on Saint Lucia. The other boat was squat and inelegant next to our trim, patrician four-master; the battle lines were instantly drawn. No amount of interior Art Nouveau tarting up of the *Maxim's des Mers* could belie its minesweeper origins. The A group—B group distinction between the two parties could not be denied by even the most generous-hearted. It carried right down to the crew of the *Wind Star,* who snubbed the crew of the *Maxim's des Mers.* "Rather like being on the wrong side of the room at '21,' " remarked a *Wind Star* passenger about the *Maxim's des Mers,* which others were already referring to as the *Mal de Mer.* The celebrity guests that Mr. Weinfeld was able to produce arrived onshore for the barbecue at the plantation. Vastly fat native women were dressed up in Aunt Jemima gear, a fourteen-piece steel band played nonstop, the elephant frolicked with the guests, and at one point Lyton and Eroline Lamontagne, got up as Scarlett O'Hara and Rhett Butler, drove down a mountain in a horse and buggy to be introduced by Lord Glenconner as his distinguished neighbors from the next plantation. Rum punch and more rum punch, and still more rum punch was consumed. And the sun beat down.

Heading Mr. Weinfeld's star list was the amply bosomed Dianne Brill, the New York underground cult figure often referred to in the gossip columns as the Queen of the Night. Although Miss Brill is a good sport, a good mixer, and a genuinely funny lady, even she could not bring about any real mixing between the passengers of the two ships. "Who do you suppose *they* are?" someone in our party asked about a trio of ladies. "In trade, I would think," said Prince Rupert Löwenstein playfully, "above a boutique and below a department store." André Weinfeld explained that because it was Thanksgiving, most of the people he had invited had backed out, and he had brought along a substitute crowd. Indeed, his wife, Raquel Welch, had not yet joined the company, but he assured us she would be along in time for her party on board the *Maxim's des Mers.*

In Mustique the inner circle widened to admit some new arrivals. Adding more than a dash of American glamour to the British festivities were two tall and sleek American beauties, Jean Harvey Vanderbilt, of New York, and Minnie Cushing Coleman, of Newport and New Orleans. On Mustique the groups within the group of the *Wind Star* began to divide up into splinter groups. "We're going to Ingrid Channon's house for lunch," said Mrs. Vyner. "We've been asked for drinks at Princess Margaret's house," said Mrs. Nutting. "We're having a box lunch at Macaroni Beach," said the ones who weren't invited to any of the private houses.

"What happens if you don't call Princess Margaret ma'am?" asked one of the new American arrivals.

"You don't get asked back," came the reply.

On the morning of Raquel Welch's party aboard the *Maxim's des Mers,* a telex arrived for Lord Glenconner from the star, saying that a contract negotiation prevented her from attending her own party. Lord Glenconner rolled his eyes in disappointment, but any attentive observer could also detect an element of anger in the eye roll. His last star had fallen by the wayside. From that moment on, Raquel Welch, who had always been referred to as Raquel in anticipation of her arrival, was referred to by one and all as Miss Welch.

"I think this is the rudest thing I have ever heard," fumed one of Lord Glenconner's guests, and then proceeded to fume against all Americans for Miss Welch's rudeness, especially since a member of the royal family had consented to attend her party.

"But Miss Welch is not American, Julian. She's English," said his wife.

"Oh dear," said her husband, calmly accepting the correction, although he had been right to begin with.

"If she can't be bothered to attend her own party, I can't be bothered to attend it either," said another guest.

"Disgraceful!"

"Movie stars always back out at the last minute."

"They're insecure in social situations."

"You don't suppose they're getting a divorce, do you, Mr. Weinfeld and Miss Welch?"

On the night of the ball, after a whole week of partying, guests ran up and down the passageways of the *Wind Star* borrowing feathers, remarking on one another's costumes, pinning and sewing up each other—all with the excitement of boarding-school students preparing for the annual spring dance. John Stefanidis had gone to Paris to borrow jewelry to wear with his Indian costume from Loulou de la Falaise, who works for Yves Saint Laurent, and indeed his pounds of pearls, rhinestone necklaces, and long drop earrings were the most elaborate jewelry at the ball—after the host's, that is.

All during the evening, Lord Glenconner's eyes shone

with the excitement of an accomplished creation—a symphony composed, an epic written, a masterpiece painted. Wearing a gold crown and ropes of pearls, he was dressed in white magnificence, his high collar and robes heavily encrusted with gold embroidery. The Glenconner house, called simply the Great House, is a Taj Mahal–like palace designed by the ultimate stage and ballet designer-fantacist, the late Oliver Messel, uncle of Lord Snowdon, former husband of Princess Margaret. Magical even in broad daylight, by night, for the ball, it was bathed in pink and turquoise fluorescent light, which gave the illusion of a Broadway-musical version of India. Handsome, almost nude black males from Saint Lucia and Mustique, their private parts encased in coconut shells painted gold, with strips of gold tinsel hanging from their shoulders to the ground, lined the pink-carpeted walkway to the house. Inside the double doors, more natives, in pink and blue Lurex fantasies of Indian dress inspired more by *The King and I* than by *The Jewel in the Crown,* stood cooling the air with giant peacock feather fans on poles.

Standing under a pink marquee, with the palm-tree-lined beach in the background and the *Wind Star,* fully lit, on the sea beyond, Lord and Lady Glenconner, with their son Charlie by their side, received their elaborately dressed guests while their son Henry called out the names as they arrived.

"Mrs. Michael Brand," called out Henry Tennant.

"I am the Honorable Mrs. Brand, not Mrs. Michael Brand," corrected Mrs. Brand.

The natives on the island of Mustique call Princess Margaret simply Princess, with neither an article preceding nor a name following. Well, Princess was late, and the procession that was to open the ball could not take place until Princess arrived, because Princess was the principal participant. The fact was, Princess had arrived at the Great House, but she was still sitting in Lady Anne's bedroom, which boasts a silver bed with silver peacocks on the head- and footboards. One story had it that Raquel Welch had also finally arrived on the island, and that Princess, not wishing to be outdone by her, as she had been the previous evening, when Miss Welch had not shown up at her own party, where Princess was an honored guest, was delaying the procession until after Miss Welch's arrival. If such was the case, Princess lost another round.

Finally, despairing of Miss Welch's ever arriving, the royal procession started. The sisters of Lady Anne, Lady Carey Basset, with one of her three sons, and Lady Sarah Walter, with her husband, Prince and Princess Rupert Löwenstein, and the Americans, Miss Jerry Hall and Mr. and Mrs. James Coleman, Jr., moved slowly from the house to the receiving tent. They were followed by Viscount Linley, in a white peacock headdress, which he never removed for the whole night, and his beautiful girlfriend, Susannah Constantine. Then came Princess Margaret, the great friend of the Glenconners. On her head, comple- menting her dress, which was a gift from Lord Glenconner, she wore a black velvet headband tiara-style, onto which her maid, that afternoon, had sewn massive diamond clips. Her resplendence had been worth the wait.

"Her Royal Highness, Princess Margaret, Countess of Snowdon," called out Henry Tennant. All the Indian-clad ladies dropped in curtsies as she passed, and all the men bowed their heads. Under the tent, Lady Anne kissed her on both cheeks before doing a deep curtsy. Then Lord Glenconner removed his crown, as did his son Charlie, and they bowed to Princess.

When Princess Margaret first saw the Indian sari that Lord Glenconner had had made for her in India, she exclaimed, "I've been dreaming of having a dress like this since I was six." During dinner a maid spilled a tray of potatoes on the dress, but Princess's dinner partners, Sir John Plumb, the eighteenth-century historian, and John Nutting, an English barrister of note, were able to right the wrong with a minimum of fuss and very little stain.

Miss Welch, the lone dissenter from Indian costume, finally arrived during dinner, dressed in a gray metallic shirred evening gown and shoulder-length metallic shirred evening gloves, which she kept on while she ate. She was seated between Prince Rupert Löwenstein, a noted wit and conversationalist, and Mr. Roddy Llewellyn, the extremely affable suitor, before his marriage, of Princess Margaret, at whose Mustique house he and his wife, Tania, were house-guests, but conversation with the film star was pretty much uphill.

"Have you read the Sinatra biography?" Prince Rupert asked her.

"No," she said, "but I made a picture with Frank. If Frank likes you, he's behind you all the way. He wrote me a letter when my father died." Then she massaged her neck with her hand and said, "My neck's out. I've been wearing a neck brace, but I couldn't wear a neck brace with this dress to Colin's party. It's stress. I've been under a lot of stress. Would you get my husband, please? I need my pills for my neck. André, would you get my pills for my neck. Two of the yellow ones."

"They're back on the boat," joked Prince Rupert. "In the Dufy suite."

"No, I'm not staying on the boat," she said. "I'm at the Cotton House."

At the far end of Lord Glenconner's enormous swimming pool stands a maharajah's pleasure palace, discovered in India, purchased in India, and then brought to Mus-

tique, along with two Indian stonemasons to put it together again. Constructed entirely of white marble, it has
lattice marble screens on all four sides, which gives the
interior constant dappled light by day. By night, for the
ball, its interior was illuminated by gold fluorescent light,
and smoke from smoke pots drifted through the lattice
screens. A plan to have Raquel Welch emerge from the
pleasure palace as part of the entertainment portion of the
evening had been scratched, and an alternative plan had
been substituted: another princess.

Princess was not the only princess at Lord Glenconner's
ball. Princess Josephine Löwenstein was there, as well as
her daughter, Princess Dora Löwenstein. And then there
was Princess Tina—just Tina, no last name. Princess Tina
provided the cabaret entertainment, appearing late in the
evening in front of the pleasure palace, doing gymnastic
gyrations while she balanced full glasses of something on
her head and pelvic area. The crowd surged out to watch
her—blacks and swells vying for the good positions from
which to view the tantalizing spectacle. One heavily wined
English lady sat in the reflecting pool in front of the pleasure palace and pulled up her skirts to the refreshing wa-
ters. "My God, look at her—she's showing her bush!"
another lady cried out.

Thrice Miss Welch upstaged Princess Margaret. She didn't
show up at her own party on the *Maxim's des Mers,* at which
Princess Margaret was a guest. She arrived later than Princess Margaret at the Peacock Ball. And on the day following the ball, at Princess Margaret's party, a picnic luncheon
on Macaroni Beach, under the same pink marquee from the
ball of the night before, transported after dawn from the
Great House, Miss Welch, accompanied by Mr. Weinfeld,

made another late entrance, as the princess and her guests were finishing dessert. Miss Welch was all smiles as she greeted her hostess. Princess inhaled deeply on her cigarette through a long holder protruding from the corner of her mouth, exhaled, pointedly looked at her watch, wordlessly established the time, and then returned the greeting with a stiff smile. One-upmanship was back in the royal corner.

That night, Lord Glenconner's party drew to a close with a farewell dinner aboard the *Wind Star.* New friends were exchanging addresses. Bags were being packed. Princess arrived on board and was seated at the right of Lord Glenconner. People said over and over again that they would never forget the week-long celebration. John Wells, who writes the "Dear Bill" column in *Private Eye,* rose and in mock-Shakespearean rhetoric recited a long poem to our host which ended with these lines addressed to Princess Margaret:

> *Your Royal Highness, may I crave*
> *Leave not only to ask God to Save*
> *The Queen, your Sister, but to bless*
> *The Author of our Happiness—*
> *This Prospero, Magician King*
> *Who makes Enchanted Islands sing;*
> *King Colin, at whose mildest Bate*
> *King Kong himself might emigrate!*
> *So charge your Glasses, Friends, to honour*
> *Our reckless Host, dear Lord Glenconner.*

Amid cheers and tears, Lord Glenconner rose. Dressed all in black, his energies spent now, his production over, he thanked the people who had helped him in his yearlong preparations: Lyton Lamontagne, Nicholas Courtney, and others. He thanked his son Charlie "for getting a little better," he thanked his son Henry and Henry's friend Kelvin for working out the treasure hunt on the island of Bequia. He thanked his daughter-in-law Tessa for her constant assistance. He did not thank Lady Anne, who seemed not to notice not being thanked. "You all say you'll never forget," he said wistfully. "But you do, you know. You do forget. I can't even remember my own wedding day."

March 1987

GRANDIOSITY
The Fall of Roberto Polo

In retrospect it's always easy to say, "Oh, yes, I knew, I always knew," about this one or that one, when this one or that one comes to a bad end or winds up in disgrace. Any number of people who knew Roberto Polo have told me that when they first heard that disaster was about to befall him, they said to the person who informed them, "I'm not surprised, are you?" and the informant invariably replied that he or she was not surprised either.

Polo, a thirty-seven-year-old Cuban-born American citizen with residences in Paris, New York, Monte Carlo, and Santo Domingo, is currently in prison in Italy, where he was arrested in June. He is wanted for questioning in Switzerland, France, and the United States concerning the alleged misappropriation of $110 million of his investors' money. At the time of his arrest, he had been a fugitive from the law for five weeks, and had been rumored either to have sought and bought refuge in Latin America or to have been murdered by the very people he was said to have swindled, on the theory that, if caught, he might reveal their identities.

"Roberto had so many personas it was hard to know which was the *real* person," one of his former employees said to me in describing him. A middle-class Cuban with dreams of glory, Polo appeared to be many things to many people, from family man to philanderer, from elegant boulevardier to preposterous phony, from fantasizer to fuckup of the American Dream. A man with the capacity to endear himself to many with his likability and charm and to enrage others with his grandiosity and pomposity, he provided uniformity of opinion among those who knew him in one thing only: He had exquisite taste.

I first met Roberto and his extremely attractive wife, Rosa, a Dominican by birth, the daughter of a diplomat and the cousin of a former president of that country, in 1984, at a small dinner for eight or ten people in New York, at the home of John Loring, senior vice president of Tiffany & Co. They were the youngest couple in the group, known to all the guests but me.

It was not until we sat down to dinner that I noticed the extraordinary ring Rosa Polo was wearing, a diamond so huge it would have been impossible not to comment on it. As one who has held up the hands and stared at the ice-skating-rink-size diamonds of Elizabeth Taylor, Candy Spelling, and Imelda Marcos, I realized that the young woman across from me was wearing one bigger and perhaps better than all of them. I asked her about it, and before she could reply Roberto called down from his end of the table and gave me the whole history of the jewel. It was the Ashoka diamond, a 41.37-carat D-flawless stone named after Ashoka Maurya, the third-century B.C. Buddhist warrior-emperor. Polo had bought it for his wife from the Mexican movie star Maria Felix.

Clearly the Polos were a young couple of consequence, but it was hard to get a line on them. Rosa was quiet, almost shy, a Latin wife who lived in the shadow of her husband, and Roberto sent out mixed signals. He was said to be a financial wizard, and he had his own company called PAMG, for Private Asset Management Group. He handled the monetary affairs of a select group of very rich foreign investors with assets in the United States.

He reclined in languid positions that first evening, and his talk was decidedly nonfinancial, about jewelry and fashion and Jacob Frères, Ltd., an antiques shop that had recently opened on Madison Avenue at Seventy-eighth Street, which was run by Rosa's brother, Federico Suro. They sold ormolu-encrusted furniture fit for palaces, and massive porcelain urns, all at prices in the hundreds of thousands of dollars. Roberto was obviously a genuine aesthete, mad about beautiful things, and his interest in fashion, which would become obsessive in the years ahead, was already evident. As a graduate student at Columbia in the early seventies, he had worked at Rizzoli, the art bookstore, and had come up with the idea of doing a show called "Fashion As Fantasy," with fashion designers showing clothes as art objects.

They were a couple in a hurry, or rather Roberto was in a hurry, and Rosa was swept along in his vortex. He had reportedly created his wife, turning her from a sweet Latin girl into a sleek and glamorous international figure. He picked out her clothes, told her what jewels to wear, chose their dinner guests, did the seating, and ordered the flowers and menu. He went to the collections in Paris with her, and in one season spent half a million dollars on clothes for her. He had a passion for jewelry and a knowledge of gemology. His role model, according to the interior designer and socialite Suzie Frankfurt, was Cosimo de' Medici.

"I didn't want it said I was just a rich boy," he said in

an early interview, before his woes, as if he were the heir to a great fortune instead of an alleged usurper of other people's money. Like a Cuban Gatsby, an outsider with his nose pressed to the window, Roberto Polo wanted it all and he wanted it quick, and he saw, in the money-mad New York of the eighties, the way to achieve his ambitions.

July 1988. The picture was improbable. A young blond girl of extraordinary loveliness, wearing a light summer dress, was leaning against the pay-telephone booth in the courtyard of the prison in Lucca, an Italian walled town between Pisa and Florence. She was reading an English novel and occasionally taking sips of Pelligrino water from a green bottle. On the roof above her, a guard with a submachine gun paced back and forth on a catwalk in the scorching Tuscan sun. There was about the girl a sense of a person waiting.

I was waiting too, reading a day-old English newspaper and leaning against the fender of a dented red Fiat. I had been waiting for a week for a permit that was never to come, from the Procura Generale in Florence, to visit the most famous detainee in the prison. Roberto Polo had been arrested by the Italian police the week before in the nearby seaside village of Viareggio, after an alleged attempt, by wrist slashing, to commit suicide. Bleeding, believing himself to be dying, Polo had made farewell telephone calls proclaiming his innocence to one of his investors in Mexico, to members of his family, and to a former associate, the man who had set the case against him in motion.

It occurred to me, watching the young girl, that we were there for the same reason. I offered her my *Daily Mail*, and she said that she hadn't seen an English paper for days. She knew a girl whose name was in Nigel Dempster's column. "She's always in the papers," she said. We exchanged names, and it turned out that I knew the mother of her stepsisters in New York.

"Why are you here?" I asked. We had stepped through rope curtains into the shade of the Caffè la Patria, a bar and tobacco shop adjacent to the prison.

"I'm with people who are seeing someone inside," she said cautiously.

"Roberto Polo?" I asked.

"Yes."

"That's why I'm here," I said.

"I supposed you were," she replied.

The previous week I had made my presence and purpose known to Gaetano Berni, the Florentine lawyer retained by Polo's family. Berni had explained to me that Polo was fighting extradition to Switzerland. "It is better for him to remain in Italy," he had said. "The Swiss will be harder on him. Besides, there is insufficient evidence to extradite him. He didn't kill. He didn't deal drugs. He's not Mafia. As the judge pointed out, he was not escaping when he was arrested."

My new friend, Chantal Carr by name, was the girlfriend of Roberto Polo's brother, Marco, a banker in Milan, where she also lived. Early that morning she had driven Marco and his father, Roberto Polo, Sr., to Lucca in her tiny Italian car. Even for the family of such an illustrious prisoner, visiting hours were restricted to one hour a week, on either Saturday or Sunday.

When Chantal Carr saw Marco Polo come out of the prison, she joined him, and I could see her telling him that I was in the bar, hoping to talk to him. Marco Polo is thirty-three, younger than his brother by four years, and handsome. His hair is black and curly, combed straight back. He has the look of the rich Italian and Latin American playboys who disco at Regine's. Standing in the hot sun, he was weeping almost uncontrollably while Chantal Carr patted him comfortingly on the back. Behind him stood his father, a smaller man with wounded eyes. Roberto Polo, Sr., seemed desolated by the disgrace that had befallen his family, as well as by the shock of having just seen his son in such awful circumstances.

"My brother is devastated. He is destroyed," said Marco when he came into the café. The prison was filthy, he told me, the food inedible. Prisoners with money could purchase food and sundries in the prison store, but they were not allowed to spend more than 450,000 lire, or $350, a month. Roberto Polo, one of the few prisoners to have that kind of money, had spent his whole month's allowance in the first few days of his imprisonment. During the time I was in Lucca, he could not even buy stamps.

"I am living in subhuman conditions . . . with murderers, thieves, drug traffickers, etc.," Polo wrote in a press release from his cell. For two hours each morning, they were allowed to pace back and forth in an enclosed patio for exercise. "He is totally incommunicado. He does not know that people have come to see him," said Marco. The only visitors he was allowed to have were his lawyers and members of his immediate family, but even they were not allowed to bring him a prescription he needed or a brand of toothpaste he requested—only food.

Marco expressed shock at the newspaper coverage of his brother's dilemma. "They have convicted him without a trial," he said.

The family was hoping to obtain Roberto's release on bail. That afternoon the lawyers were due, Gaetano Berni from Florence and Jacques Kam from Paris. It seemed in keeping with the glamorous aspects of Roberto Polo's recent life that Maître Kam, the principal lawyer he had picked to defend his interests at the time the warrant for his arrest was issued, was also the lawyer of Marlene Dietrich, the late Orson Welles, Dior, and Van Cleef & Arpels. "Speed is of the essence," said Marco. "Everything comes to a standstill in August. The judicial system closes down. Of course, even if bail is granted, all his money has been frozen."

All around us in the café, waiting for the afternoon visiting hours to start, were prisoners' relatives, many with small children. Looking at them, Marco said, "Roberto wants to see Marina, his daughter. But Rosa and he have decided that it is best she not come. She is five. She would remember."

I asked about Rosa, who was expected in Lucca the following day from Paris, and whom I had spoken with a few days earlier. "Rosa has not cried once," replied Marco, and there was an implied criticism in his voice. It is a known fact among all their friends that Rosa Polo and her husband's mother have never gotten along. Rosa, however, who had every reason to be outraged at the position she found herself in, had been staunchly loyal to her beleaguered husband when I spoke with her. She is, after all, the daughter of a diplomat. Shortly after her husband's disappearance five weeks before his arrest, the French police confiscated $26 million in paintings and furnishings from the couple's Paris apartment, leaving Rosa and her daughter only mattresses on the floor to sleep on. "This whole thing has been a double cross," she had told me. "We know who has been feeding everything to the press. When the press destroys you, it is hard for anyone to ever believe you." The person who she believed had double-crossed her husband was Alfredo Ortiz-Murias, the former associate of Roberto Polo who had received one of his farewell calls. "We are united," she had said to me about Roberto and her.

Marco and his father were also scornful about Alfredo Ortiz-Murias. "He was always jealous of my brother," Marco said. Ortiz-Murias was the principal witness in the suit brought against Polo by Rostuca Holdings, Ltd., an offshore company operating out of the Cayman Islands, whose money was managed by Polo's company, PAMG. It came out in the conversation that the man behind the company known as Rostuca was the governor of one of the poorest states in Mexico. I remembered Gaetano Berni saying to me a few days earlier, about this same man, "What kind of person has $20 million in U.S. dollars *in cash* outside his own country? Even Mr. Agnelli or Mr. Henry Ford, when he was alive, did not have $20 million in cash." He had grimaced and shaken his head. The implication was clear.

"Will you tell me the circumstances of Roberto's arrest?" I asked Marco.

"I have heard three stories. I do not know which one is the truth," he replied, dismissing the subject.

I had heard several stories too, the first from Alfredo Ortiz-Murias in New York, about his farewell call from Roberto. According to Ortiz-Murias, who had blown the whistle on Polo, Roberto had said to him, "Good-bye, Alfredo. It's 6:30 A.M. in Europe. I am sorry you felt that way about me. Good-bye." When I asked Ortiz-Murias what his reaction to the call was, he said, "He was trying to make me feel guilty."

I had also heard from Pablo Aramburuzabala, one of Polo's investors, a well-to-do Mexican businessman whose wife is the godmother of the Polos' daughter, that Roberto had called his house four times to say that he was going to commit suicide. "The first three times I was out, but my wife spoke to him. He was calling from a public telephone. When I talked with him, he said he had never done anything wrong. He gave me the address in Viareggio and said that I could call Interpol if I wanted. He said he was full of blood and didn't have too much time. Then he must have called his mother. She called me to say that Roberto was dead. She said she didn't know where to go to claim his body. I gave her the address in Viareggio. Then the brother, Marco, called from Tokyo. Marco said that Roberto had been picked up by an ambulance and was in the hospital in Viareggio."

Roberto Polo gave his own version of his arrest in a press release: "I ate some fish which apparently made me very sick, because early in the morning, I called my brother (who lives in Milan), who speaks Italian, in order to ask him to call the police station to have them send a doctor because I felt like I was dying. My brother, who has a friend in Viareggio, asked his friend to call the police in order that they send a doctor to see me. By the time the doctor arrived, I had already vomited and had some tea: I felt much better. However, the doctor took my blood pressure, stated that it was a bit high, then left. A few hours later (I was already dressed to go to the beach on my bicycle), the police returned without the doctor and asked me to go with them to the station. . . . I was interrogated. . . . After that I was taken, handcuffed, to the prison where I am in Lucca."

It seems odd that a person wanted by the police in three countries would call his brother in Milan to call the police in Viareggio to get a doctor for an attack of food poisoning. According to Gaetano Berni, the Florentine lawyer, Roberto himself called for an ambulance. It seems odd also that nowhere in Polo's account of the events in Viareggio does he mention Fabrizio Bagaglini. Only Gaetano Berni would speak about Bagaglini when I brought

up the name. He said, "Fabrizio stayed until the arrest."
We will come to Fabrizio Bagaglini.

"Were you separated by a screen when you saw your
brother?" I asked Marco Polo.

"No, we were able to embrace him."

"Was he wearing the ribbon?" Chantal Carr asked
Marco.

"Yes," he replied.

Three weeks before Polo vanished, the French government had made him a Commander of the Order of the Arts
and Letters in gratitude for his having donated to the Louvre Museum Fragonard's painting *The Adoration of the Shep-
herds* and a crown of gold, emeralds, and diamonds that had
belonged to the Empress Eugénie.

"Does he wear a prison uniform?" I asked.

"No, he wears his own clothes. His body is clean. His
clothes are clean. The place is filthy and horrible, but my
brother looks classy. My brother is the classiest person I
know."

In 1982 the Polos moved from a one-bedroom apartment
on Lexington Avenue to a large Park Avenue apartment, for
which they spent $450,000. That move signaled the begin-
ning of their rise. They had a Botero in the dining room
and a picture by Mary Cassatt of a woman reading *Le
Figaro,* which Roberto later sold at Christie's for $1 mil-
lion. "He took to buying paintings and then selling them a
year later," said Alfredo Ortiz-Murias. "He had no attach-
ment to anything. Everything he bought was for sale."
Their only child, Marina, was born in 1983, while they
were living in the Park Avenue apartment. The child's
godfather was the Count of Odiel, whose wife is a cousin of
the King of Spain. Early in 1984, Roberto bought a five-

story town house on East Sixty-fourth Street for $2.7 million. Four years later, Ramona Colón, Polo's administrative assistant and office manager at the time of this purchase, stated in an affidavit filed with a New York civil suit, "I first became suspicious that not all of the clients' money was being invested as required. At that time Roberto directly or indirectly purchased a town house . . . and directed [an assistant] to transfer money, in the approximate amount of the purchase price of the town house, from clients' time deposits maturing at that time to an account at European American Bank on 41st Street, New York, and then to an account in the name of ITKA, at Crédit Suisse in the Bahamas. I believe that the ITKA account was Roberto Polo's personal account."

The redecorating of the new house from top to bottom —a job that would have normally taken anywhere from a year to two years—was done in six weeks, and Roberto was his own decorator. His men worked seven days a week, at the same frantic pace that his near neighbor Imelda Marcos had set when she did over her new town house on East Sixty-sixth Street in time to give a party for the international arms dealer Adnan Khashoggi. He brought special upholsterers from England to install the green damask on the library walls. People who watched Polo during this period said that he worked like a man possessed in creating the perfect setting, as if he knew that his good fortune couldn't last. The dark-paneled dining room on the first floor was large enough to seat thirty-six comfortably, and the living room on the floor above was the size of a small ballroom, with a white damask banquette along one wall and ample space to hang the young couple's astonishing and ever-growing art collection. He sold his Impressionist art to make room for his new and even more impressive collection of eighteenth-century French paintings, Fragonards and Bouchers and Vigée-Lebruns, mostly purchased through the Wildenstein gallery in New York. In order to get insurance for the paintings, he had to have steel shutters installed on all the windows; at the push of a button, these dropped and plunged the interior of the house into total darkness.

He also moved his offices. He had started PAMG in the bedroom of his apartment. Then he had shared a small office with several other people. Next he had taken space at 101 Park Avenue. Now he rented grand offices on the forty-third floor of the General Motors Building on Fifth Avenue.

More and more, Roberto Polo began to be talked about. His antiques buying at auctions and in shops in New York and Paris was nonstop, and he always paid the top prices. A former associate of his described Roberto on a spree in Paris, going from shop to shop, buying $3 million worth of antiques to stock Jacob Frères. On one occasion Rosa wore $6 million in emeralds. On another, she pushed her baby's stroller through Central Park wearing a T-shirt and jeans, the Ashoka diamond, and a million-dollar strand of pearls. Roberto, no slouch in the jewelry department himself, wore a ring with a 10.5-carat Burmese ruby worth over $1 million. He was so meticulous that when he bought a picture for his office he would have a picture hanger come from Wildenstein to install it. He was a terror at home; one out-of-place ashtray or a table not dusted properly could drive him into a rage. On the other hand, when he had people to lunch at the town house, in the midst of all that grandeur he might serve his guests grilled-cheese sandwiches on paper plates, which a servant would pick up from a nearby luncheonette. He could not stand to be alone; he even took people on the Concorde with him so that he would not have to fly alone. He ran his multimillion-dollar business mainly from his house, on one rotary telephone without even call waiting, and held meetings there in darkened rooms.

My second encounter with the glamorous Polos was at a charity ball for Casita Maria, the oldest Hispanic settlement house in New York. Apart from the ball for the Spanish Institute, the Casita Maria Fiesta is considered to be *the* Latin party of the year in New York. A new and interesting way for rich social aspirants to get their name known in smart circles is to underwrite charity parties, and in 1985 Polo underwrote the Casita Maria ball. It was the custom of Casita Maria to present three prominent people with gold medals, and in previous years honored guests had included Placido Domingo and Dame Margot Fonteyn. That year the honorees were the Colombian painter Fernando Botero, former secretary of the treasury William Simon, and the film star Maria Felix, who was enormously popular in Mexico but, unlike her sister star Dolores Del Rio, little known in the United States. People say that Polo had an obsession with this septuagenarian actress, whom he had met through his mother, and from whom he had purchased the Ashoka diamond as well as a diamond snake necklace of extraordinary workmanship made by Cartier, both of which adorned Rosa Polo that night.

At the last minute, Maria Felix canceled, informing the committee that she had broken her ankle. So Polo and his brother-in-law, Federico Suro, put together an eleven-minute montage of Felix's film clips as a substitute for the no-show star. He had promised the glittering crowd a celebrity, and he delivered instead badly edited clips, far too long and in Spanish. Soon the audience in the Grand Ballroom of the Plaza Hotel grew bored, and began to talk and laugh as if the film were not going on. Polo became petulant, then furious, and at the end of the film he went up to the microphone and berated the audience for their bad manners. He said he was glad Maria Felix was not there.

At this outburst, looks were exchanged across the tables, the kind of looks that clearly said, Who the hell is this little upstart to lecture us on manners? To make matters worse, Roberto's mother, who he had told people had once been an opera singer at La Scala, rose and applauded her son's speech.

"That night Roberto was finished in New York," said a Venezuelan society woman who resides in the city. Actually, he wasn't finished in New York that night. People with vast sums of money are never finished in social life as long as they keep picking up the checks, and Roberto Polo continued to pick up the checks for large dinners at Le Cirque and other fashionable restaurants, where he would sometimes order wine that cost a thousand dollars a bottle and take only a sip or two of it.

Some people are mesmerized by money. It covers all defects. Even people who suspected that something was not quite right about Polo overlooked his flaws and listened to him with rapt attention. Like a peacock, as soon as he met someone he wanted to impress, he would spread his feathers and show off all his colors, telling of his paintings, his furniture, his wife's jewels, his financial acumen, his social achievements. Often he would close this self-congratulatory catalog with the words "and only thirty-six"—his age at the time.

These same people, however, were beginning to speculate about who Roberto Polo was and where all his money came from. "We manage money for wealthy individuals," he would say. But talk was rampant that some of the money he managed was dirty money, meaning that he was laundering money, or drug-trafficking, or running arms. One former associate, however, who subsequently broke with him, told me he firmly believes that the clients' money was clean. The company served as financial adviser to a group of Mexicans, Latin Americans, and Europeans who happened to have money—often a great deal of money—in the United States. In most cases, however, it was illegal for these clients to have money invested secretly outside of their own country. In Spain, for instance, the government can confiscate all the Spanish holdings of an individual who has undeclared investments in the United States. At Citibank, where Polo had worked before founding PAMG, he became an account executive, but several times he was passed over for assistant vice president even though he attracted business to the bank. In 1981 he left to found his own company, which would serve the same function as the bank but with more personalized attention given to clients than the bank gave. PAMG arranged financial transactions for investors, and most of the money was in time deposits.

Although some former clients—Pablo Aramburuzabala, for one—say that they did not authorize Polo, or PAMG, to invest their money in art, Polo did entice new business to PAMG with a glossy brochure picturing his specialty in investments: paintings, jewels, and real estate. "Otherwise, his clients could have gone to Morgan Guaranty," said his lawyer Jacques Kam.

One of the great titans of Wall Street, who later refused to comment on his statement, is reported to have said about Roberto Polo, after meeting him at a small dinner party and listening to him talk, "There's something wrong. If there's that much money, I would have heard about him." He was echoing the old saying, "If they have the right kind of money, they're known at the bank."

"All of us, we may not know each other, but we know who each other is," said a New York social figure from a prominent Latin-American family, "and no one, not a single soul, knew anything about Roberto Polo or his family. Ask any of the Cubans we know. Never *heard* of Roberto Polo."

A New York fashion designer who was thinking of bringing out a fragrance backed by Polo was warned, "Do not touch him with the end of a barge pole."

Shortly after completing the town house, Polo gave a dinner for Amalita Fortabat, who is said to be the richest woman in Argentina. Many New York social figures attended. "Where did you get that fabulous Fragonard, Roberto?" someone asked him. "My parents brought it with them out of Cuba," he replied. People knew that wasn't the truth, but no one called him on it. "He bought the Fragonard at Wildenstein's, but he liked the old-money, old-family sound of his version of the acquisition," said a person who was present. Often he would point out a piece of his furniture by saying, "The twin to that is in Versailles."

Upper-class Cubans in New York and Florida are amazed by the stories Roberto Polo would tell of his family's background. "There is no mention of the Polo family in the old Social Registers from the days before Castro," said a Cuban lady in New York. Another said, "We know our own. The Polos were not in the clubs, and the boys did not go to either of the two schools everyone we know went to." Still another said, "He learned everything so fast. Just seven years ago, he was wearing black shoes and white socks." She paused and added, "He was always polite, very well mannered. I think he is to be admired for the myth he has created about himself. He really does think his family built all the oil refineries in Cuba. His family was perfectly nice—an engineer, or something like that, his father was—but they were certainly not a family that went about in social circles.

Like Imelda Marcos, who has spent a lifetime upgrading the circumstances of her birth, Polo had a tendency to paint a more aristocratic picture of his family than the truth would bear out. Even in stir, facing a long incarceration and sharing a cell and a toilet that doesn't work with two other prisoners, he issued a press release emphasizing the grandeur of his background. He quotes from early magazine articles written about him in which he was described as "the darkly handsome, wealthy Cuban refugee, son of Countess Celis de Maceda." He describes his father as having been, "like his father before him," a "very rich playboy" in Cuba, as if—even if it were true, which it appears not to be—it were an admirable thing to be the son and grandson of wealthy playboys. He also says, "On my father's side of the family the wealth came from the construction business; they built various oil refineries and industrial plants for Standard Oil Company, the Bacardi plants in Nassau and Puerto Rico, and parts of the United Fruit Company in Costa Rica. . . . My mother's family was wealthy, but less than my father's. However, whatever wealth they missed (compared to my father's family) they made up in a more aristocratic, artistic, and generally more socially prominent background. . . . My mother's nobiliary title came to her as the oldest child in her family through her grandmother; I inherited this title, which I have never used nor pretend to (even though there are those who want to make me a social climber, hardly necessary given my higher education, refinement, and family upbringing relative to my American counterparts), because I am the oldest child in my family."

Roberto Polo was born in Havana on August 20, 1951,

the older of two sons of Roberto Polo, an engineer, and his wife, Maria Teresa. The family fled Cuba in the wake of Castro and moved to Peru, where they suffered serious financial losses when the government nationalized their business. They then moved to Miami, where Roberto and Marco went to school. Their mother, a trained opera singer, became a hospital nutritionist after they left Cuba. An aspiring artist, Roberto attended the Corcoran School in Washington on a scholarship from age fourteen to eighteen, and then graduated from the American University in Washington, where he met his future wife's brother, Federico Suro. He studied philosophy and art. He moved to Montreal in order to avoid the draft for the Vietnam War, but he was later classified 4-F due to curvature of the spine and flat feet. He then got a master's degree in painting and sculpture at Columbia University, and while he was there he took his first job, at Rizzoli. After Columbia, he joined Citibank.

In an article in *Women's Wear Daily* this year, he said of his wife's family, "My in-laws are very wealthy. My wife's uncle was the president of the Dominican Republic. His name was Antonio Guzman. His brother died of cancer and left a huge fortune. I left Citibank to oversee that money." In fact, the Suro family is intellectually prominent and highly respected, but it is not a rich family. Dario Suro, Rosa Polo's father, is considered to be one of the greatest Dominican painters. He became the cultural attaché at the embassy in Washington in 1963, under Ambassador Enriquillo Del Rosario, who is now an ambassador to the United Nations. Rosa Polo's mother, Maruxa Suro, was the first cousin of the late president Antonio Guzman, but since the pay at the embassy was low, Mrs. Suro, in order to provide her children with a good education, worked for a time in the dress department of Lord & Taylor in Washington. Rosa, after moving to New York, studied first at the Harkness School of Ballet and then at the Joffrey Ballet school until she married Roberto in 1972.

Soon after Polo started in business for himself, old friends began to notice a change in him. A grand Spanish lady who had been one of his investors said, "Several times I saw Roberto Polo in Le Cirque. A kid like that showing off at Le Cirque, pretending he was rich. Uh-uh." She withdrew her money from his management. An old friend of his wife's family, who had thought of himself as a friend of Roberto's as well, found that Roberto stopped speaking to him. "I often saw him in the company of the flashy type of Latin, wealthy but not of the top social class."

People began to say that the bubble was going to burst. Roberto was traveling more and more, leaving Rosa and the baby behind. Beneath the bravado was a man very unsure of himself. His look changed constantly. He didn't seem to know who he was. His hair was short, then it was long. One week he wore English clothes, the next week he wore Italian. I ran into him in the lobby of the Plaza-Athénée Hotel in Paris in 1986 and didn't recognize him when he spoke to me. He was wearing his hair in a ponytail, and either he was in the process of growing a beard or he was affecting an exaggerated version of the Don Johnson–*Miami Vice* look. Even his eyes looked different, and later I learned that he had taken to wearing blue contact lenses. He appeared at one evening party in a sort of bolero jacket, and people told me he had hoped to start a trend for bolero jackets in the evening. Close friends of Rosa said that she never looked happy. She complained that Roberto was constantly entertaining people from Mexico. She was always on call.

In May 1986, Polo moved his firm to Geneva and his family to Paris, so abruptly that it seemed as if he were

leaving New York in a hurry. A Cuban lady who had followed his activities for several years said, "Roberto was
disappointed with New York. You see, he was never really
accepted by either the Latins or the Anglos. No matter how
hard you try, very few Latins are really accepted in New
York. He thought that that would not be true in Europe."

Polo claimed that the United States had cooperated
with the governments of Haiti and the Philippines in revealing what assets were held in this country by the recently deposed Baby Doc Duvalier and Ferdinand and
Imelda Marcos. He stated publicly that he thought President Reagan was throwing Duvalier and the Marcoses to
the lions, and that PAMG investors deserved more discreet
treatment than the U.S. government was offering. He sent
a letter to his clients saying that Swiss banks offered them
greater secrecy than other banks.

Several former associates have different views of Polo's
quick move to Europe: "If you have more than fifteen clients that you are giving advice to, you need a license with
the SEC. If the SEC had come to investigate after he
bought the house on East Sixty-fourth Street, they would
have known." Or: "He may have thought that by moving
to Switzerland he could hide under the Swiss secrecy laws."
Or: "He had placed some time deposits in savings and
loans in Maryland that went bankrupt. Jumbo CDs. The
SEC was investigating those S&Ls."

Before leaving New York, Polo presented a Marisol
sculpture to the Metropolitan Museum. He also did what
had been in the cards for him to do for years: He entered
the world of fashion. The dress designer Polo had always
admired most was the brilliant and ill-fated British-Ameri-
can Charles James, whose dresses he thought of as pieces of
sculpture. In James's declining years, when he was living

in near destitution in the Chelsea Hotel, Polo had sent him $200 a week.

In December 1985 he purchased the fashion house of a designer named Miguel Cruz, a fellow Cuban whom he had met through Maria Felix. A second-echelon but respected designer with a faithful following, Cruz had been established in Rome since the 1960s. When he approached Polo to borrow money from him for his business, Polo is supposed to have said, "I don't lend money. I'll buy you." Fashion had always been a business that fascinated him. Now it became the business that would destroy him.

In Paris, he bought a fourteen-room apartment at 27 Quai Anatole-France which surpassed in elegance and grandeur the house on East Sixty-fourth Street. A Marisol sculpture of Rosa and Marina stood in the hallway. A Toulouse-Lautrec, Van Dongens, Fragonards, and Bouchers lined the walls. Following in the steps of such other Latin American collectors who had lived in Paris as Arturo Lopez-Willshaw, Antenor Patino, and Carlos de Beistegui, Polo filled his apartment with the rarest of rare furniture, including pieces that had once belonged to Marie Antoinette. He tried to charm his way into French society with gifts and flowers, and he took tables in restaurants for fifteen or twenty people. Rosa became best friends with the wife of the antiques dealer Jean-Marie Rossi, who is the granddaughter of the late General Franco of Spain.

Polo hired the fashion consultant Eleanor Lambert to advise him on the buyout of the Miguel Cruz company. Cruz was paid a salary of $120,000 a year and a royalty on gross sales, although Polo claimed in an interview with *Women's Wear Daily* that he paid Cruz a minimum annual salary of $500,000. His intention was to vault Cruz into the ranks of the elite international designers of expensive ready-to-wear and to rival the houses of Giorgio Armani and Gianni Versace.

To launch the venture, Polo made an agreement with a retailer named Scarpa to turn her shops in Venice and Milan into Miguel Cruz boutiques. Scarpa received merchandise on consignment. Polo made a similar deal with a boutique owner on the island of Capri, and he paid $300,000 for the renovation of the shop. By the time the business opened, Polo had three boutiques, an office in the General Motors Building in New York with a rent of approximately $12,000 a month, and a showroom and warehouse in Milan. In spite of this huge overhead, Polo decided to launch an enormous advertising campaign. In the first season he spent $700,000 for media (media means buying space) and $30,000 on production. For the spring 1986 collection, there was an $800,000 advertising budget. For the fall 1986 collection, Polo spent $900,000 on advertising.

Consider, now, PAMG's contract with its investors: PAMG received a fee of one-half of 1 percent for managing an account. So on a $1 million account the annual fee would be $5,000. On a $100 million account, the fee would be $500,000. Therefore, people who worked for PAMG naturally began to wonder where the money was coming from to run the Miguel Cruz dress business as well as to cover Polo's continued buying of art and jewelry.

From the beginning, Polo played an active part in advertising and promotion, hiring the models, flying them to New York to be photographed, even staging the fashion shows. Fashion experts say that the campaign didn't work commercially, even if the photography was sometimes great. Like so much about Roberto Polo, his advertising sent out mixed signals; there was confusion as to whether he was selling his wares or his models. He claimed that he would make the name of Miguel Cruz known through the shock value of the ads. "We're living in a society that wants to be shocked," he told one interviewer. A Robert Mapplethorpe photograph for the Miguel Cruz men's line showed the back of a seated naked man removing a sweater over his head. For the women's line, a two-page ad showed a dimly lit female model in a black jeweled evening dress with one fully lit naked man behind her and another sitting on the floor in front of her.

It enraged Polo that while no one questioned the propriety of Calvin Klein's massively nude advertising campaign, which was going on at the same time, his own campaign was labeled prurient and offensive. "They object to my ads but not to Calvin Klein's." The advertisement showing the bull's-eye picture with the male rump may have offended one segment of the public, but a more lurid segment bombarded the New York office for copies of it.

Polo always knew more about everything than the experts. Soon he started directing Mapplethorpe's photo sessions, and Mapplethorpe, a bit of a prima donna himself, resented the interference. Eventually there was a falling-out, and Mapplethorpe resigned the account. Not to be topped, Polo wrote the photographer a letter firing him, and sent copies to several prominent people in New York.

Despite all the fanfare and hype, the Miguel Cruz line was a disaster almost from the beginning. The clothes were often badly made, delivery dates were missed, and orders were canceled. "I don't care about your four pages in *Vogue* —the clothes are not in my store" became a common complaint. It got to the point where the company was doing $1 million in advertising and only $100,000 in sales. In the fall of 1987, when all the collections of all the designers in Paris, New York, and Milan were showing skirts above the knee, Miguel Cruz was showing skirts down to the ankle. At that point Polo stepped in to give Cruz artistic advice on how the clothes should look, and he began writing memos telling him what colors and fabrics to use.

Unlike Polo's art acquisitions, which could be sold at a profit, the Miguel Cruz fashion venture was a bottomless pit. It is estimated that Polo lost between $12 million and $15 million on it, but he remained adamant in his belief that the clothes were beautiful and that the company was going to be a big success. He didn't want anyone to tell him the truth. He had a blind spot about Miguel Cruz, and he could not accept criticism. He thought that if he spent an enormous amount of money on advertising he should be rewarded with good reviews. He wrote irate letters to Polly Mellen of *Vogue* and Carrie Donovan of the *New York Times* threatening to pull his ads when they criticized the collections, and he had to be restrained from mailing a mocking letter to Hebe Dorsey, the late beloved fashion editor, demanding a retraction because she had mistakenly said Miguel Cruz designed in Rome in the fifties when she meant the sixties. He had the idea that American editors could be bought. One of the most powerful women in fashion, who asked that she not be identified, told me that on the morning after one of the collections was shown in Milan she received in her hotel room a box containing a full-length black coat lined in sable. She tried it on, modeled it in front of a mirror, wrapped it up again, and returned it to Roberto Polo at the Miguel Cruz office. A former employee told me that Hebe Dorsey had returned many such gifts.

Peter Dubow, the owner of a company called European Collections Inc., was hired by Polo as a consultant to use his retailing contacts to penetrate the American stores. Dubow, who, like a lot of Roberto Polo's employees, is still owed a great deal of money in salary and expenses, says,

"The easy speculation is that Roberto didn't care if the collections weren't good, that he was simply getting dirty money back into circulation. But he did care. He cared passionately."

One day in Paris, in the magnificent apartment on Quai Anatole-France, Dubow said to Polo, "We need someone to stage the fashion shows. We need an art director for the advertising."

"That's what I do," replied Roberto quietly.

Trying another tack, Dubow said about the latest collection, "It's not good enough. It's totally lacking in commerciality." He even went a step further. "It is ugly, Roberto."

Polo said, "How many Fragonards do you own?"

"None," replied Dubow.

With a gesture, Polo indicated his possessions in the drawing room where they were seated. "Do you own furniture like this?"

"No," said Dubow.

"Well, I think Miguel's collection is beautiful," said Polo, in his superiority, settling the matter. "I cannot imagine how ready-to-wear can be any more beautiful than this."

It is a curious quirk of Roberto's business sense that he gave priority to the evening dresses he presented as free gifts to society women in New York to wear to publicized social functions at a time when stores he depended on for business were not getting their shipments on time and orders were being canceled. To set things right, Roberto hired his brother, Marco, to be chief of production for the fashion house. There had always been a rivalry between the two brothers, particularly for the affection of their mother, and it was she who asked Roberto to take Marco into the company. Marco had wanted to go into the investment side of Roberto's business, not the fashion side, because he thought he knew more about banking than Roberto did. "When I was a kid, I used to beat the shit out of my brother, and now he's this big man ordering me around," Marco complained to an American employee of the business. At Miguel Cruz, Marco did a good job of putting the business in order, but the quality of the workmanship remained poor and orders were rarely delivered on time.

Late in 1987, at a party in Milan for the opening of a collection, Polo met Fabrizio Bagaglini. A sometime actor, sometime model, the twenty-five-year-old Bagaglini became a dominant figure in the life of Roberto Polo over the next seven months, right up until Polo's actual arrest in Viareggio. Shortly after meeting Fabrizio, Polo hired him to do his public-relations work, although Bagaglini was not known to have any experience or skill in that field.

In an interview conducted before the warrant went out for Polo's arrest, but published after, Nadine Frey of *WWD* wrote, "As a last gesture, [Polo] gave a mini-tour of his apartment, as Barry White blared out of a speaker somewhere and a handsome Roman aide de camp hustled out to make a lunch reservation." Roberto showed off Fabrizio as if he were a painting. He told people that he wanted to make Fabrizio the vice president of the perfume company he was planning to start, to be called Le Parfum de Miguel Cruz. Bagaglini began wearing Roberto's wristwatch, an eighteen-karat-gold Breitling, and Polo gave him a Ferrari Testarossa, worth $134,000, at a time when the unpaid bills and salaries at the Miguel Cruz office in New York amounted to $600,000. On several occasions, Polo said to his friends, "I have had three passions in my life: my wife, Rosa, my daughter, Marina, and Fabrizio." However, he persistently claimed that the friendship with Fabrizio was no more than a friendship.

Glamorous pictures of the glamorous Polos began appearing in all the fashionable magazines in France, usually showing them elegantly posed amid their museum-quality possessions. Elsewhere in the world, meanwhile, Mexican, Latin American, and European investors in PAMG were demanding to know where all the Polo money was coming from. "Roberto took too high a profile. He was too much in the papers, lived on far too grand a scale. His investors didn't like it, especially as he was living on a far grander scale than they," said Alfredo Ortiz-Murias, Polo's associate. Ortiz-Murias had at one time been Roberto's superior at Citibank. He had left the bank to form his own money-management firm, but, according to Polo, it had not done well, and he later joined PAMG, bringing his own clients with him. Ortiz-Murias claims to have introduced Roberto Polo to everyone in New York, but Polo says otherwise. The former associates are now bitter enemies.

Polo's behavior became more and more extreme. According to an employee of Miguel Cruz's men's wear in Milan, "The stories he told about himself became more and more fantastic, brilliant strokes of genius—how he had bought things at one price and sold them a short time later at enormous profits, like a pearl he bought for half a million dollars and resold for a million. He said, 'I always have $10 million in cash on hand.' "

Once, he showed up in the lobby of the Hotel Palace in Milan and requested twenty-five rooms for important people he was flying in to see the Miguel Cruz collection. The hotel, part of the CIGA hotel group, owned by the Aga Khan, was totally booked for the fashion week of the Milan collections and therefore unable to provide these accommodations. Polo made a loud scene. "Get the Aga Khan on the telephone!" he screamed indignantly.

He met Grace Jones and signed her up as a runway

model for three shows. At a time when the company was in serious trouble, he offered her $50,000 for each appearance. Jones wisely insisted on being paid in advance before each show.

He became a confider of intimate secrets, assuring each confidant that he or she was the only person he could trust. "I find that I wake up in a different bed each morning," he told an associate, who later discovered he had shared the same intimacy with his publicist and a number of friends. In October 1987, during the collections, he called several people, some he didn't even know very well, sobbing, saying he was getting a divorce. Rosa was said to be jealous of the female models in the shows, and at one point she packed and left Milan for Paris. There she remembered she had left her jewelry behind in the hotel safe, so she returned, and everything was all right between them again.

One observer told me that Polo got "weirder and weirder." He dieted down to 145 pounds and began to dye the hair on his chest.

Last February, amid persistent widespread rumors of imminent financial troubles, he appeared at a sale in Monte Carlo with Fabrizio Bagaglini and a whippet dog and paid $500,000 for a pair of chairs by the French furniture-maker Sené, chairs so rare that they could not be taken out of France.

That same month, Pablo Aramburuzabala, who had been Roberto Polo's first major client and who had a sort of father-son relationship with him, flew from Mexico to Paris to confront him about all the rumors. "The investors were nervous and not happy hearing all the publicity he was getting, being described as a Cuban-American millionaire," he told me. "He didn't have time to make that kind of money unless he was doing something wrong. People start to do little things and get away with it, and then start to take more and more. I gave him his chance. My wife is the godmother of his daughter. I met Roberto at Citibank. Then he started being money manager with me. It was just a matter of calling several banks to see which bank gave the best interest. I would see him four times a year, and he would tell me how my portfolio was. In February I asked him, 'Do you have financial problems?' He said no. He said that Mr. Ortiz-Murias was making trouble. I said to him, 'I don't think you have that kind of money.' I never authorized him to deal with art. He said that he had a syndicate of people for buying art. He told me he was managing a billion dollars. When I commented on Rosa's jewels, I was told that some of her jewels were lent by jewelers as a way of advertising. I said to him, 'I need some money. You have to give me some money back.' After a while I received part of it, not even 30 percent of the amount. Later, another small part, even smaller than the previous payment. I realized that things were in terrible shape. He promised to come to Mexico to straighten things out, but he never came."

The New York office of Miguel Cruz was run on money that was sent each month from Geneva. It took approximately $200,000 a month to keep the New York end of the business going, and more often than not only half that amount was sent. Salaries and bills went unpaid. By the end of 1987 there were bills in excess of $1 million. "A lot of people have been hurt by the unpaid bills, including Miguel Cruz himself," said Peter Dubow. "Miguel always paid his bills, and the matter was highly embarrassing for him."

In the fall of 1987, Roberto Polo made his biggest play for social recognition, as well as a last-ditch bid to promote the flailing fashion line, by underwriting two famous balls, the Save Venice ball in Venice to help restore the Church of

Santa Maria dei Miracoli, followed seventeen days later by the Chantilly Ball in France to benefit the Institute of France. They attracted the crème de la crème of international society. With rumors everywhere that he was financially strapped, Polo spent over $600,000—some say closer to a million—on the two events. In addition, it was reported in society columns that he flew guests from all over the world by private jet to attend the parties. The talk of the Save Venice ball was Rosa Polo's jewels, in all the colors. She swam each day in the swimming pool of the Hotel Cipriani in a different bathing suit with a necklace of precious stones to match. Meanwhile, the people in the warehouse in Milan had to pass the hat to pay for the gasoline to get the collection to the Chantilly Ball. After that they sent the collection to New York for the fashion week there, but the New York office didn't have the money to get it out of customs.

Polo's hope, apparently, was that his new perfume company would rescue his collapsing empire. At a cost of nearly $1 million, he built a new office for Le Parfum de Miguel Cruz on Avenue Marceau in Paris. He hired as the president of the company Jacques Bergerac, the fifties movie star, who had been married to Ginger Rogers and Dorothy Malone, and who had more recently—before the takeover by Ronald Perelman—been a high-ranking executive at Revlon. He also hired the New York architectural and design firm of de Marsillac Plunkett to design the bottles and packaging. He himself played an important part in choosing the scents for the perfume. The perfume business, however, is considered a seven-to-one shot for success, and it usually takes two to three years before profits begin to show. To finance Le Parfum and perhaps to settle with his disgruntled investors, who were beginning to demand their money back, Polo is reported to have sold $22 million in jewels between February and May.

He drew more international press by announcing that he had donated to the Louvre the Empress Eugénie crown, valued at $2.5 million, and Fragonard's *The Adoration of the Shepherds,* valued at between $2.5 million and $5 million. At a well-publicized ceremony attended by sixty guests in evening clothes, the French government expressed its gratitude by making him a Commander of the Order of Arts and Letters.

Next Polo announced that he was putting his famous collection of eighteenth-century French paintings up for sale. In what is thought to have been an I'll-pat-your-back-if-you-pat-mine gesture, Pierre Rosenberg, the distinguished curator of paintings at the Louvre, wrote the preface to the catalog for the sale, even though it is frowned on in museum circles for museum people to become involved in such commercial enterprises. To counteract the speculation that he was selling his collection to meet the demands of his investors, or to save his failing dress business, or to finance his perfume business, Roberto Polo wrote the foreword to the beautiful catalog, in which he said, "Collectors can be divided into two groups: those who satisfy their appetite by the endless accumulation of things and those who are most excited by the 'hunt,' the search and research of things. The latter kind of collector satisfies his appetite and curiosity for the collectible once he has it and squeezes out of it, as from a ripe fruit, all the juice that it has to give, then moves on to a different collectible . . . I am one of those collectors." Polo said he expected the sale to bring in between $18 million and $20 million.

·   ·   ·

When Alfredo Ortiz-Murias returned home from the Venice and Chantilly balls, he observed to Ramona Colón that he had seen a change in Roberto's personality. Ramona Colón told him that she thought Roberto had been transferring clients' money to "third parties." Ortiz-Murias claims that that was his first knowledge of malfeasance on the part of Polo. Colón stated in her affidavit that Polo would direct her to transfer a client's time deposit to the PAMG-NY account and then to the ITKA account. "I noticed that some client time deposit cards were marked 'PAMG' in Roberto's handwriting. Although these time deposit cards were regularly updated and statements sent to the clients continued to report these time deposits, I believe that the entries and statements were fraudulent and that the time deposits no longer existed. . . . Sometime in mid-1984, I calculated the total shown on all cards marked 'PAMG' and the total was about $37 million." Colón also stated in her affidavit, "I saw Roberto take home shopping bags full of client transfer records and other client information. Since I worked with the files on a daily basis, I know he never brought the records or information back. On one occasion, when Alfredo Ortiz-Murias requested some information on one of his clients and the record could not be found, Roberto explained that he had probably burned it in his fireplace by mistake. Also, during that time, Roberto instructed me to erase all the time deposit computer records. He told me that if they could not be erased, he would throw the computers into the river. Following Roberto's instructions, I contacted a man at Commercial Software, Inc., and he instructed me on how to erase the computer records, which I did."

Alfredo Ortiz-Murias began to notify his own clients and others that there was trouble, and the clients began to place calls on their assets, meaning, in layman's terms, they wanted their money back, immediately. In one of his letters from prison, Polo has said, "Rostuca advised PAMG in December 1987 that it wished to terminate its relationship; the other clients did the same in April and May of 1988; this means that PAMG was in the obligation to repay its clients between December of 1988 and June of 1989, at the earliest. Now as before this scandal, PAMG is prepared to pre-pay, but Alfredo is not interested, because as he said, 'I hate Roberto. I only want his blood.' "

When too many of Polo's investors demanded their money at the same time, it was like a run on the bank. He could not meet their demands. But that, his defenders say, did not make him a crook.

A Swiss arrest warrant was issued on April 30. The Swiss were expecting Polo to appear at the opening of the exhibition of twenty-six paintings that were to be auctioned on May 30, but he didn't show up. In the meantime the Swiss judge got in touch with the French police, and an international arrest warrant was issued. At that time Polo made a call from Paris to Milan from a street telephone. "Don't call me at home," he said. "The telephones are tapped."

On May 8, Roberto Polo and Fabrizio Bagaglini were in Haiti. Polo intended to start a new collection of pictures to replace his collection of French masterpieces. An American friend, Kurt Thometz, and his wife were in Paris at the time. They visited the Polo apartment and said there were already between thirty-five and forty Haitian paintings in one room. Roberto was also buying Dominican art, including some new works by his father-in-law.

On May 11, Polo was seen at a jewel auction in Geneva, selling.

On May 12, he was seen in the South of France with Rosa, Fabrizio, the child, the nanny, and Julio Cordero,

Rosa's cousin, who was the manager of the Geneva office, and his wife.

On May 15, the group was in Monte Carlo, and Polo's life seemed out of control. With an international warrant out for his arrest, he arrived that afternoon at the Hôtel de Paris apartment of Baby Monteiro de Carvalho, the richest man in Brazil, to watch the Grand Prix, which raced by in the square below. He was accompanied by Rosa, Marina, and Fabrizio, and other guests commented that he seemed harassed.

On May 16, police entered the office of the Miguel Cruz perfume company in Paris and told the staff that Roberto Polo was under arrest. The feeling, according to Ortiz-Murias, is that perhaps the employees alerted Polo. He and his family returned from the South of France that night. Rosa and the child went to the apartment, but Roberto did not. Instead he went to a hotel.

On May 17, Roberto disappeared.

On May 18, at nine o'clock in the morning, the police and detectives walked into the Polo apartment. Rosa was there. The police seized $26 million in furniture and paintings, leaving her with only two mattresses on the floor. Rosa asked the police if she could keep her engagement ring, and they let her.

The Ferrari Testarossa was seized in Monte Carlo.

In the days that followed, several people in New York had direct-dial overseas calls from Polo. Eleanor Lambert told me, "He didn't give his name. He simply said, 'You know who this is, don't you?' I said yes, and he went on to say that all the stories about him were lies spread by Alfredo Ortiz-Murias, and that in time his name would be cleared." People who knew him best said that he would not allow the police to catch him, that he would take sleeping pills.

"I wouldn't be surprised if he was dead," said an antiques dealer in New York.

"A suicide?" I asked.

"No, murdered."

"Murdered?"

"You must understand that there are a lot of people who don't want him to be found, because he could incriminate them."

In addition to the investors who did not want to be identified, several of the antiques dealers Polo did business with in Europe were said to have been paid partially in their own country and partially in Switzerland, a practice not only frowned upon but considered criminal in some countries.

The whereabouts of Roberto Polo and Fabrizio Bagaglini between May 16 and the end of June, when they turned up in Viareggio, remains a mystery, although the most persistent speculation at the time, later proved incorrect, was that they were in Peru, Chile, or Brazil. Alfredo Ortiz-Murias believes that Polo was hiding out in an apartment in Paris, because Rosa Polo, who was then under surveillance, left her apartment each afternoon and went to the Hôtel Ritz on the Place Vendôme to use the public telephone, presumably to call her husband. In one of the press releases Polo wrote from the prison in Lucca, he says about this period, "Prior to going to Viareggio, I had been in my apartment in Monte Carlo, at the Hôtel de Paris (also in Monte Carlo), at the Hôtel Hermitage (also in Monte Carlo), at Hôtel Le Richemond in Geneva (registered in my name), and before that in Port-au-Prince in Haiti with friends and Santo Domingo, Dominican Republic, with family." There is no doubt that he was in all those places, but earlier than May 16. There is further speculation that the French police did not want to make the arrest in France because a nephew of President Mitterand, Maxime Mitterand, was an employee in the Geneva office of PAMG, Ltd.

On May 30, the auction of Polo's French masterpieces went on in Paris as scheduled. Five days earlier, Ader Picard Tajan, the auctioneer, had called a press conference to explain that the sale would be a "forced one" and that he would be the "receiver" for the courts. Surprisingly, the highly publicized sale did not draw crowds. The $14 million realized from it was $3.4 million less than had been expected. There was talk in art circles that if the works donated to the Louvre by Polo had been purchased with money that was not his own the Louvre would have to return them.

After Polo's arrest in Viareggio, Fabrizio Bagaglini returned to Rome, where he remained for two weeks. From there he went to Paris and then on to London with a rich Argentinean girlfriend.

As of this writing, Roberto Polo has been denied bail by the Italians. Here in America, in addition to the ongoing investigations reportedly being conducted by the IRS and the SEC, the FBI is now allegedly involved in collecting evidence to see if there has been mail fraud, if, as Ramona Colón claimed in her affidavit, Polo sent false statements to his investors each month. On East Sixty-fourth Street in Manhattan, the gray stucco Italianate front of the Polo's town house is cracked and peeling. Inside, the lights stay on day and night. All the furniture is gone except for a set of six upholstered chairs, a chaise longue, and a sofa, all covered in chintz, that were left behind in the sitting room of the master bedroom, and an Aubusson rug, folded in one corner. On the front door is a notice that says, "Warning:

"U.S. Government seizure. This property has been seized for non-payment of internal revenue taxes, due from Roberto Polo, by virtue of levy issued by the District Director of the Internal Revenue Service."

From prison Roberto Polo wrote me saying he was reading *One Hundred Years of Solitude* while awaiting the determination of his fate. He also issues communiqués and ultimatums, as if he were in the best bargaining position. In response to the criticism that his life-style surpassed that of the people whose money he handled, he wrote, "It is quite stupid to state that my lifestyle is better than that of my clients: I have a better education and sense of the quality of life, as well as make more money than any of them singly! Does the President or Chairman of the Board of Citibank, for example, live better than most of the bank's clients? Of course he does! PAMG, Ltd. has clients who are worth U.S. $20,000,000, but who don't know any better than to buy their clothes at Alexander's when they visit New York or who dine at coffee shops!"

From Mexico City, Pablo Aramburuzabala said, "Yesterday Polo said that if we didn't accept his offer to accept the money that had already been frozen he was going to tell everyone who we were. I said that my money is not dirty money. He can go ahead and tell."

In New York, Alfredo Ortiz-Murias says he has received irate calls from Roberto Polo's mother in Miami. She says she will not rest until she sees Alfredo in jail. Chantal Carr has become engaged to Marco Polo. Rosa Polo continues to live with Marina in the stripped-down apartment in Paris. The Miguel Cruz fashion house is defunct, and the perfume company is at a standstill. Everyone is waiting.

Jacques Kam, Polo's French lawyer, told me when he was in New York on the case, "There are many things in the stories that are quite wrong, 100 percent wrong." He added, "It is not the round that counts. It is the match. This whole case could boomerang."

Like the people who danced the nights away in the various discotheques of Imelda Marcos and then, after her fall from grace, pretended not to have known her, or claimed to have only met her, many of the recipients of Roberto Polo's largess act now as if the Polos had been no more than passing acquaintances, although they attended their parties and accepted free evening dresses from the ill-fated Miguel Cruz collections. Such is life in the fast lane. There are those, however, who remember Roberto Polo differently, for example the Chilean painter Benjamin Lira and his artist wife, Francisca Sutil. "The Roberto Polo we know doesn't match with this man we have been reading and hearing about," Lira said. They remember their friend Roberto as a devout family man and a loving and generous friend, with whom they went to concerts and films and galleries, and with whom they spent long evenings in their loft or in the Polos' town house, discussing art.

"Roberto's understanding of art goes far beyond taste," said Francisca Sutil. Eleanor Lambert agreed: "He was not just showing off. He was someone with real destiny. He could have been one of the great authorities on art, another Bernard Berenson."

October 1988

DANSE MACABRE
The Rockefeller and
the Ballet Boys

⟳

THERE IS NO ONE, not even his severest detractor, and let me tell you at the outset of this tale that he has a great many severe detractors, who will not concede that Raymundo de Larrain, who sometimes uses the questionable title of the Marquis de Larrain, is, or at least was, before he took the road to riches by marrying a Rockefeller heiress nearly forty years his senior, a man of considerable talent, who, if he had persevered in his artistic pursuits, might have made a name for himself on his own merit. Instead his name, long a fixture in the international social columns, is today at the center of the latest in a rash of contested-will controversies in which wildly rich American families go to court to slug it out publicly for millions of dollars left to upstart spouses the same age as or, in this case, younger than the disinherited adult children.

The most interesting person in this story is the late possessor of the now disputed millions, Margaret Strong de Cuevas de Larrain, who died in Madrid on December 2, 1985, at the age of eighty-eight, and the key name to keep in mind is the magical one of Rockefeller. Margaret de

Larrain had two children, Elizabeth and John, from her first marriage, to the Marquis George de Cuevas. The children do not know the whereabouts of her remains, or even whether she was, as a member of the family put it, incinerated in Madrid. What they do know is that during the eight years of their octogenarian mother's marriage to Raymundo de Larrain, her enormous real-estate holdings, which included adjoining town houses in New York, an apartment in Paris, a country house in France, a villa in Tuscany, and a resort home in Palm Beach, were given away or sold, although she had been known throughout her life to hate parting with any of her belongings, even the most insubstantial things. At the time of her second marriage, in 1977, she had assets of approximately $30 million (some estimates go as high as $60 million), including 350,000 shares of Exxon stock in a custodian account at the Chase Manhattan Bank. The location of the Exxon shares is currently unknown, and documents presented by her widower show that his late wife's assets amount to only $400,000. Although these sums may seem modest in terms of today's billion-dollar fortunes, Margaret, at the time of her inheritance, was considered one of the richest women in the world. There are two wills in question: a 1968 will leaving the fortune to the children and a 1980 will leaving it to the widower. In the upcoming court case, the children, who are fifty-eight and fifty-six years old, are charging that the will submitted by de Larrain, who is fifty-two, represents "a massive fraud on an aging, physically ill, trusting lady."

Although Margaret Strong de Cuevas de Larrain was a reluctant news figure for five decades, the facts of her birth, her fortune, and the kind of men she married denied her the privacy she craved. However, her children, Elizabeth, known as Bessie, and John, have so successfully guarded their privacy, as well as that of their children, that they are practically anonymous in the social world in which they were raised. John de Cuevas, who has been described as almost a hermit, has never used the title of marquis. He is now divorced from his second wife, Sylvia Iolas de Cuevas, the niece of the art dealer Alexander Iolas, who was a friend of his father. His only child is a daughter from that marriage, now in her twenties. He maintains homes in St. James, Long Island, and Cambridge, Massachusetts, where he teaches scientific writing at Harvard. Bessie de Cuevas, a sculptor whose work resembles that of Archipenko, lives in New York City and East Hampton, Long Island. She is also divorced, and has one daughter, twenty-two, by her second husband, Joel Carmichael, the editor of *Midstream,* a Zionist magazine so reactionary that it recently published an article accusing the pope of being soft on Marxism. Friends of Bessie de Cuevas told me that she was never bothered by the short financial reins her mother kept her on, because she did not fall prey to fortune hunters the way her sister heiresses, like Sunny von Bülow, did.

Margaret Strong de Cuevas de Larrain, the twice-titled American heiress, grew up very much like a character in a Henry James novel. In fact, Henry James, as well as William James, visited her father's villa outside Florence when she was young. Margaret was the only child of Bessie Rockefeller, the eldest of John D. Rockefeller's five children, and Charles Augustus Strong, a philosopher and psychologist, whose father, Augustus Hopkins Strong, a Baptist clergyman and theologian, had been a great friend of old Rockefeller. A mark of the brilliance of Margaret's father was that, while at Harvard, he competed with fellow student George Santayana for a scholarship at a German

university and won. He then shared the scholarship with
Santayana, who remained his lifelong friend. Margaret was
born in New York, but the family moved shortly thereafter
to Paris. When Margaret was nine her mother died, and
Strong, who never remarried, built his villa in Fiesole, outside Florence. There, in a dour and austere atmosphere,
surrounded by intellectuals and philosophers, he raised his
daughter and wrote scholarly books. His world provided
very little amusement for a child, and no frivolity.

Each year Margaret returned to the United States to see
her grandfather, with whom she maintained a good relationship, and to visit her Rockefeller cousins. Old John D.
was amused by his serious and foreign granddaughter, who
spoke several languages and went to school in England.
Later, she was one of only three women attending Cambridge University, where she studied chemistry. Never,
even as a young girl, could she have been considered attractive. She was big, bulky, and shy, and until the age of
twenty-eight she always wore variations of the same modest sailor dress.

Her father was eager for her to marry, and toward that
end Margaret went to Paris to live, although she had few
prospects in sight. Following the Russian Revolution there
was an influx of Russian émigrés into Paris, and Margaret
Strong developed a fascination for them that remained with
her all her life. She was most excited to meet the tall and
elegant Prince Felix Yusupov, the assassin of Rasputin,
who was said to have used his beautiful wife, Princess Irina,
as a lure to attract the womanizing Rasputin to his palace
on the night of the murder. In Paris, Prince Yusupov had
taken to wearing pink rouge and green eyeshadow, and he
supported himself by heading up a house of couture called
Irfé, a combination of the first syllables of his and his wife's
names. Into this hothouse of fashion, one day in 1927,

walked the thirty-year-old, prim, studious, and unfashionable Rockefeller heiress. At that time Prince Yusupov had working for him an epicene and penniless young Chilean named George de Cuevas, who was, according to friends who remember him from that period, "extremely amusing and lively." He spoke with a strong Spanish accent and expressed himself in a wildly camp manner hitherto totally unknown to the sheltered lady. The story goes that at first Margaret mistook George de Cuevas for the prince. "What do you do at the couture?" she asked. "I'm the saleslady," he replied. The plain, timid heiress was enchanted with him, and promptly fell in love, thereby establishing what would be a lifelong predilection for flamboyant, effete men. The improbable pair were married in 1928.

From then on Margaret abandoned almost all intellectual activity. She stepped out of the pages of a Henry James novel into the pages of a Ronald Firbank novel. If her father had been the dominant figure of her maidenhood, George de Cuevas was the controlling force of her adult existence. Their life became more and more frivolous, capricious, and eccentric. Through her husband she discovered an exotic new world that centered on the arts, especially the ballet, for which George had a deep and abiding passion. Their beautiful apartment on the Quai Voltaire, filled with pets and bibelots and opulent furnishings, became a gathering place for the *haute bohème* of Paris, as did their country house in St.-Germain-en-Laye, where their daughter, Bessie, was born in 1929. Their son, John, was born two years later. Along the way the title of marquis was granted by, or purchased from, the King of Spain. The Chilean son of a Spanish father, George de Cuevas is listed in some dance manuals as the eighth Marquis de Piedrablanca de Guana de Cuevas, but the wife of a Spanish grandee, who wished not to be identified, told me that the title was laughed at in Spain. Nonetheless, the Marquis and Marquesa de Cuevas remained a highly visible couple on the international and artistic scenes for the next thirty years.

When World War II broke out, they moved to the United States. Margaret, already a collector of real estate, began to add to her holdings. She bought a town house on East Sixty-eighth Street in New York, a mansion in Palm Beach, and a weekend place in Bernardsville, New Jersey. She also acquired a house in Riverdale, New York, which they never lived in but visited, and one in New Mexico to be used in the event the United States was invaded. In New York, Margaret always kept a rented limousine, and sometimes two, all day every day in front of her house in case she wanted to go out.

Although Margaret had inherited a vast fortune, she was to inherit a vaster one through the persistence of her husband. George de Cuevas's wooing of his wife's grandfather, old John D. Rockefeller, turned Margaret from a rich woman into a very rich woman. While John D. had bestowed liberal inheritances on his four daughters during their lifetimes, he believed in primogeniture, and in his late seventies he turned over the bulk of his $500 million fortune to his only son, John D. Rockefeller, Jr., the father of Abby, John D. III, Nelson, Laurence, Winthrop, and David. He retained the income for himself. Margaret at that time was indifferent to her inheritance, but George, for whom the prospect of Rockefeller millions had surely been a lure in his choice of a life mate, was not one to sit back and watch what he felt should be his wife's share pass on to her already very rich Rockefeller cousins. He set about to charm his grandfather-in-law, and charm him he did. He even became his golfing companion. Rockefeller had never come across such a person as this eccentric bird of paradise that his granddaughter had married. Surprisingly, he not only was amused by him but genuinely liked him. The family legend goes that one day George took Bessie and John by the hand to the old man and said, "Do you want to see your great-grandchildren starve because their mother has not been taken care of the way the rest of the Rockefellers have been?" The tycoon calmly assured him that Margaret would be provided for. Old John D. then began investing his enormous income in the stock market and in the last years of his life made a second fortune, the bulk of which he left to Margaret on his death, when she was forty years old.

In 1940, in Toms River, New Jersey, George de Cuevas became an American citizen and renounced his Spanish title, claiming he would henceforth be known as merely George de Cuevas. However, he continued to be referred to by his title, and once his role as a ballet impresario grew to international prominence, he changed the name of the company associated with him throughout his career from the Ballet de Monte Carlo to the Grand Ballet du Marquis de Cuevas. From 1947 to 1960 the marquis toured the company all over the world, with the financial support of his wife, who donated 15 percent of her income to his troupe. He introduced American dancers to France and French dancers to America, and soon became a beloved figure in the dance world. The impresario Sol Hurok in his biography described him as "a colorful gentleman of taste and culture . . . perhaps the outstanding example we have today of the sincere and talented amateur in and patron of the arts."

Actually, de Cuevas is better remembered for one episode of histrionics and temperament than for any of his productions. In 1958 the dancer and choreographer Serge Lifar, then fifty-two years old, became angry when the marquis's company changed the choreography of his ballet *Black and White.* After a heated exchange of words the marquis, who was seventy-two at the time, slapped Lifar in the face with a handkerchief in public and then refused to apologize. Lifar challenged de Cuevas to a duel, and the marquis accepted. Although neither of the combatants was known as a swordsman, épées were chosen as the weapons. The location of the duel was to be kept secret because dueling was outlawed in France, but more than fifty tipped-off reporters and photographers showed up at the scene. The encounter was scheduled to last until blood was drawn. For the first four minutes of the duel Serge Lifar leapt about while the marquis remained stationary. In the third round the marquis forced Lifar back by simply advancing with his sword held straight out in front of him, and pinked his opponent. It was not clear, according to newspaper accounts of the duel, whether skill or accident brought the marquis's blade into contact with Lifar's arm. "Blood has flowed! Honor is saved!" cried Lifar. Both men burst into tears and rushed to embrace each other. Reporting the event on its front page, the *New York Times* said that the affair "might well have been the most delicate encounter in the history of French dueling."

As a couple, the Marquis and Marquesa de Cuevas became increasingly eccentric. "It was unconventional, their marriage, but, curiously, it worked," said Viscountess Jacqueline de Ribes, who was a frequent guest in their Paris apartment. "There were always people waiting in the hall to have an audience—it was like a court," said one family member. Another longtime observer of the inner workings of the de Cuevas household, Jean Pierre Laclocle, said, "Margaret was always in her room during the parties. She hated coming out, but usually she finally did. She gave in to all of George's pranks. She didn't care. He made life interesting around her." George de Cuevas often received visitors lying in bed wearing a black velvet robe with a sable collar and surrounded by his nine or ten Pekingese dogs, while Margaret grew more and more reclusive and slovenly in her dress. She always wore black and kept an in-residence dressmaker to make the same dress for her over and over again. When she traveled to Europe, she would book passage on as many as six ships and then be unable to make up her mind as to which she wanted to sail. If she wanted to go from Palm Beach to New York, she would book seats on every train for a week, and then not be able to make the commitment to move. Once, unable to secure a last-minute booking on a Paris-Biarritz train and determined to leave, no matter what, she piled her daughter, her maid, ten Pekingese dogs, and her luggage into a Paris taxicab and had the driver drive her the five hundred miles to Biarritz. The trip took three days.

George de Cuevas liked to entertain, and he filled their homes with society figures, titles, celebrated artists and dancers, and a constant flow of Russian émigrés. "At the Cuevas parties were such as the Queen Mother of Egypt, Maria Callas, and, of course, Salvador Dalí, who was a regular in the house," said Mafalda Davis, an Egyptian-born public-relations woman who was a great friend of George de Cuevas. George was a giver of gifts. He bought old furs and jewels from the poor Russians in Paris and gave them away as presents. He gave the Viscountess de Ribes a sable coat, and he gave Mrs. Gurney Munn of Palm Beach a watch on which he had had engraved "May the ticking of this watch remind you of the beauty of a faithful heart."

Somehow, in the midst of this affluent chaos on two continents, Bessie and John de Cuevas were raised. A relative of the family told me that Margaret had a good and strong relationship with her children. "Not a peasant-type relationship," he said, "not conventional," meaning, as I understood him, not many hugs and kisses, but strong in its way. Another relative said, "After a short period with her children—and later with her grandchildren—she was ready to send them out to play or to turn them over to their nanny. Margaret, who throughout her life was notorious for never being on time, arrived so late for her daughter's coming-out party at the Plaza Hotel in New York, which was attended by all of her Rockefeller relations, that she almost missed it. When Bessie was seventeen she met Hubert Faure, who became her first husband. "She was an extraordinary-looking person," said Faure about his former wife, with whom he has retained a close friendship. "English-American in intellect with a Spanish vitality behind that." Hubert Faure, now the chairman of United Technology, was not at the time considered a catch by the Marquis de Cuevas, who wanted his daughter to marry a Spanish grandee and possess a great title. But Bessie exhibited an early independence: she went ahead and married Faure in Paris in 1948, when she was nineteen, with no family and only another couple in attendance. John, her brother, was also married for the first time at an early age. The children, as Bessie and John are regularly referred to in the upcoming court case with Raymundo de Larrain, have at times shown a bemused attitude about their life. Once, when questioned about her nationality, Bessie described herself as a third-generation expatriate. John, during a brief Wall Street career, was asked by a colleague if he could possibly be related to a mad marquesa of the same name. "Yes," he is said to have replied, "she is a very distant mother."

The apex of the social career of George de Cuevas was reached in 1953 with a masked ball he gave in Biarritz; it vied with the Venetian masked ball given by Carlos de Beistegui in 1951 as the most elaborate fete of the decade. France at the time was paralyzed by a general strike. No planes or trains were running. Undaunted, the international nomads, with their couturier-designed eighteenth-century costumes tucked into their steamer trunks, made their way across Europe like migrating birds to participate in the *tableaux vivants* at the Marquis de Cuevas's ball, an event so extravagant that it was criticized by both the Vatican and the left wing. "People talked about it for months before," remembered Josephine Hartford Bryce, the A&P heiress, who recently donated her costume from the ball to the Metropolitan Museum of Art. "Everyone was dying to go to it. The costumes were fantastic, and people spent most of the evening just staring at each other." As they say in those circles, "everyone" came. Elsa Maxwell dressed as a man. The Duchess of Argyll, on the arm of the duke, who would later divorce her in the messiest divorce in the history of British society, came dressed as an angel. Ann Woodward, of the New York Woodwards, slapped a woman she thought was dancing too often with her husband, William, whom she was to shoot and kill two years later. King Peter of Yugoslavia waltzed with a diamond-tiaraed Merle Oberon. And at the center of it all was the Marquis George de Cuevas, in gold lamé with a headdress of grapes and towering ostrich plums, who presided as the King of Nature. He was surrounded by the Four Seasons, in the costumed persons of the Count Charles de Ganay; Princess Marella Caracciolo, who would soon become the wife of Fiat king Gianni Agnelli; Bessie, his daughter; and her then husband, Hubert Faure. As always, Margaret de Cuevas did the unexpected. For days beforehand, her costume, designed by the great couturier Pierre Balmain, who had paid her the honor of coming to her for fittings, hung, like a presence, on a dress dummy in the hallway of the de Cuevas residence in Biarritz. But Margaret did not appear at the ball, although, of course, she paid for it. She may have been an unlikely Rockefeller, but she was still a Rockefeller, and the opulence, extravagance, and sheer size (four thousand people were asked and two thousand accepted) of the event offended her. She simply disappeared that night, and the party went on without her. She did, however, watch the arrival of the guests from a hidden location, and a much repeated, but unconfirmed story is that she sent her maid to the ball dressed in her Balmain costume.

George de Cuevas increasingly made his life and many homes available to a series of young male worldlings who enjoyed the company of older men. In the early 1950s Margaret de Cuevas purchased the town house adjoining hers on East Sixty-eighth Street in New York. The confirmation-of-sale letter from the realty firm of Douglas L. Elliman & Co. contained a cautionary line: "The Marquesa detests publicity and would appreciate it if her name weren't divulged." An unkind novel by Theodora Keogh, called *The Double Door,* depicted the marriage of George and Margaret and their teenage daughter. The double door of the title referred to the point of access between the two adjoining houses, beyond which the wife of the main character, a flamboyant nobleman, was not permitted to go, although the houses were hers. The drama of the novel revolved around the teenage daughter's clandestine romance with one of the handsome young men beyond the double door. Inevitably, the marriage of George and Margaret de Cuevas began to founder, and for the most part they occupied their various residences at different times. They maintained close communication, however, and Margaret would often call George in Paris or Cannes from New

York or Palm Beach to deal with a domestic problem. Once when the marquesa's temperamental chef in Palm Beach became enraged at one of her unreasonable demands and threw her breakfast tray at her, she called her husband in Paris and asked him to call the chef and beseech him not only to quit but also to bring her another breakfast, because she was hungry. George finally persuaded the chef to recook the breakfast, but the man refused to carry it to Margaret. A maid in the house had to do that.

At this point in the story, Raymundo de Larrain entered the picture. "Raymundo is not just a little Chilean," said a lady of fashion in Paris about him. "He is from one of the four greatest families in Chile. The Larrains are aristocratic people, a better family by far than the de Cuevas family." Whatever he was, Raymundo de Larrain wanted to be something more than just another bachelor from Chile seeking extra-man status in Paris society. He was talented, brilliant, and wildly extravagant, and soon began making a name for himself designing costumes and sets for George de Cuevas's ballet company. A protégé of the marquis's to start with, he soon became known as his nephew. An acquaintance who knew de Larrain at that time recalled that the card on the door of his sublet apartment first read M. Larrain. Later it became M. de Larrain. Later still it became the Marquis de Larrain.

In Bessie de Cuevas's affidavit in the upcoming probate proceedings, she emphatically states that although various newspapers have described de Larrain as the nephew of her father and suggested that he was raised by her parents, there was no blood relation between the two men. In a letter to an American friend in Paris, she wrote, "He is not my father's nephew. I think he planted the word long ago in Suzy's column. If there is any relationship at all, it is so remote as to be meaningless." Yet as recently as November, when I spoke with de Larrain in Palm Beach, he referred to George de Cuevas as "my uncle." That fact of the matter is that Raymundo de Larrain has been described as a de Cuevas nephew and has been using the title of marquis for years, and he was on a familiar basis with all members of the de Cuevas family. Longtime acquaintances in Paris remember Raymundo calling Margaret de Cuevas Tante Margaret or, sometimes, perhaps in levity, Tante Rockefeller. In her book *The Case of Salvador Dalí,* Fleur Cowles described the Dalí set in Paris as follows: "On May 9, 1957, the young nephew of the Marquis de Cuevas gave a ball in honor of the Dalís. According to Maggi Nolan, the social editor of the *Paris Herald-Tribune,* the Marquis Raymundo de Larrain's ball was 'unforgettable' in the apartment which had been converted . . . into a vast party confection," with "the most fabulous gala-attired members of international society." Fleur Cowles then went on to list the guests, including in their number the Marquis de Cuevas himself, without his wife, and M. and Mme. Hubert Faure, his daughter and son-in-law. Although Cowles did not say so, George de Cuevas almost certainly paid for Raymundo's ball.

Along the way de Larrain met the Viscountess Jacqueline de Ribes, one of the grandest ladies in Paris society and a ballet enthusiast to boot. "Before Jacqueline, no one had ever heard of Raymundo de Larrain except as a nephew of de Cuevas. Jacqueline was his stepping-stone into society," said another lady of international social fame who did not wish to be identified. The viscountess became an earlier admirer of his talent, and they entered into a close relationship that was to continue for years, sharing an interest in clothes and fashion as well as the ballet. Raymundo de

Larrain is said to have made Jacqueline de Ribes over and given her the look that has remained her trademark for several decades. A famous photograph taken by Richard Avedon in 1961 shows the two of them in exotic matching profiles. At a charity party in New York known as the Embassy Ball, chaired by the Viscountess de Ribes, Mrs. Winston Guest, and the American-born Princess d'Arenberg, Raymundo de Larrain's fantastical butterfly décor was so extravagant that there was no money left for the charity that was meant to benefit from the event. In time the viscountess became known as the godmother of the ballet, and she, more than any other person, pushed the career of Raymundo de Larrain.

After the publication of *The Double Door*, the de Cuevases were often the subject of gossip in the sophisticated society in which they moved, but somehow they had the ability to keep scandal within the family perimeter. The relationship of both husband and wife with the unsavory Jan de Vroom, however, almost caused their peculiar habits to be open to public scrutiny. A family member said to me that at this point in Margaret de Cuevas's life she fell into a nest of vipers. Born in Dutch Indonesia, Jan de Vroom was a tall, blond adventurer who dominated drawing rooms by sheer force of personality rather than good looks. A wit, storyteller, and linguist, he had an eye for the main chance, and like a great many young men before him looking for the easy ride, he attached himself to George de Cuevas. De Vroom was quick to realize on which side the bread was buttered in the de Cuevas household, and, to the distress of the marquis, who soon grew to distrust him, he shifted his attentions to Margaret, whom he followed to the United States. At first Margaret was not disposed to like him, but, undeterred by her initial snubs, he schooled himself in Mozart, whom he knew to be her favorite composer, and soon found favor with her as a fellow Mozart addict. He got a small apartment in a brownstone a few blocks from Margaret's houses on East Sixty-eighth Street and was always available when she needed a companion for dinner. She set him up in business, as an importer of Italian glass and lamps. From Europe, George de Cuevas tried to break up the deepening intimacy, but Margaret, egged on by her friend Florence Gould, ignored her husband's protests. As the friendship grew, so did de Vroom's store of acquisitions. He was a sportsman, and through Margaret de Cuevas's bounty he soon owned a sleek sailing boat, a fleet of Ferrari cars, a Rolls-Royce, and—briefly, until it crashed —an airplane. He also acquired an important collection of rare watches.

Raymundo de Larrain and Jan de Vroom detested each other, and Jan, in the years when he was in favor with Margaret, refused to have Raymundo around. De Vroom had no wish to join the ranks of men who made their fortune at the altar; he was content to play the role of son to Margaret, a sort of naughty-boy son whose peccadilloes she easily forgave. A mixer in the darker worlds of New York and Florida, he entertained her with stories of his subterranean adventures. Often, in her own homes, she would be the only woman present at a dining table full of men who were disinterested in women.

In 1960 the Marquis de Cuevas, in failing health, offered Raymundo de Larrain, with whom he was now on the closest terms, the chance to create a whole new production of *The Sleeping Beauty,* to be performed at the Théâtre des Champs Élysées. De Larrain's *Sleeping Beauty* is still remembered as one of the most beautiful ballet productions of all time, and it was the greatest box-office success the company had ever experienced. The marquis was permitted by his physicians to attend the premiere. "If I am going to die,

I will die backstage," he said. After the performance he was pushed out onto the stage in a wheelchair and received a standing ovation. George de Cuevas attended every performance up until two weeks before his death. He died at his favorite of the many de Cuevas homes, Les Délices, in Cannes, on February 22, 1961. Margaret, who was in New York, did not visit her husband of thirty-three years in the months of his decline. In his will George left the house in Cannes to his Argentinean secretary, Horacio Guerrico, but Margaret was displeased with her husband's bequest and managed to get the house back from the secretary in exchange for money and several objects of value.

Although Margaret had never truly shared her husband's passion for the ballet, or for the ballet company bearing his name, which she had financed for so many years, she did not immediately disband it after his death. Instead she appointed Raymundo de Larrain the new head of the company. There was always a sense of dilettantism about George de Cuevas's role as a Maecenas of the dance— not dissimilar to the role Rebekah Harkness would later play with her ballet company. The taste and caprices of the marquis determined the policy of the company, which relied on the box-office appeal of big-star names. This same sense of dilettantism carried over into de Larrain's contribution. The de Cuevas company has been described to me by one balletomane as ballet for people who normally despise ballet, ballet for society audiences, as opposed to dance audiences.

De Larrain's stewardship of the company was brief but not undramatic. In June 1961 he played a significant role in the political defection of Rudolf Nureyev at the Paris airport when the Kirov Ballet of Leningrad was leaving France. The story has become romanticized over the years, and everyone's version of it differs. According to de Larrain,

Nureyev had confessed to Clara Saint, a half-Chilean, half-Argentinean friend of de Larrain's, that he would rather commit suicide than go back to Russia. In one account, Clara Saint, feigning undying love for the departing star, screamed out to Nureyev that she must have one more kiss from him before he boarded the plane and returned to his homeland. Nureyev went back to kiss her, jumped over the barriers, and escaped in a waiting car as the plane carrying the company took off. De Larrain says that Clara Saint had alerted the French authorities that there was going to be a defection, and she advised Nureyev during a farewell drink at the airport bar that he must ask the French police at the departure gate for political asylum. He says that Nureyev spat in the face of the Russian security official. For a while Nureyev lived in de Larrain's Paris apartment, and the first time he danced after his defection was for the de Cuevas company, in de Larrain's production of *The Sleeping Beauty*. "He danced like a god, but he also had a spectacular story," de Larrain told me. At one of his first performances the balcony was filled with communists, who pelted the stage with tomatoes and almost caused a riot. People who were present that night remember that Nureyev continued to dance through the barrage, as if he were unaware of the commotion, until the performance was finally halted.

In Raymundo de Larrain's affidavit for the probate, he assesses his role in Nureyev's career in an I'm-not-the-nobody tone: "With the help of Margaret de Cuevas we made him into one of the biggest stars in the history of ballet." The professional association between de Larrain and Nureyev, which might have saved the de Cuevas ballet, did not last, just as most of de Larrain's professional associations did not last. "Raymundo and Rudolf did not have the same point of view on beauty and the theater, and they fought," explained the Viscountess de Ribes in Paris recently.

"Raymundo had great talent and tremendous imagination. He had the talent to be a stage director, but neither the health nor the courage to fight. He was very unrealistic. He didn't know how to talk to people. He was too grand. What Raymundo is is a total aesthete, not an intellectual. He wanted to live around beautiful things. He was very generous and gave beautiful presents. Even the smallest gift he ever gave me was perfect, absolutely perfect," she said. Another friend of de Larrain's said, "Raymundo had more taste and knowledge of dancing than anyone. His problem was that he was unprofessional. He couldn't get along with people. He had no discipline over himself." When the Marquesa de Cuevas decided in 1962 not to underwrite the ballet company any longer, it was disbanded. Then, under the sponsorship of the Viscountess de Ribes, de Larrain formed his own ballet company. He began by producing and directing *Cinderella,* in which he featured Geraldine Chaplin in a modest but much publicized role. The viscountess, however, couldn't afford for long to underwrite a ballet company, and withdrew after two years. Raymundo de Larrain then took to photographing celebrities for *Vogue, Town & Country,* and *Life.* His friends say that he had one obsession: to "make it" in the eyes of his family back in Chile. He mailed every newspaper clipping about himself to his mother, for whom, de Ribes says, "he had a passion."

For years Margaret de Cuevas's physical appearance had been deteriorating. Never the slightest bit interested in fashion or style, she began to assume the look of what has been described to me by some as a millionairess bag lady and by others as the Madwoman of Chaillot. "Before Fellini she was Fellini," said Count Vega del Ren about her, but other assessments were less romantic. Her nails were uncared for. Her teeth were in a deplorable state. She had knee problems that gave her difficulty in walking. She covered her face with a white paste and white powder, and she blackened her eyes in an eccentric way that made people think she had put her thumb and fingers in a full ashtray and rubbed them around her eyes. Her hair was dyed black with reddish tinges, and around her head she always wore a black net scarf, which she tied beneath her chin. She wrapped handkerchiefs and ribbons around her wrists to hide her diamonds, and her black dresses were frequently stained with food and spilled white powder and held together with safety pins. For shoes she wore either sneakers or a pair of pink polyester bedroom slippers, which were often on the wrong feet. Her lateness had reached a point where dinner guests would sit for several hours waiting for her to make an appearance, while Marcel, her butler of forty-five years, would pass them five or six times, carrying a martini on a silver tray to the marquesa's room. "She drank much too much for an old lady," one of her frequent guests told me. Finally her arrival for dinner would be heralded by the barking of her Pekingese dogs, and she would enter the dining room preceded by her favorite of them, Happy, who had a twisted neck and a glass eye and walked with a limp as the result of a stroke.

Her behavior also was increasingly eccentric. In her bedroom she had ten radios sitting on tables and chests of drawers. Each radio was set to a different music station—country-and-western, rock 'n' roll, classical—and when she wanted to hear music she would ring for Marcel and point to the radio she wished him to turn on. For years she paid for rooms at the Westbury Hotel for a group of White Russians she had taken under her wing.

In the meantime Jan de Vroom had grown increasingly alcoholic and pill-dependent. "If someone's eyes are dilated, does that mean they're taking drugs?" Margaret asked a friend of de Vroom's. "I've been too kind to him. I've spoiled him." Young men—mostly hustlers and drug dealers—paraded in and out of his apartment at all hours of the day and night. In 1973 two hustlers, whom he knew, rang the bell of his New York apartment. On a previous visit they had asked him for a loan of $2,000, and he had refused. When de Vroom answered the bell, they sent up a thug to frighten him and demand money again. Jan de Vroom, in keeping with his character, aggravated the thug and incited him to rage. A French houseguest found de Vroom's body: his throat had been cut, and he had been stabbed over and over again. Although he was known to be the person closest to Margaret de Cuevas at that time in her life, her name was not brought into any of the lurid accounts of his murder in the tabloid papers. De Vroom's body, covered from the chin down to conceal his slit throat, lay in an open casket in the Westbury Room of the Frank E. Campbell Funeral Chapel at Madison Avenue and Eighty-first Street. Except for a few of the curious, there were no visitors. A little-known fact of the sordid situation was that, through the intercession of Margaret de Cuevas, the body was laid to rest in the Rockefeller cemetery in Pocantico Hills, the family estate, although subsequently it was shipped to Holland. The killers were caught and tried. There was no public outcry over the unsavory killing, and they received brief sentences. It is said that one of them still frequents the bars in New York.

Into this void in the life of the Marquesa Margaret de Cuevas moved Raymundo de Larrain. People meeting Margaret de Cuevas for the first time at this point were inclined to think that the cultivated lady was not intelligent, because she was unable to converse in the way people in society converse, and they suspected that she might be combining sedatives and drink. The same people are uniform in their praise of Raymundo de Larrain during this time. For parties at her house in New York, Raymundo would invite the guests and order the food and arrange the flowers, in much the same way that her late husband had during their marriage, and no one would argue the point that Raymundo surrounded her with a better crowd of people than Jan de Vroom ever had. He would choreograph a steady stream of handpicked guests to Margaret's side during the evening. " 'Go and sit with Tante Margaret and talk with her, and I will send someone over in ten minutes to relieve you,' " a frequent guest told me he used to say. "He was lovely to her." Another view of Raymundo at this time came from a New York lady who also visited the house: "He was so talented, Raymundo. Such a sense of fantasy. But he got sidetracked into money-grubbing." Whatever the interpretation, Margaret de Cuevas and Raymundo became the Harold and Maude of the Upper East Side and Palm Beach. Bessie de Cuevas, in her affidavit, acknowledges that "Raymundo was always attentive and extremely helpful to my mother, particularly in her social life, which consisted almost exclusively of gatherings and entertainments at her various residences."

On April 25, 1977, at the oceanfront estate of Mr. and Mrs. Wilson C. Lucom in Palm Beach, the Marquesa Margaret de Cuevas, then eighty years old, married Raymundo de Larrain, then forty-two, in a hastily arranged surprise ceremony. The wedding was such a closely guarded secret that Margaret de Cuevas's children, Bessie and John, did not know of it until they read about it in Suzy's column in the New York *Daily News*. Bessie de Cuevas's friends say that she felt betrayed by Raymundo because he had not told her of his plans to marry her mother. Among the prominent guests present at the wedding were Rose Kennedy, Mrs. Winston Guest, and Mary Sanford, known as the queen of Palm Beach, who that night gave the newlyweds a wedding reception at her estate. In her affidavit Bessie de Cuevas states, "I had visited with my mother at some length at her home in New York just about two months before. She was clearly aging but we talked along quite well about personal and family things. She said she would be leaving soon to spend some time at her home in Florida. She did not in any way suggest that she was considering getting married. After I read the article, I called her at once in Florida. She could only speak briefly and seemed vague. I assured her that of course my brother John and I wanted anything that would make her comfortable and happy, but why, I asked, did she do it this way. Her reply was simply, 'It just happened.' "

Wilson C. Lucom, the host of the wedding, was also married to an older woman, the since-deceased Willys-Overland automobile heiress Virginia Willys. Lucom, who had trained as a lawyer, never practiced law but had served on the staff of the late secretary of state Edward Stettinius. Shortly after the wedding, in response to an inquiry from the Rockefeller family, he sent a Mailgram to John D. Rockefeller III, the first cousin of Margaret Strong de Cuevas de Larrain, stating his position as the representative of the marquesa and now of de Larrain. "Do not worry about her or be concerned about any rumors you may have heard," the Mailgram read. "She was married at our house with my wife and myself as witnesses. It was a solemn ceremony, and she was highly competent and knew precisely that she was being married and did so of her own free will being of sound mind." Bessie de Cuevas says in her affidavit, "I had never met or heard my mother speak of Mr. Lucom."

For the wedding, Raymundo told friends, he gave his bride a wheelchair and new teeth. He also supervised a transformation of her appearance. "You must understand this: Raymundo cleaned Margaret up. Why, her nails were manicured for the first time in years." He got rid of the white makeup and blackened eyes, and he supervised her hair, nails, cosmetics, and dress. "Margaret was never better cared for" is a remark made over and over about her after her marriage. De Larrain would invite people to lunch or for drinks and wheel her out to greet her guests; he basked in the compliments paid to his wife on her new appearance. However, lawyers for the Chase Manhattan Bank, which represents Bessie and John de Cuevas's interests, told me that the two health-care professionals who cared for the marquesa at different times in 1980 and 1982 recalled that de Larrain did not spend much time with his wife, and that she would often ask about him. But when attention was paid by him, it would be lavish; he would send roses in great quantity or do her makeup. Since he had arranged it so that no one would become close to his wife, "she was particularly vulnerable to such displays of charm and affection." During her second marriage, she became known as Margaret Rockefeller de Larrain. Although this was illustrious-sounding, it was incorrect, for it implied that she was born Margaret Rockefeller rather than Margaret Strong. "The snobbishness and enhancement were de Larrain's," sniffed a friend of her daughter's.

Shortly after the marriage, Sylvia de Cuevas, the then wife of John de Cuevas, took the marquesa's two granddaughters to visit her in Palm Beach. She says she was stopped at the front door by an armed guard, who would not let them enter until permission was granted by Raymundo. Soon other changes began to take place. Old servants who had been with the marquesa for years, includ-

ing her favorite, Marcel, were fired by de Larrain. Bessie de
Cuevas claims in her affidavit that he accused them of steal-
ing and other misdeeds. Long-term relationships with
lawyers and accountants were severed. Copies of correspondence to the marquesa from Richard Weldon, her lawyer
for many years, and Albert Remmert, her secretary and
financial adviser for many years, reflect that her directives
to them were so unlike her usual method of communication that they questioned the authority of the letters.
Shortly thereafter both men were replaced. Another longtime secretary, Lillian Grappone, told Bessie de Cuevas
that her mother had complained of the fact that there were
constantly new faces around her. During this period the
many houses of the marquesa were sold or given to charity,
among them her two houses on East Sixty-eighth Street in
New York, which had always been her favorite as well as
her principal residence. Bessie de Cuevas claims in her affidavit that her mother sometimes could not recall signing
anything to effect the transfer of these houses. At other
times she would talk as if she could get them back. On one
occasion she acknowledged having signed away the houses
but said she had been talked into it at a time when she was
not feeling well. Her father's villa in Fiesole, where she had
grown up, was given to Georgetown University. The house
in Cannes was given to Bessie and John de Cuevas. Her
official residence was moved from New York to Florida, but
she was moved out of her house of many years on El Bravo
Way in Palm Beach to a condominium on South Ocean
Boulevard. Several people who visited her at the condominium said that she seemed confused as to why she should be
living there instead of in her own house. Other friends
explain the move as a practical one: The house on El Bravo
Way was an old Spanish-style one on several floors and

many levels, badly in need of repair, and for an invalid in a wheelchair life was simpler in the one-floor apartment.

During this period the financial affairs of the marquesa were handled more and more by Wilson C. Lucom, the host at the wedding. Bessie de Cuevas states in her affidavit, "I think my mother's belief that Lucom would safeguard her interests against de Larrain only highlights her lack of appreciation for the reality of her circumstances." Bessie de Cuevas tells of an occasion when she visited her mother at the Palm Beach condominium and Lucom "taunted" her by boasting that he and de Larrain were drinking "Rockefeller champagne." "My mother's total dependence on de Larrain is reflected in an explanation she gave for why she did not accompany de Larrain to Paris on a trip he made concerning her holdings there. De Larrain told her no American carrier flew to Paris any longer, and since my mother did not care for Air France, it was best for her not to go. Plainly, my mother had lost any independent touch with the real world."

Access to her mother became more and more difficult for Bessie de Cuevas. When she called, she was told her mother could not come to the telephone. Some friends who visited the marquesa say that she would complain that she never heard from her daughter. Others say that messages left by Bessie were never given to her. In 1982 Raymundo de Larrain took his wife out of the country, and they began what lawyers representing the de Cuevases' interests call an "itinerant existence." She never returned. They went first to Switzerland, then to Chile, where he was from and where they had built a house, and finally to Madrid, where de Larrain was made the cultural attaché at the Chilean embassy. There Margaret died in a hotel room in 1985. Bessie de Cuevas saw her mother for the last time a few weeks before she died. Neither Bessie nor her brother has any idea where she is buried.

Certainly there was trouble between the Rockefeller family and the newlywed de Larrains from the time of the marriage. After the change of residence from New York to Florida, David Rockefeller urged his cousin to donate her two town houses at 52 and 54 East Sixty-eighth Street to an institution supported by the Rockefeller family called the Center for Inter-American Relations. The appraisal of the two houses was arranged by David Rockefeller, and the appraiser had been in the employ of the Rockefellers for years. He evaluated the two houses at $725,000. Subsequently Margaret de Larrain was distressed to hear that these properties, which she had donated to the Center for Inter-American Relations, were later sold to another favorite Rockefeller forum, the Council on Foreign Relations, for more than twice the amount of money they had been appraised at.

Raymundo de Larrain, in his affidavit for the probate proceedings, says that his wife's male Rockefeller cousins discriminated against the females of the family. "Not only did her cousin-trustee [John D. Rockefeller III] want to dominate her life and tell her how to spend her trust income, but wanted also to dictate and approve how she spent her non-trust personal principal and income. My wife strongly resented their intrusion in her personal life. . . . Her position was that her money was hers outright, not part of her trust, and that she and she alone was to decide how she spent it or what gifts she—not they—would make." Later in the affidavit, de Larrain says that his wife's trustees "wanted her to give virtually all her personal wealth away to her children long before she even thought of dying. Then they would control her through their control of her trust income."

De Larrain said that his wife had been generous with her two children, but that they were not satisfied with her gifts of millions to them. "They wanted more and more." After giving her children more than $7 million, she refused to transfer her personal wealth to them. Even after her gift of $7 million, he claimed, the trustees cut her trust income. "My wife was shocked and distressed at the unjust and cruel and illegal actions of the cousin-trustees in pressuring her to give millions to her children and then breaking their agreement not to cut her trust income. This further alienated her from her family. She felt cheated and a victim of a plan by the family and the Chase Manhattan Bank."

On February 21, 1978, a year after her marriage, Margaret de Larrain, at age eighty-one, revoked all prior wills and codicils executed by her. "I have personally destroyed the original wills in my possession, namely, two original wills dated February 14, 1941, and an original will dated April 26, 1950, and an original will dated May 14, 1956, and an original will dated May 17, 1968, and an original will dated June 11, 1968." Thereafter, Margaret de Larrain added two codicils to a new will of November 20, 1980. In the first, she stated that she had already transferred her fortune to her husband, and she made him the sole beneficiary and sole personal representative of her estate. In the second, she expressed her specific wish that her only two children and two grandchildren receive nothing. De Larrain ended his affidavit with this statement: "There is abundant testimony that my wife was entirely competent when she later added the two codicils which expressed that she wanted to give the property to me, her husband. She did this because her children neglected her and she had provided abundantly for them in her lifetime by giving them approximately $7 million in gifts."

It might be added that Margaret's will did not set a precedent in the stodgy Rockefeller family. Her mother's sister, Edith Rockefeller McCormick, who divorced her husband, Henry Fowler McCormick, heir to the International Harvester fortune, and then engaged in a series of flamboyant affairs with male secretaries, which caused her father great embarrassment, in 1932 bequeathed half of her fortune to a Swiss secretary.

Pending the upcoming court case, Raymundo de Larrain has dropped out of public view. When he is in Paris, he lives at the Meurice Hotel, but even his closest friends there, including the Viscountess de Ribes, do not hear from him, and he has dropped completely out of the smart social life that he once pursued so vigorously. On encountering Hubert Faure, the first husband of Bessie de Cuevas, in the bar of the Meurice recently, he turned his back on him. In Madrid he stays sometimes at the Palace Hotel and sometimes at less well-known ones. He has been seen dining alone in restaurants there. Sometimes he nods to former acquaintances, but he makes no attempt to renew friendships. He has also been seen in Rabat and Lausanne. In the past year he has made two substantial gifts to charity. He gave a check for $1 million to the Spanish Institute in New York, and, as a member of the board of the Spanish Institute said at a New York party, "The check didn't bounce." He also recently gave a check for $500,000 to Georgetown University to supplement the gift of his late wife's father's villa in Fiesole to Georgetown. "You have to figure that if Raymundo gave a million dollars to the Spanish Institute *before* the trial, he must have already squirreled away at least $10 million," said a dubious Raymundo follower in Paris recently.

This is not a sad story. The deprived will not go hungry. If the courts are able to ascertain what happened to

Margaret Strong de Cuevas de Larrain's fortune in the years of her marriage and to decide on an equitable distribution of her wealth, already rich people will get richer. As a woman friend of Raymundo de Larrain said to me recently, "Raymundo will be bad in court, nervous and insecure. If there's a jury, the jury won't like him." She thought a bit and then added, "It's only going to end up wrong. If you don't behave correctly, nothing turns out well. I mean, would you like to fight the Rockefellers, darling?"

February 1987

THE WINDSOR
EPILOGUE

On April 2, 1987, in Geneva, A. Alfred Taubman, the Michigan mall millionaire who has become the *grand seigneur* of the auction world, put on an auction which, for sheer showmanship, rivaled the finest hours of the late P. T. Barnum, the *grand seigneur* of the circus world, who immodestly called his circus the greatest show on earth. Mr. Taubman, no shrinking violet himself, pitched his tent, or rather his red-and-white-striped marquee, on the banks of Lake Geneva and papered the house with some of the grandest names in the *Almanach de Gotha*—nonbidders, to be sure, but the swellest dress extras in auction history. Sprinkled among the princesses, the countesses, the baronesses, and an infanta were the buyers who meant business: dealers from New York and London, Japanese businessmen, a Hollywood divorce lawyer, representatives of the Sultan of Brunei and Prince Bernhard of the Netherlands, not to mention a battery of bidders who, because they did not wish to travel or like to be looked at, were connected by phone to Sotheby's in New York and Geneva. Under the red-and-white-striped marquee, after six months of an un-paralleled publicity blitz, the gavel was finally raised on the opening lot of the sale of the jewels and love tokens of the late Duchess of Windsor, the American woman from Baltimore for whom a king gave up his throne. What followed was a jewel auction against which all jewel auctions to come will be compared.

In the month preceding the sale, the jewels, which I heard an English woman in Geneva describe as "frighteningly chic," traveled from Paris, where they had been under the protectorship of Maître Suzanne Blum, the Duchess's lawyer and a key figure in the story, to Palm Beach and New York—all with great fanfare and hype generated by Sotheby's, the 243-year-old London-based auction house which took over New York's Parke-Bernet Galleries in 1964, in order to woo the rich Americans who were expected to be the chief buyers in Geneva. In both cities, Alfred Taubman, the owner and chairman of Sotheby's since 1983, hosted smart parties so that all the right people, like Mrs. Astor and Malcolm Forbes and the other heavy hitters, might have a leisurely view of the treasure trove that a besotted monarch had showered on his twice-divorced ladylove. Mr. Taubman, a hale and hearty sixty-two, whose assets are estimated in the *Forbes*-magazine list of the four hundred richest people in America at $800 million, and his beautiful younger wife, Judy, a former Miss Israel who once worked behind the counter at Christie's, the rival auction house, handing out catalogs, are high-profile figures on the New York and Palm Beach Social circuits. "Selling art is a lot like selling root beer," he once said.

Duchess fever swept New York. "The romance of the twentieth century," we heard over and over. In actual fact, it was not a romance that can bear very close scrutiny: the love story of a masculine woman of middle age, who was probably never once called beautiful in her life, and a Peter Pan king, who resisted responsibility and composed embarrassing love letters. "A boy loves a girl more and more and is holding her so tight these trying days of waiting," he wrote to her when he was forty-two. Be that as it may, royal romance was in the air. By day the hoi polloi, willing to wait in line for three or four hours just to pass by the jewel-filled vitrines, turned out in such record numbers that the *New York Times* reported the event on its front page. Public interest was so great that Sotheby's desisted from running advertisements in the newspapers and cut back plans to show the jewels on local television shows because the security force at the auction house could not handle any more people than were already jamming its halls.

Although the British press reported even more avidly than ours every detail of the presale hype, the traveling jewel show bypassed England. From a public-relations point of view, Sotheby's felt it best not to open old wounds or to stir up adverse criticism when such big bucks were at stake. Fifty years after Edward VIII gave up his throne for the woman he loved, his duchess, even in death, remains a controversial figure in that country, still disliked and still unforgiven by a generation that blames her for taking away from them a beloved king. A close friend of Princess Margaret, brimming with insider information straight from the palace, informed me, "The royal family hated her. Simply hated her."

Her American admirers felt very differently, of course. As one of them said to me in Geneva, "The English didn't get her. The English still don't get her. They should erect a statue to Wallis Windsor in every town in the realm for taking away their king."

．　　．　　．

The Duchess's sale lasted two days. The Hôtel Beau-Rivage, where Sotheby's is, was where the action was, but the Hôtel Richemond, directly next door, was unmistakably smarter. That was where the Taubmans stayed. The sale of the Duchess's jewelry was also the occasion of a Sotheby's board-of-directors meeting, and the Sotheby's board of directors, as assembled by Alfred Taubman, is the swellest board of directors in big business today, boasting such illustrious names as Her Royal Highness the Infanta Pilar de Borbón, Duchess of Badajoz, who happens to be the sister of the King of Spain, for starters, as well as the Right Honourable the Earl of Gowrie, the Earl of Westmorland, and Baron Hans Heinrich Thyssen-Bornemisza de Kaszon, who has the largest private art collection in the world after the Queen of England's, and such Americans as Henry Ford II, Mrs. Gordon Getty, and Mrs. Milton Petrie.

Society girls in the employ of Sotheby's, wearing black dresses and single strands of pearls, bristled with self-importance as they manned the telephones, dispensed press badges, sold catalogs, and gave terse replies to queries. The bars in both hotels were never not full, and the gossip was terrific, although not always reliable. "Absolutely not!" one indignant upper-class voice, overbrandied, rang out. "I don't care what you've heard! The Duchess of Windsor was not a man!"

Always, following the death of a prominent person, individuals come forward claiming to have had a closer acquaintance with the deceased than the facts would bear out. One favorite preoccupation among the insiders was minimizing the degree of familiarity certain people claimed to have had with the late Duke and Duchess. "So-and-so," they said, talking about a highly profiled man in

New York, "was not nearly so close to the Duchess as he says he was. The Duke would never have had him around." Or, "I visited the Duchess for years and I never once heard her mention So-and-so," naming an international lady.

A thousand smartly dressed people piled into the tent to find their ticketed seats, all carrying the glossiest and most gossipy auction catalog ever printed. At fifty dollars a copy, it promptly sold out, and is now a collector's item. Friends met. Men greeted men with kisses on both cheeks, and women did the same. On closed-circuit television sets around the tent a film was shown, but no one watched, because they were all looking at one another. "The world was fascinated by them," intoned a voice on the sound track, "and they were obsessed with each other. . . . The Prince of Wales's father, George V, had Mrs. Simpson's past investigated and decided she was not a suitable companion for his son. . . . Queen Mary called her an adventuress." Year after year of newsreels of their glittering and empty life flashed by: weekends at Fort Belvedere when the Duke was still king, their somber wedding at the Château de Candé, the two of them arriving here, arriving there, fashion plates both, stepping out of limousines, waving from the decks of ocean liners, sweeping into parties, relentlessly up to the moment, in all the very jewels that were about to be sold, the Duchess leading, the Duke following, she gleaming, he scowling, or smiling sadly. Behind it all, a voice sang, "The party's over. It's all over, my friend." But no one was listening either, because they were all talking to each other. The Princess of Naples, married to Victor Emmanuel, who would have been the king of Italy if history had gone another way, chatted up Prince Dimitri of Yugoslavia, who works for Sotheby's jewelry department, while his brother, Prince Serge of Yugoslavia, chatted up the Baroness Tita Thyssen-Bornemisza, ablaze in sapphires, who chatted up the Countess of Romanoes, who was wearing the diamond bracelet she had inherited from the Duchess of Windsor and who in turn chatted up the Infanta Beatriz of Spain, who chatted up Grace, Countess of Dudley, who chatted up Princess Firyal of Jordan, who chatted up Judy Taubman, while her husband, Alfred Taubman, the *grand seigneur,* radiating power and importance, carried a huge unlit cigar and smiled and waved and greeted.

Then the auction began.

From the first of the 306 lots, a gold-ruby-and-sapphire clip made by Cartier in Paris in 1946, the air in the tent was charged with excitement. A few moments later, lot 13, a diamond clip lorgnette by Van Cleef & Arpels, circa 1935, which was estimated to bring in $5,000, went to a private bidder for $117,000. The excitement began to build. Two lots later, when a pair of pavé diamond cuff links and three buttons and a stud, estimated to go for $10,000, went for $440,000 to a mysterious, deeply tanned man who was said to be bidding for the Egyptian who has taken over the Windsors' house outside Paris, the first applause broke out in the tent. People realized they were present at an event, engaged in the heady adventure of watching rich people acting rich, participating in a rite available only to them, the spending of big money, without a moment's hesitation or consideration. The sable-swathed Ann Getty, who wanted it known that she was there because of the board-of-directors meeting and not to bid, changed her seat from the fifth row to the first in order to be closer to the arena. By lot 91, a pair of yellow-diamond clips by Harry Winston, 1948, that went to the London jeweler Laurence Graff, one of the royal family's jewelers, for over $2 million, financial abandon filled the air with an almost erotic intensity, and it never lessened during the remaining hours of the sale. Powdered bosoms heaved in fiscal excitement at big bucks being spent. Each time the bidding got into the million-dollar range, for one of the ten or so world-class stones in the collection, the tension resembled the frenzy at a cockfight. Sotheby's employees manning the telephones waved their hands frantically to attract the auctioneer. People rose in their seats to get a better look at the mysterious Mr. Fabri, who bid and bid— money no object—on all the pieces directly linked to the love affair between Edward and Wallis. "The Duke would have hated all this," said a friend of the Duke's, shaking his head. "I'm surprised they're not auctioning off his fly buttons."

The auctioneer, like the judge at a trial, has the power to enthrall his audience. At the podium in Geneva was the tall and debonair Nicholas Rayner. It was he who first approached Maître Suzanne Blum, the keeper of the Windsor flame, about the disposition of the Duchess's jewels. A notoriously difficult woman, the octogenarian Maître Blum is said to have been charmed by Rayner, and because of him she entrusted the jewels to Sotheby's. The charm that captivated Maître Blum captivated all the women in the tent as well. "Divine," said one woman about Rayner. "And separated," said another, as if that fact added to his glamour. Although he was criticized by a few purists for several times allowing the bidding to continue after he had dropped the gavel—he said that since the money was going to charity the ordinary rules did not apply—he won over far more people than he alienated. He had a sense of theater, realized that he was in a leading role, and understood exactly how to keep this audience in the palm of his hand. Graceful, witty, he was Cary Grant at forty, giving the kind of performance that turns a good actor into a major star. At the end of the second day, when the total sales had reached $50 million, the audience rose and gave Rayner a standing ovation which rivaled any that Lord Olivier ever received.

It was a sad disappointment to auction voyeurs that they could not turn around and stare at Miss Elizabeth Taylor raising her already jeweled hand to bid $623,000 for a diamond clip known as the Prince of Wales feathers brooch, which Richard Burton had once admired on the Duchess, for the simple reason that Miss Taylor had chosen to make her bid by telephone while sun-tanning next to her swimming pool in Bel-Air, California. They could not watch the multimillionaire dress designer Calvin Klein either, as he bid by telephone from New York $733,000 for a single-row pearl necklace by Cartier, or $198,000 for another single-row pearl necklace by Van Cleef & Arpels, or a mere $102,600 for a pearl-and-diamond eternity ring by Darde & Fils of Paris, or $300,600 for a pearl-and-diamond pendant by Cartier, for which he outbid the Duchess's friend and frequent New York hostess Estée Lauder, the cosmetics tycoon, and all for his beauteous new wife, Kelly. Expensive, yes, but Van Cleef & Arpels had told Calvin Klein it would take ten years to match pearls for the necklace he had in mind and cost several million dollars. He told the press that he was not going to wait for a special day to give them to Kelly. "The best presents just happen," he said.

Under the marquee, only Marvin Mitchelson, the Hollywood divorce lawyer, who built his fortune on the failed marriages of the famous, broke the rules of anonymity and had himself announced as the purchaser of the Duchess's amethyst-and-turquoise necklace for $605,000. He further wanted it announced that he dedicated the purchase to the memory of his mother, who had worked to put him through law school. Mitchelson also purchased a huge sapphire brooch for $374,000 for someone else, a client whom he would not name, although he tantalized the press by hinting that it was Joan Collins, whom he was representing in her latest divorce.

In seats every bit as good as the seats occupied by the Princess of Naples and Princess Firyal of Jordan sat two dark-haired beauties in Chanel suits—real Chanel suits, not knockoffs—who were there to bid, not gape. They scrutinized their catalogs, and they had mink coats folded over their knees. Their stockings had seams, a subtle signal to the cognoscenti of such things that they were wearing garter belts, not panty hose. Ms. X and Ms. Y, two international ladies of the evening, told me they were staying at the Richemond, where they felt as at home as they do at the Plaza Athénée or the Beverly Hills Hotel. Ms. X had her heart set on lot 26, a pavé diamond heart with a gold-and-ruby crown and the initials W. and E., for Wallis and Edward, intertwined in emeralds. It had been the twenti-eth-wedding-anniversary present of the Duke to the Duch-ess. Ms. Y had *her* heart set on lot 31, a single-row diamond bracelet with nine gem-set Latin crosses hanging from it. The Duchess had worn it on her wedding day in 1937 and had once remarked that the crosses represented the crosses she had to bear. Ms. X said about Ms. Y, jok-ingly, that she wanted the bracelet with the crosses to wear on her whipping hand. Used to the best, Ms. Y has a custom-made bag by Hermès to carry her whips in. She didn't get the bracelet with the crosses, which went for $381,000. Ms. X didn't get the pavé diamond heart either. It went for $300,000. "The prices just got out of hand. We were a couple of zeros too short," Ms. X told me during a break. "That heart probably belongs to Candy Spelling by now. Come and have tea tomorrow. We're free until ten."

Of course there was the inevitable Japanese, with millions at his disposal, who said he would have gone even higher than the $3.15 million he paid for the Duchess's solitary diamond. Hours later, no one could remember his name or his face.

There will be other jewel sales, even better jewel sales, but that night in Geneva, the jewel capital of the world, people wanted, at any price, no holds barred, something about which they could say, "This belonged to the Duchess of Windsor," because they knew that they were buying romance and history. Nowhere was this so evident as in lot 68, a pearl-and-diamond choker, which Nicholas Rayner carefully pointed out was imitation. The choker then sold for $51,000. The sale of the Duchess's jewels, coming as it did only a few days after the $39.9 million sale of a Van Gogh sunflowers painting, whose chrome yellow paint had turned brown, made one realize the enormous amount of money there is in the world waiting to be spent, even for the imperfect, if the credentials are OK.

In the back of the tent, unknown to most of the people there, sat Georges Sanègre and his wife, Ofélia, the long-time butler and maid to the Duke and Duchess, quietly watching the personal possessions of their former employers make auction history. Not physically present, but prominently there in spirit, was the old and elusive Maître Blum, called Mrs. Blum by her detractors, who are legion. Maître Blum, who had met the Windsors in Portugal during World War II and then been their French lawyer for forty years, followed every moment of the auction by telephone from Paris and knew minute by minute everything that was going on.

Maître Blum's relationship with the former king and his duchess was strictly a business one. Social contact was limited to two dinners or lunches a year, and those in the context of business courtesy rather than friendship. The Duke was thought to have more regard for her than the Duchess, who, friends say, wanted to fire her after the Duke's death, but whose increasing mental confusion made this impossible.

"She lost her mind, you know," people told me about the Duchess, "during the last decade of her life." Or, "She was gaga." Or, "A veg." The *on-dit*, as these people say, meaning the gossip, or inside story, is that the Duchess insisted on having a final face-lift even though she was advised not to because of her age. Plastic surgeons in England and France declined to perform the operation, and warned her about the effects of anesthesia on people over seventy. Determined, she persevered. A plastic surgeon from another country performed the operation, in the course of which there was a technical difficulty with the anesthesia and the air to the Duchess's brain was briefly cut off. This is widely said to be the cause of the derangement that came on her after her husband's death. During her stay at Buckingham Palace at the time of the Duke's funeral, she often thought she was in Paris, and she mistook the Queen Victoria fountain, which she could see from the palace windows, for the Place de la Concorde. The Duke, before he died, aware that the Duchess's mind had begun to wander, entrusted her care to Maître Blum.

Shortly after the Duke's death, when the Duchess was in a confused and vulnerable state, all his private papers were confiscated, possibly under the direction of his cousin Lord Mountbatten, acting on behalf of the royal family. These papers now reside in the archives of Windsor Castle, unavailable to the public. Georges, the butler, is said to have hidden the love letters of the Duke and Duchess to prevent their being carried off in the same swoop. The letters he rescued were later published under the title *Wallis and Edward, Letters 1931–1937: The Intimate Correspondence of the Duke and Duchess of Windsor*.

It was the Duke's wish, so stated in his will, that the Duchess's jewels be removed from their settings after her death so that the pieces could never be worn by any other woman, but such was not the Duchess's wish. People who have had access to the Duchess's private papers tell me that several Americans tried to persuade the Duchess, because she was American, to leave her jewels, in whole or in part, to the Smithsonian Institution in Washington. Another suggestion was that she leave her jewels to the White House, as a permanent collection for the First Lady of the United States to wear. Although Maître Blum is most often blamed for nixing these American plans for the disposition of the collection, it was the Duchess herself who decided that France, the country that had given her refuge for fifty years, should be the beneficiary. There are unkind people who will tell you that if the Duchess had had her way, all her money would have been left to a dog hospital. The truth is, Maître Blum prevailed upon the Duchess to leave the money to the Pasteur Institute, the leading medical-research institution in France.

People familiar with the Windsors noticed, looking at the jewelry, that a great many pieces were missing. "What happened to all the Fulco di Verdura pieces?" they asked, referring to the designs of the Sicilian Duke di Verdura, whose scrapbooks show a great number of pieces he made for the Duchess which were not in the auction. Or, one heard in Geneva and later in New York, "All those marvelous things on her tables—her bibelots—what has become of those, we wonder?" The implication, each time the rhe-

torical question is asked, is that malfeasance was afoot.
Michael Bloch, who edited the book of the couple's love
letters, is adamant in his defense of Maître Blum. He af-
firms that she has not profited at all in the disposal of the
estate, and his strong feelings are borne out by several other
people close to the couple.

The Duchess had, in effect, an almost ten-year death,
with nurses around the clock. The family fortune, in terms
of hard cold cash, at the time of the Duke's death was
around $1 million—not a great deal of money for people
with their standard of living. The high cost of a royal death
was prohibitive, and, curiously, the Duchess did not have
medical insurance. From time to time during the years of
the long illness, Maître Blum sold off pieces of jewelry, sets
of china, or the odd Bergère chair or ormolu table to pay off
the medical costs. Several years ago, for instance, Mrs. São
Schlumberger of Paris bought a ruby necklace. A Sotheby's
official assured me that the price she paid was at the top of
the market at the time. Nate Cummings, the late American millionaire, collector, and friend of the Duke and
Duchess, bought, among other things, a set of vermeil
plates. Maître Blum also sold some bead necklaces in emeralds, rubies, and sapphires to the London firm of Hennell,
who traveled to Beverly Hills with their wares before the
auction. Candy Spelling, the wife of the television mogul
Aaron Spelling and the possessor of one of the most spectacular jewel collections in the country, bought one of the
necklaces. Another was sold to Mrs. Muriel Slatkin, the
former owner, with her sister, Seema Boesky, the wife of
the Wall Street swindler Ivan Boesky, of the Beverly Hills
Hotel. A third was sold to Mrs. Marvin Davis, the wife of
one of the country's richest men, who is, incidentally, the
new owner of the Beverly Hills Hotel. Also, the Duchess

gave away several pieces of her jewelry before she died. Princess Alexandra, a favorite niece of the Duke, received a piece. Princess Michael of Kent, whose own popularity in the royal family is on a par with the Duchess's, won the heart of her husband's aunt by marriage by calling her in a letter "Dear Aunt Wallis," thereby likening her own marriage to that of the Windsors, and she too was rewarded.

The Duchess in her will mentioned certain people, like the American-born Countess of Romanoes, who received a diamond bracelet with an inscription from the Duke to the Duchess engraved on the back of it. When the item to be inherited was not specified, it was left to the discretion of Maître Blum, and in this role the mighty *maître* exerted her authority to the fullest. One lady of haughty bearing irritated Maître Blum exceedingly at the time of the Duchess's funeral by assuming too important a position and attitude among the mourners. Months later, her bijou of inheritance still undelivered, the haughty lady is said to have wailed to her friends, "Why does Maître Blum hate me so?" Her inheritance was the last to be distributed and the least important of the lot in both beauty and value.

No one lingers in Geneva. At fifteen minutes before eight the morning after the sale, Alfred Taubman, a huge unlit cigar balanced between his teeth, paced back and forth in front of the Hôtel Richemond, impatience in his every step. The auction was over, history made, he wanted to be gone. The jacket of his double-breasted gray flannel suit was unbuttoned. A cashmere scarf was wrapped Dickensian-style around his neck against the brisk lake breezes. By the curb three dark blue Mercedeses were being loaded with first-rate luggage, and he was directing the operation. Nervous minions offered assistance.

"How much . . . ?" someone started to ask him, meaning how much had the auction grossed.

"Forty-nine million plus," he answered, interrupting the question before it was finished. It was not the first time he had been asked the question since the night before, and he was proud of the figure.

"Call upstairs to Mrs. Taubman," he told the hall porter, walking back into the lobby of the hotel. "I left my yellow handkerchief behind. Tell her to find it." He walked back out to the street again. "C'mon. Let's get this show on the road." He did not like to be kept waiting. "Between Judy and Princess Firyal . . ." he said, shaking his head in exasperation at the delays women cause. Finally all was ready. "We're going to General Aviation, where my plane is," he said to the driver of the lead car.

The party was over, my friend.

In the six weeks that followed, two other notable jewel auctions took place. At Sotheby's in New York, the jewels of Flora Whitney Miller, the daughter of Gertrude Vanderbilt Whitney, were auctioned along with the jewels of a Romanian princess and the singer-actress Pia Zadora, among others. Back in Geneva, at Christie's, certain jewels of the Hon. Mrs. Reginald Fellowes, known as Daisy Fellowes, were sold in combination with jewelry from what the catalog listed merely as "various sources."

Unlike the Duchess of Windsor, both Mrs. Miller and Mrs. Fellowes, her contemporaries, were born to great wealth and great families. Mrs. Fellowes was the daughter of a French duke and a Singer-sewing-machine heiress. It was said that every time Mrs. Fellowes passed an advertisement for Singer sewing machines she crossed herself. Historically Daisy Fellowes is little more than a footnote in the memoirs and diary entries of social historians, although in fact she was just as relentlessly chic as the Duchess, far richer, and equally witty. She owned one of the largest yachts in the Mediterranean, the *Sister Anne,* one which the Windsors once sailed. Stories about her are endless. Once, a former footman with exceptional good looks, who had advanced himself from his position behind a dining-room chair to a seat at some of the best tables in the South of France, Palm Beach, and Beverly Hills, asked Daisy Fellowes if she missed her yacht, which she had recently sold. She looked at the fellow and answered, "Yes. Yes, I do. I miss it very much. Do you miss your tray?"

The auction of her jewels and the auction of the jewels of Flora Whitney Miller were dispirited occasions in comparison with the Windsor sale. "This won't be anything like that," a Christie's executive told me shortly before the Fellowes jewelry auction. "In all my years in the auction business," she said wistfully, in remembrance of things past, "I never saw anything like the Duchess's sale."

In the weeks following the sale, the Duchess's jewels began appearing on fashionable necks, wrists, and bosoms. Elizabeth Taylor arrived at Malcolm Forbes's party-of-the-year in Far Hills, New Jersey, wearing her Prince of Wales Plumes, and Mrs. Milton Petrie, who, when she was the Marquesa de Portago, was a great friend of the Duchess, walked into New York hostess Alice Mason's party for former president and Mrs. Jimmy Carter wearing the Duchess's articulated tourmaline-and-quartz necklace.

At another dinner party in New York, I heard Mr. Taubman describing, not immodestly, how he had restructured Sotheby's and made it a profitable company. "I computerized it. I got rid of the advertising department entirely. They were doing institutional advertising. I said to them, 'This isn't an institution. This is a business.' I didn't do wholesale firing, as everyone said. I kept the best people, but I brought in experts to go over every department. Now we have a working operation. When I took over the company, they were doing 350, 375 million a year. Last year we did 900 million. By the end of this year, I expect we'll do something like a billion two, a billion five, around there."

As far as the auction world is concerned, Mr. Taubman hit a peak with the sale of the Duchess's jewels. He made it the greatest show on earth. He took an estate appraised by his own experts at $7 million tops and, by means of hype and romance and showmanship, made it bring in over $50 million.

No matter how you slice it, though, Maître Blum emerges as the heroine of this tale. The Duchess of Windsor, unlike other ladies of the royal family she married into, was not a patroness of the arts or sciences. No orphanage or hospital ever knew her as a benefactress. Instead, she was the woman who defined the meaning of a life in society for her time. "Chic" and "stylish" were her adjectives of description. Her servants' livery was made by the same uniform maker who made the uniforms of General de Gaulle. Her days were spent preparing for the evening, telephoning friends, being massaged, being manicured, being coiffed, having fittings for her vast and ever-changing wardrobe, seating her dinners, choosing her china, ordering her flowers, having steamer trunks packed for their endless peregrinations in pursuit of pleasure. But fate stepped in to give a final importance to her life when Maître Blum suggested that the Pasteur Institute be the beneficiary of her will. At the time, no one could know that the Pasteur Institute would become the leading French medical institution involved in finding a cure for AIDS. Today, however, when the whole world is gripped with the fear of AIDS, the $45 million that the Pasteur Institute will receive from the sale of the Duchess's jewelry gives a sort of poetic finality to her life. Even, perhaps, the nobility that always eluded her.

August 1987

Robert Mapplethorpe's Proud Finale

"No one expected him to live for the opening, and there he was, on a high," said Tom Armstrong, the director of the Whitney Museum of American Art in New York. Whether the artist would or would not be present was the question that occupied the minds of all the people involved, in the days preceding the highly publicized and eagerly anticipated vernissage of the work of Robert Mapplethorpe, the photographer who took his art to the outer limits of his own experience, at the Whitney last July.

For nearly two years the rumors of Robert Mapplethorpe's illness had been whispered in the New York art and social circles in which he moved as a celebrated and somewhat notorious figure. The death in January 1987 of the New York aristocrat and collector Sam Wagstaff from AIDS had brought the matter of Mapplethorpe's illness with the same disease out into the open. Mapplethorpe, the principal inheritor of Sam Wagstaff's fortune, had once been Wagstaff's lover and later, for years, his great and good friend. The inheritance, believed to be in the neighborhood of $7 million—some say more, depending on the value of his art and silver collection—made the already much-talked-about Mapplethorpe, a famed figure of the night in the netherworld of New York, even more talked about, especially when the will was contested by the sister of Sam Wagstaff, Mrs. Thomas Jefferson IV of New York. Mapplethorpe has never avoided publicity; indeed, he has carefully nurtured his celebrity since his work first came to public notice in the mid-seventies.

That summer night at the Whitney Museum, there were sighs of relief when he did arrive for the opening, having been released from St. Vincent's Hospital only days before. He was in a wheelchair, surrounded by members of his entourage, carrying a cane with a death's-head top and wearing a stylish dinner jacket and black velvet slippers with his initials embroidered in gold on them—a vastly different uniform from the black leather gear that had been his trademark. For those who had not seen the once-handsome figure in some time, the deterioration of his health and physical appearance was apparent and quite shocking. His hair looked wispy. His thin neck protruded from the wing collar of his dinner shirt like a tortoise's from his shell. But even ill, he was a man who commanded attention, and who expected it. A grouping of furniture had been placed in the center of the second of the four galleries where the exhibition was hung, and there he sat, with his inner circle in attendance, receiving the homage of his friends and admirers, a complex olio of swells and freaks, famous and unknown, that makes up the world of Robert Mapplethorpe. His eyes, darting about, missed nothing. He nodded his head and smiled, speaking in a voice barely above a whisper. "It's a wonderful night," person after person said to him, and he agreed. He was enjoying himself immensely. On the wall facing him hung *Jim and Tom, Sausalito,* his 1977–1978 triptych of two men in black leather, adorned with the accoutrements of sadomasochistic bondage and torture. In the photographs, Jim, the master, is urinating into the willing, even eager, mouth of Tom, the tied-up slave. "Marvelous," said one after another of the fashionable crowd as they surveyed the work. "Surreal" was the word that came to my mind.

However much you may have heard that this exhibition was not a shocker, believe me, it was a shocker. Robert Mapplethorpe was described by everyone I interviewed as the man who had taken the sexual experience to the limits in his work, a documentarian of the homoerotic life in the 1970s at its most excessive. Even his floral photographs are erotic; as critics have pointed out, he makes it quite clear that flowers are the sexual organs of plants. But the crowds that poured in that night, and kept pouring in for the following three months that the exhibition remained up, had not come just to see the still lifes of stark flowers, or the portraits of bejeweled and elegant ladies of society, like Carolina Herrera and Princess Gloria von Thurn und Taxis and Paloma Picasso, and of artist friends, like David Hockney and Louise Nevelson and Willem de Kooning, which are also very much a part of Mapplethorpe's *oeuvre.* They had come to see the sexually loaded pictures, freed of all inhibitions, that were hanging side by side with the above in the galleries of the Whitney, like the startling *Man in Polyester Suit,* in which an elephantine-size black penis simply hangs out of the unzipped fly of a man whose head is cropped, or the even more startling *Marty and Veronica,* in which Marty makes oral love to a stockinged and girdled Veronica, whose upper body is cropped off at her bare breasts. Mapplethorpe was a participant in the dark world he photographed, not a voyeur, a point he made clear by allowing a self-portrait showing his rectum—rarely considered to be one of the body's beauty spots—to be hung on the wall of the museum, with a bullwhip up it. The Mapplethorpe sexual influence is so great that in the otherwise scholarly introduction to the catalog of the show, Richard Marshall, an associate curator of the Whitney, made reference to this same photograph as the *"Self Portrait* with a whip inserted in his ass." That night, and on two subsequent visits to the exhibition, I watched the reactions of the viewers to the more graphically sexual pictures. They went from I-can't-believe-what-I'm-seeing-on-the-walls-of-the-Whitney-Museum looks to nudges and titters, to nervous, furtive glances to the left and right to see if it was safe to really move in and peer, and, finally, to a subdued sadness, a wondering, perhaps, of how many of the men whose genitalia they were looking at were still alive.

"On the opening night this amazing strength came to Robert," said Flora Biddle, the granddaughter of Gertrude Vanderbilt Whitney, who is the chairman of the board of trustees of the Whitney Museum, which her grandmother started. "At the end of the evening he got up and walked out, after he had come in a wheelchair."

Later, Mapplethorpe told me his feelings about the opening. "It was pretty good. I kept thinking what it would have been like if I'd been feeling better."

"You've become really famous, Robert," I said. "How does that feel?"

"Great," he said quietly, but shook his head at the same time. "I'm quite frustrated I'm not going to be around to enjoy it. The money's coming in, though. I'm making more money now than I've ever made before."

Today Mapplethorpe charges $10,000 for a sitting. His one-of-a-kind pictures sell for an average of $20,000 each. A Mapplethorpe print from the Robert Miller Gallery, his dealer in New York, starts at $5,000.

"I seem to read something about you every day in the press," I said.

"I do love publicity," he replied. "Good publicity."

In a sense, Sam Wagstaff created Robert Mapplethorpe, but anyone who knows Robert Mapplethorpe will tell you that he was ready and waiting to be created. They met over the telephone when Mapplethorpe was twenty-five and Sam was fifty. "Are you the shy pornographer?" Wagstaff asked when he telephoned him. Robert had heard of Sam before the call. "Everyone said there was a person in the art world I should meet. So Sam came over to look at my etchings, so to speak."

At the time the totally unknown Mapplethorpe was sharing an apartment in Brooklyn with the then totally unknown poet and later rock 'n' roll star Patti Smith, who has remained one of his closest friends. Although he was, in his own words, "doing photographs of sexuality" with a Polaroid camera back then, he did not yet consider himself a photographer. The Polaroid camera had been purchased for him by John McKendry, the curator of prints and photographs at the Metropolitan Museum. Mapplethorpe had become a sort of adopted son to McKendry and his wife, Maxine de la Falaise, the daughter of the English portrait painter Sir Oswald Birley, and was taken about by them into the smart circles of people who later became his friends and patrons. Wagstaff and Mapplethorpe became positive influences on each other's lives. The handsome and patrician Wagstaff, who graduated from Yale and once worked in advertising, had long since moved away from the Upper East Side and New York society world of his birth into the bohemian world downtown. A former museum curator, he had become more and more of a reclusive figure, involved with a group devoted to self-fulfillment called Arica, and sometimes, according to Mapplethorpe, observing whole days of silence. Wagstaff encouraged Mapplethorpe in his photography, and Mapplethorpe persuaded Wagstaff to start collecting photographs. "He became obsessed with photography," said Mapplethorpe. "He bought with a vengeance. It went beyond anything I imagined. Through him, I started looking at photographs in a much more serious way. I got to know dealers. I went with him when he was buying things. It was a great education, although I had my own vision right from the beginning. If you look at my early Polaroids, the style was then what I have now."

Richard Marshall states in his introduction in the catalog that Mapplethorpe "did not feel a strong ideological commitment to photography; rather it simply became the medium that could best convey his statement." Explaining this, Marshall said, "He wasn't a photographer who found his subject. The camera became the best way for him to express himself. Before that he was into collage, drawings, et cetera. He took up the camera to play with, and found that it was what he was looking for."

Barbara Jakobson, who was one of Mapplethorpe's first avid supporters as well as an old friend of Wagstaff's, said, "When I become enthusiastic about an artist, I do not keep my mouth shut. Within five minutes the jungle drums are beating. I like to see people I admire succeed. That was when our friendship started. Robert really saved Sam Wagstaff's life. At the beginning of the seventies, anyone who knew Sam said that he was virtually a recluse. Robert is the one who got him interested in collecting photography. Sam revolutionized the way we look at photographs. When he sold his collection to the Getty Museum, his position in photography was forever assured."

Mapplethorpe does not stint in his acknowledgment of his late friend's patronage. "I was a real hippie. Sam was a real hippie too. Financially he certainly helped me. He was very generous. We never actually lived together. I had a loft on Bond Street, which he bought for me. He had a loft on Bond Street too. We were lovers as well. I think if you're going to do a story, you should get all the facts. It lasted a couple of years. Then we became best friends. I even introduced him to James Nelson, who became his boyfriend after me." He paused before he added, "He's sick at this point too."

"With AIDS?"

"Yes. He's going through all his money. He's spending like crazy. He rents an apartment at Number One Fifth Avenue, where he and Sam lived, but Sam's apartment in that building has been sold."

Shortly after we talked, Jim Nelson died. Nelson, a former hairstylist for the television soap opera "All My Children," inherited 25 percent of Wagstaff's residuary estate, and Mapplethorpe inherited 75 percent. Nelson, aware that he was dying, wanted his money immediately, so Mapplethorpe, through their lawyers, bought out Nelson's share. As Nelson's life neared its end, he fulfilled a long-held dream and rented two suites on the *Queen Elizabeth 2,* one for himself and one for a companion, and sailed to England, where he stayed in a suite at the Ritz Hotel, and then took the Concorde back to New York. He spent the last day of his life making up a list of people he wanted to be notified of his death and another list of people he did not want to be notified, one of these being the person who told me this story.

Barbara Jakobson said, "It was great to observe Robert

and Sam together. Sam got such a kick out of Robert, and Robert allowed Sam to be indulgent. Sam was a Yankee with cement in his pocket, but he was very generous with Robert. Sam always meant for Robert to have his money. I was very unhappy over the publicity about the will after Sam died."

Another close woman friend of both men, who did not want to be named, said, "Robert was looking for a patron, and along came Sam. Sam made Robert's career. He showed Robert this other way of life. Robert was into learning more than anyone I ever knew. When Robert met Sam, all the doors opened for him. Sam was his sugar daddy in a way."

Most of Wagstaff's money came from his stepfather, Donald Newhall, who left him and his sister shares of the Newhall Land and Farming Company in California, which later went public. Over the years, Wagstaff sold off some of his shares to buy his art, photography, and silver collections. In his will he left bequests of $100,000 each to the Museum of Modern Art, the Metropolitan Museum, and the New York Public Library, as well as $10,000 and the family silver to his sister, Mrs. Jefferson, and $10,000 to each of her three children.

"She's enormously rich," said Mapplethorpe about Mrs. Jefferson. "She didn't need the money."

"Then why did she contest the will?"

Mapplethorpe shrugged. "She needed entertainment," he said. In the long run, the litigation never went to trial; Wagstaff's sister decided against proceeding with the suit on the day of jury selection. Several subsequent lawsuits over Wagstaff's million-dollar silver collection, in which Mapplethorpe charged the New York Historical Society with "fraudulent conduct" in obtaining a five-year loan of Wagstaff's silver as he lay dying, were settled out of court.

Mapplethorpe's lawyer, Michael Stout, who handles many prominent people in the creative arts, said about him, "Robert is the most astute businessman of any of my clients. If there is a decision to be made, he understands the issues and votes the right way."

Although I had known Sam Wagstaff for years, my contact with Robert Mapplethorpe was minimal, no more than an acquaintanceship, so I was surprised when he asked me to write this article, and more surprised when he asked to photograph me. Two years ago, right after Sam Wagstaff died, when the rumors of litigation between his family and his heir over his will were rampant, I had thought of writing an article on the subject for this magazine. Mapplethorpe, however, let it be known through his great friend Suzie Frankfurt, the socialite interior decorator, that he did not wish me to write such a piece, and I immediately desisted. Later I saw him at the memorial service for Sam that was held at the Metropolitan Museum. Already ill himself, he made a point of thanking me for not writing the article.

I had met Mapplethorpe for the first time several years earlier, at a dinner given by the Earl of Warwick at his New York apartment. Although Mapplethorpe was then famous as a photographer, the celebrity that was so much a part of his persona was due equally to his reputation as a leading figure in the sadomasochistic subculture of New York. Indeed, he was the subject of endless stories involving dark bars and black men and bizarre behavior of the bondage and domination variety. He arrived late for the dinner, dressed for the post-dinner-party part of his night in black leather, and became in no time the focus of attention and unquestionably the star of Lord Warwick's party.

He was at ease in his surroundings and, surprising to me, up on the latest gossip of the English smart set, telling stories in which Guinness and Tennant names abounded. When coffee was served, he took some marijuana and a package of papers out of his pocket, rolled a joint, lit it, inhaled deeply, all the time continuing a story he was telling, and passed the joint to the person on his right. It was not a marijuana-smoking group, and the joint was declined and passed on by each person to the next, except for one guest who, gamely, took a few tokes and then passed out at the table, after saying, "Strong stuff." Unperturbed, Mapplethorpe continued talking until it was time for his exit. After he was gone, those who remained talked about him.

Like everything else about Robert Mapplethorpe, the studio where he now lives and works on a major crosstown street in the Chelsea section of New York, which was also purchased for him by Wagstaff, is enormously stylish and handsomely done. In 1988 it was photographed by *HG* magazine, and Martin Filler wrote in the accompanying text, "Mapplethorpe's rooms revel in the pleasures of art for art's sake and reconfirm his aesthetic genealogy in a direct line of descent from Oscar Wilde and Aubrey Beardsley through Christian Bérard and Jean Cocteau." There are things to look at in every direction, a mélange of objects and pictures, but everything has its place. Order and restraint prevail. "You create your own world," said Mapplethorpe. "The one that I want to live in is very precise, very controlled." It fits in with his personality that he pays his bills instantly on receiving them.

Each time we met, we sat in a different area. In the back sitting room of the floor-through loft space, the windows have elegant brown-black taffeta tieback curtains designed by Suzie Frankfurt, which seem both incongruous and not at all incongruous. Frankfurt, who maintains a complicated friendship with him, said, "Robert lives in the middle of a contradiction—part altar boy and part leather bar." That day he was wearing a black dressing gown from Gianni Versace, the Italian designer, and his black velvet slippers.

At one point he went into a paroxysm of coughing, and from the look he gave me I realized he didn't want me to see him like that. "Would you excuse me for a minute," he said. I got up and went to another part of the apartment until he called me back.

"Oh, I'm so sick," he said. "I've been throwing up all night. The nights are awful."

"When did you first know you had AIDS?" I asked.

"It was diagnosed as AIDS two years ago in October."

"Did you suspect beforehand that you had it?"

"Every faggot suspects beforehand."

He said that he had two nurses on twelve-hour shifts that cost him a thousand dollars a day. "But I'm lucky. I have insurance." He has been on AZT almost from the beginning. He worries constantly about friends who are less fortunate, specifically his black friends. In a conversation with Marlies Black, who assembled the Rivendell Collection of modern art and photography, which contains the largest selection of Mapplethorpe's work in the world, he once said, "At some point I started photographing black men. It was an area that hadn't been explored extensively. If you went through the history of nude male photography, there were very few black subjects. I found that I could take pictures of black men that were so subtle, and the form was so photographical." Now, musing on that, he said, "Most of the blacks don't have insurance and therefore can't afford AZT. They all die quickly, the blacks. If I go through my *Black Book,* half of them are dead."

When I sat for him to be photographed, I was nervous, even though he had asked me to sit. It was on a day that he was not feeling well. He had not slept the night before. He coughed a great deal. His skin was very pale. We sat on the sofa and talked while Brian English, his assistant, set up the camera and chair where I would sit for the picture. Although ill, Mapplethorpe kept working most days. He showed me pictures he had taken a day or two before of the three-year-old daughter of the actress Susan Sarandon, and he had arranged to photograph Carolina Herrera, the dress designer, as soon as he was finished with me. I was talking about anything I could think of, mostly about people we both knew, to postpone the inevitable. Finally, I told him I was nervous. "Why?" he asked. "I just am," I said. "Don't be," he said quietly. I was struck as always by his grace and manners, which seemed such a contradiction to the image most people have of Robert Mapplethorpe. Finally Brian placed me in the chair, and Robert got up and walked very slowly over to where the Hasselblad camera was set up. He looked in the viewfinder. He asked Brian to move a light. He made an adjustment on a lens opening. "Look to the left," he said. "Keep your head there. Look back toward me with your eyes." He was in charge.

Another time, I remarked that he was looking better. He told me that he was finally able to eat something called TPN, a totally nutritious substance which gave him 2,400 calories a day. "I don't actually eat. I'm fed mostly by tube. If I hadn't found this, I'd be dead by now. I couldn't keep any food down." And then he said a line I heard him say over and over. "This disease is hideous."

"My biggest problem now is walking. I have neuropathy, like when your foot's asleep. It's constant. It's in my hands too. If it weren't for that, I'd go out." His eyes moved toward the window. "I'd like to go to Central Park to see the new zoo. And I'd like to go back to the Whitney to see the show. I hear there are lines of people to see it."

He was born in a middle-class suburban neighborhood called Floral Park, which is on the edge of Queens, New York, the third of six children in a Catholic family of English, German, and Irish extraction. His mother is a housewife. His father does electrical work. He went to a public school in Floral Park, but he would have preferred to go to the Catholic school, which his younger brothers went to. Although he now says that Floral Park was a perfect place for his parents to raise a family, early yearnings in nonconformist directions brought his family life to a halt. "I wanted to have the freedom to do what I wanted to do. The only way to do that was to break away. I didn't want to have to worry about what my parents thought. When I was sixteen, I went to college at the Pratt Institute. That was when I began to live elsewhere."

Except for his brother Edward, the youngest of the six, who was at the studio each time I was there, he has not been close to his family for years, although he said that they are "closer since I told them I was sick, which was not too long ago."

"Did your parents come to see your show at the Whitney?" I asked him.

He shook his head no. "They intend to," he said. Then he added, "But they have come to see me here."

While still in school, he began living with Patti Smith, whom he met in Brooklyn. Maxine de la Falaise McKendry remembered that when Robert first met Smith he kicked a hole through from his apartment to hers so that they could communicate better. "Patti and I built on each other's confidence. We were never jealous of each other's work. We inspired each other. She became recognized first. Then she had a record contract. She pushed ahead. There was a parallel happening to each career." Patti Smith, who is now married with two children, lives in Detroit. "We talk to each other all the time," he said.

"S&M is a certain percentage of Robert's work, and necessary to show, to give a representation of his work," said Richard Marshall. He told me that when they put the exhibition together there had never been any idea of censorship, or any reservation about including offensive material, although, he added, "there are some stronger pictures which do exist, some more explicitly graphic pictures, the uh, penetration of the arm." What Marshall was referring to was what Mapplethorpe calls his fist-fucking file. "Call Suzanne," he said to me, speaking of his lovely young secretary, Suzanne Donaldson, "and ask her, if you want to see the fist-fucking file, or the video of me having my tit pierced." When certain of these photographs were shown at an art gallery in Madrid, the gallery owner, who has since died of AIDS, was sent to jail.

"There were some letters of protest about the show, but not in great numbers at all," said Marshall. "We put up signs in three or four locations, warning parents that the show might not be applicable for children."

Flora Biddle concurs. "I went on a tour of the show the night before it opened with the Whitney Circle, which is the highest category of membership. Richard Marshall talked about the pictures to the group, dealing with the pictures you could call the most sexual, and spoke beautifully about them. The people in the Circle were attentive and open to them. Afterward, people came up and said they thought it was so wonderful the Whitney was hanging this show."

Barbara Jakobson said, "Sometimes I'd drive downtown in my yellow Volkswagen to have dinner with Robert. Then, later, I'd drop him off at the Mineshaft, or one of those places. God forbid he be seen having a woman drop him off, so I'd leave him a block away. I had no desire to see inside, but I once asked Robert to describe what it was like, in an architectural way. He said there were places of ritual. He told me how the rooms were divided, without telling me what actually went on. Once he showed me a sadomasochistic photograph. I said to him, 'I can't believe that a human being would allow this to be done.' He replied, 'The person who had it done wanted it to be done. Besides, he heals quickly.' Robert would find these people who enjoyed this. The interesting part is that they posed for him."

When I discussed this conversation with Mapplethorpe, he said, "I went to the Eagles Nest and the Spike to find models. Or I'd meet people from referrals. They'd hear you were good at such and such a thing, and call. I was more into the experience than the photography. The ones I thought were extraordinary enough, or the ones I related to, I'd eventually photograph."

"Were drugs involved?"

"Oh, yes. I've certainly had my share of drug experiences, but I don't need drugs to take pictures. They get in the way. However, drugs certainly played a big factor in sex at that time. MDA was a big drug in all this. It's somewhere between cocaine and acid.

"Most of the people in S&M were proud of what they were doing. It was giving pleasure to one another. It was not about hurting. It was sort of an art. Certainly there were people who were into brutality, but that wasn't my take. For me, it was about two people having a simultaneous orgasm. It was pleasure, even though it looked painful.

"Doing things to people who don't want it done to them is not sexy to me. The people in my pictures were doing it because they wanted to. No one was forced into it.

"For me, S&M means sex and magic, not sadomasochism. It was all about trust."

"If his S&M work were heterosexual, it wouldn't be acceptable," I was told by a world-famous photographer, who, because of Mapplethorpe's illness, did not wish to be quoted by name making critical remarks about him. "The smart society that has accepted his work has done so because it is so far removed from their own lives."

Even before the AIDS crisis, though, Mapplethorpe had begun to move away from the S&M scene as subject matter for his photography. One of his closest associates said to me, "Robert had gotten more and more away from being a downtown personality. He had been observing the uptown life for some time, and I think he wanted to become a society photographer. Once, leaving someone's town house on the Upper East Side, he said, 'I wouldn't mind living like that.' "

Carolina Herrera, the subject of one of Mapplethorpe's earliest and most celebrated society portraits, has known him for years, "long before he was famous." They met on the island of Mustique in the Caribbean in the early 1970s, when Herrera and her husband were guests of Princess Margaret, and Mapplethorpe, along with his English friend

Catherine Tennant, was a guest of Tennant's brother Colin, who is now Lord Glenconner. Tennant remembers Mapplethorpe at the time wearing more ivory bracelets up his arms than the rebellious Nancy Cunard wore in the famous portrait Cecil Beaton took of her in 1927. When Mapplethorpe took Herrera's picture in a hotel room in New York, he had only a minimum of photographic equipment and no assistant. Herrera's husband, Reinaldo, had to hold the silver umbrella reflector for him. Mapplethorpe photographed Herrera wearing a hat and pearls, against a blank ground, and since then his style in social portraiture has remained as stark as in his nude figures, mirroring the sculptural influence of Man Ray more than the ethereal settings of Cecil Beaton.

On Friday evening, November 4, 1988, Robert Mapplethorpe gave a large cocktail party at his studio to celebrate his forty-second birthday. Incidentally, November 4 was also the birthday of Sam Wagstaff. Birthday celebrations have always been important to Mapplethorpe, according to Barbara Jakobson. She remembered other birthday parties in the past that Sam had given for Robert. " 'Sam is going to give me a party,' Robert would say way in advance."

At the peak of the birthday party, nearly two hundred people milled through the vast studio, among them the film stars Susan Sarandon, Sigourney Weaver, and Gregory Hines, all of whom had been photographed by Mapplethorpe. In the crowd were Prince and Princess Michael of Greece, the Earl of Warwick, Tom Armstrong of the Whitney Museum, gallery owner Mary Boone, Bruce Mailman, who was a managerial partner in the St. Marks Baths until it was closed down in the wake of the AIDS epidemic, and Dimitri Levas, the art director and principal stylist on Mapplethorpe's fashion shoots, who is said to be one of his heirs, as well as well-known figures from the magazine, gallery, auction, and museum worlds. And collectors. And people who were just friends. Inevitably, there were men in black leather, some wearing master caps, standing on the sidelines, watching. Everyone mixed.

Everybody brought gifts, wonderfully wrapped, and soon there was a mountain of them on a bench by the front door. Bouquets of flowers kept arriving throughout the party, including one of three dozen white roses in a perfect crystal vase. Waiters in black jackets moved through the crowd, carrying trays of fluted glasses of champagne. On several tables were large tins of beluga caviar, and Robert kept leaning over and helping himself.

Although there was certainly a sense that this was Robert Mapplethorpe's farewell party for his friends, there were no feelings of sadness in the studio that night. Robert, continually indomitable, provided his guests with an upbeat and optimistic celebration. He looked better than he had looked in weeks. He sat in his favorite chair, missing nothing, receiving guest after guest who came and knelt by his side to chat with him. Toward the end of the evening, he stood up and walked.

"This is Robert. This is his life. Everybody beautiful. Everybody successful," said one of the guests whom I did not know.

"Robert has style," said Prince Michael of Greece, surveying the event. "Personal style is not something you learn. It's something you have."

One of the most frequently asked questions these days is where Robert Mapplethorpe will leave his money when he dies. His lawyer, Michael Stout, refused to answer the question. But it is known that the photographer has recently set up the Robert Mapplethorpe Foundation, with a board of directors. Besides specific bequests to friends, the foundation will probably give money to the arts as well as to the American Foundation for AIDS Research (AmFAR), an organization with which Mapplethorpe had been associated since Sam Wagstaff's death. In a letter he sent out asking friends and acquaintances to pay $100 each to attend a private viewing of Sam Wagstaff's silver collection prior to its sale at Christie's in January, he wrote, "I have asked AmFAR to use the funds raised from this benefit to support community-based trials of promising AIDS drugs, a pilot program which will greatly increase patient access to treatments that may help extend their lives."

February 1989

THE LIGHT
OF HUSSEIN

❧

PEOPLE CAME because she was beautiful, and were then awed by her brilliance. She had dispelled the fairy-tale image. "This is no fairy tale. This is not a fairy tale at all," said Sarah Pillsbury, the Hollywood film producer, about her Concord Academy classmate Queen Noor al Hussein after the queen had spoken in the United States in October, defending the controversial role of her husband, King Hussein of Jordan, in the Middle East crisis. The Arab kingdom is precariously situated, bordered by Iraq, Israel, Syria, and Saudi Arabia. Should a war erupt, Jordan could become a battlefield. But in Amman, the capital, there was no overt sense of turbulence, or of a country close to war, during my visit two weeks later.

Foreign correspondents, on their way to and from Baghdad or Riyadh, talked in the bar of the Inter-Continental Hotel of atrocities and war, but taxi drivers and shopkeepers did not. Over dinner, the minister of information, speaking for the king, told a group of American journalists, "We don't want war. We are extremely nervous about military action in the area. We cannot afford to have a war. Jordan will be destroyed." But life seemed to go on as usual. In Petra, "the rose-red city half as old as time," I asked a Bedouin guide, "Don't you worry about the crisis?" "No," he replied, "we live our life in crisis. We have our faith. We're not afraid of death."

I had come hoping to see the American queen, whom I had heard speak several weeks earlier at the Brookings Institute in Washington, D.C., but my visit began inauspiciously. Checking into the Inter-Continental Hotel, I was confronted by a figure from the palace, Fouad Ayoub, who informed me that there were obstacles. The appointment for an interview with Her Majesty, he said, was unfixed, uncertain, and unpromised. There was a reluctance to let me meet with her until certain guidelines had been agreed upon, guidelines that were never going to be agreed upon. The best I was able to muster up was an evening visit with the only female member of the Jordanian senate, Laila Sharaf. An unpromising interview, of real interest to neither Mrs. Sharaf nor me.

The taxi driver who took me from the Inter-Continental to Mrs. Sharaf's house, high up on a hill on the outskirts of the city, spoke English but resisted all my attempts at conversation. There was, I was soon to discover, an underlying dislike of Americans in the country. In the taxi was a photograph of King Hussein next to one of Iraqi president Saddam Hussein, the man described by President Bush as worse than Hitler. King Hussein, who for many years positioned Jordan as a "moderate" Arab monarchy—who, indeed, has long been one of Washington's staunchest allies in the region—refused to join the anti-Saddam coalition. The surface reasons were apparent: Palestinians, who have sided with Iraq, account for more than half of Jordan's population, and the king could ill afford to ignore their interests. Even those Jordanians opposed to the brutal policies of Saddam Hussein are more opposed to the presence of American troops in the area. Although Jordan has abided by the U.N. sanctions against Iraq, the king's position severely strained his relations with the Bush administration and Saudi Arabia, which reacted by cutting off oil shipments to Jordan, leaving Iraq as its only supplier, and deepening the economic crisis.

At Mrs. Sharaf's large and handsome villa, the scent of night-blooming jasmine filled the air. The flower garden was in full bloom, and birds in great profusion sang on the roof. It was a setting of Middle Eastern luxe, marred only by the presence of an armed guard in a sentry box. I asked the taxi driver to wait for me in the courtyard. He was reluctant until I assured him that I would pay for his waiting time.

Laila Sharaf, the widow of a prime minister, is a distinguished woman in her own right, involved in cultural affairs. With the queen, she was active in starting the Jerash Festival of Culture and Arts, an annual program of dance, poetry, and music held in an ancient Roman amphitheater. The festival brought thousands of tourists to the country and was a boon to the economy, but with the beginning of the Gulf crisis, tourism became nonexistent overnight. Her butler brought a tray with glasses of lemonade, orange juice, cola, and water. We settled on comfortable sofas, and she began to describe to me the duties and accomplishments of the American queen.

A fiercely private woman until the recent events in the Middle East focused attention on her, Queen Noor has never captured the imagination of the American public in the way that Princess Grace of Monaco, her obvious counterpart, did. Comparisons to the late princess are said to disconcert, even annoy, her. In London recently, she attended the play *Love Letters* with her great friend Tessa

Kennedy, the interior designer who decorated several residences of the Jordanian royal family. After the show, the queen went backstage to visit one of the stars, another old American friend, Stefanie Powers. A friend of mine who sat behind the queen said she was virtually unrecognized by the audience. She has never become a fashion darling of the international paparazzi in the manner of the Princess of Wales, the Duchess of York, and the two princesses of Monaco. However, since Iraq invaded Kuwait in August, the queen has had a much higher profile, becoming the most visible woman in the Middle East. She played a major role in helping to organize aid for the nearly three-quarters of a million refugees who fled from Kuwait and flooded into her adopted country. The presence of the refugees placed an enormous burden on Jordan's already stricken economy. Her main priority was to help get the refugees home, and to accomplish that she personally enlisted the aid of Richard Branson, the British music and entertainment entrepreneur, who owns Virgin Atlantic Airways. The queen had recently returned from the United States, where she had spoken publicly in New York and Washington and had been interviewed by Barbara Walters on "Nightline." On that program she evidenced her skill in evading ticklish questions. When Walters asked her to describe her impression of Saddam Hussein, she replied that she had met him only once, very briefly. When Walters continued, "When your husband comes home after he's had these meetings, how does he describe him?" the queen replied, "My husband and I discuss issues more than personalities."

She was criticized in Jordan by those who felt it was not the natural role of the wife of the king to give speeches about foreign policy. In addressing such criticism, Mrs. Sharaf said, "The queen not only understands the facts, but she has put herself on the same perspective as the Arabs. Her way of thinking is very Western, but she has absorbed the Arab side."

Outside the house, arrival sounds could be heard. The butler hurried into the room and spoke excitedly to Mrs. Sharaf in Arabic. "She is here," Mrs. Sharaf said, surprised.

"Who?" I asked.

She rose and rapidly made her way to the hall and opened the door. A BMW motorcycle was driving into the courtyard. On it was King Hussein, the longest-ruling leader in the Arab world. Sitting behind him on the seat, arms around his waist, was Queen Noor. A military vehicle filled with soldiers came up behind them.

Suddenly feeling like an intruder, I said, "Would you like me to leave?"

"No, no. Wait in that room," my hostess told me.

I retreated to the salon and listened as she greeted the king and queen. The royal couple said they had been out for an evening spin in the hills above Amman and had decided to call on Mrs. Sharaf. Then I heard the lowered voice of Mrs. Sharaf explaining my presence in the adjoining room.

Suddenly the door opened, and the queen walked into the salon where I was standing. She is thirty-nine years old, tall, slender, and exceptionally good-looking. She was wearing blue jeans and a loose-fitting light blue sweater, but her carriage was as regal as if she had been in coronation regalia. Her long honey-colored hair fell to her shoulders, kept in place by a headband. Despite the informality of her dress and the situation we found ourselves in, however, the formal distance of royalty prevailed. She had come to pay an impromptu call on a friend and had found an unexpected visitor. "Sir," she said in greeting. Later I discovered she addresses most men as "sir."

Her looks are American. Her handshake is American. Her eye contact is American. And yet, somehow, she is ceasing, or has even ceased, to be American. In Washington earlier in the month, when she spoke at the Brookings Institute, she had several times said, "Speaking as an Arab . . ." Lisa Halaby, Princeton '74, has truly become, during the twelve years of her marriage, the Queen of Jordan. Her voice is American, but her manner of speech is not. So deliberate is her prose style that at times I had the ridiculous feeling that she was translating in her mind from Arabic to English. She often interjects phrases such as "if you will" and "as it were." There is no chitchat. There are no short answers. Every sentence is carefully thought out and spoken in a modulated, complicated, sometimes convoluted manner.

Behind her, a moment later, the king appeared. He, too, was dressed for biking, in a black leather jacket and aviator glasses, but even though his attire was informal, his history enveloped him. The thirty-eighth-generation descendant of the Prophet, he has been on the throne of the Hashemite kingdom of Jordan for thirty-eight years. At the age of fifteen, he witnessed the assassination of his grandfather King Abdullah during a visit to the Al Aqsa Mosque in Jerusalem. The same assassin then fired at him, but the bullet was deflected by a medal on the tunic of his military-school uniform. Two years later, he succeeded his mentally unstable father, King Talal, to the throne. If he was distressed at finding a reporter present during a rare private moment in his overcast life, he gave no indication of it. We shook hands. In all the official photographs that hang in the shop windows and office buildings of Amman, the king stands considerably taller than the queen. In reality, the queen is taller than the king by almost a head. Mrs. Sharaf motioned us to sit, and the butler reappeared with his tray of juices and cola. In the awkward moments that followed, I said that although I had hoped to meet them I had never expected to encounter them on a motorcycle.

"We courted on a motorcycle," said the queen. I was struck by the old-fashioned word "courted." "It was the only way we could get off by ourselves." Then she added, with a slight nod of her head to the courtyard outside, where the king's guards were, "Of course, we were always followed."

They discussed the Nobel Peace Prize, which had been awarded that day to Mikhail Gorbachev. The king had sent him a telegram of congratulations. They discussed Vaclav Havel. The queen said she had never met Havel, but would like to. She added that their days of travel were limited, at least for the time being. Invariably, the conversation returned to the Gulf crisis. It is a constant in everyone's mind. It is the dark cloud over their country and monarchy. "The country has never been more united," she said.

Although she is a beautiful woman, her intelligence rather than her beauty is her dominant force. She has weathered gossip and criticism, but even those salon ladies, as they are called, meaning the upper-class ladies of Amman, who most disliked her in the beginning have a grudging respect for the manner in which she recently presented the views of her country in the United States. Her husband, who has been on the throne since his wife was one year old, is at the peak of his popularity in his country. Several times during the visit, he looked over at her and smiled. There is an open affection between them. When she returned from her recent trip abroad in the royal family's Gulfstream jet, the king was at the airport to meet her.

In the course of the conversation, the queen mentioned that she would visit the new site of the Jubilee School the next day. The Jubilee School is one of her pet projects, a three-year coeducational boarding school for the most gifted high-school students in the region, providing them with scholarships to develop their leadership potential.

After fifteen minutes I departed, leaving them to their visit. Outside, in the courtyard, the king's motorcycle had been parked by the front door. Eight soldiers carrying assault rifles hovered by the guardhouse waiting for their monarch. My taxi driver, who had been heretofore so disagreeable, was now wide-eyed with awe. He was convinced that the king had arrived by motorcycle at the hilltop villa specifically to meet with me in secret conference. I did nothing to dissuade him of his misperception. The following morning a call came from the palace, inviting me to go along with the queen on her visit to the Jubilee School. In the days that followed, every time I encountered the taxi driver at the taxi stand in front of the hotel, we shook hands and chatted amiably, but by that time I was being picked up by silver Mercedes sedans with soldier-chauffeurs provided by the palace, and had no more need of taxis.

Queen Noor al Hussein was born Lisa Najeeb Halaby on August 23, 1951, into a prominent Arab-American family. Her well-known father, Najeeb Halaby, known as Jeeb, was of Syrian descent. He headed the Federal Aviation Administration during the Kennedy-Johnson years and was at one time the president of Pan American World Airways. Lisa was fashionably educated at the National Cathedral School in Washington, D.C., and the Concord Academy in Massachusetts before entering Princeton University in its first coeducational freshman class. She wore a black armband to protest the Vietnam War and became one of the first women cheerleaders. "She wore white ducks. She was the most gorgeous thing you ever saw, with her long hair," recalled television producer Gillian Gordon, one of her classmates and still a close friend. After her sophomore year, she took a year off and moved to Aspen, Colorado, where she supported herself as a waitress. She also did work in the library of the Aspen Institute and indulged her passion for skiing. Returning to Princeton, she took her degree in architecture and urban planning. Her graduation yearbook picture shows a rather plain girl with long, stringy hair and a quizzical, faraway look in her eyes. Beside their pictures, most of her classmates have a paragraph about themselves, describing academic accomplishments and future dreams. But not Lisa Halaby. Beside her picture is a blank white space, startling in retrospect, as if her past had already been put behind her and her future as the queen of a Middle Eastern country was too unfathomable even to imagine.

After Princeton she traveled to Australia and Iran, where she was hired as an assistant by Marietta Tree, the director of the American branch of the British architectural and planning firm of Llewelyn-Davis, Weeks. The firm had been commissioned by the late Shah of Iran to replan the city of Teheran, and Lisa Halaby lived there for six months doing architectural drafting. From Teheran she went to Jordan, where her father was closely connected with the head of Alia, the Jordanian airline, to work on a plan for the creation of an Arab air university. She was introduced to King Hussein when he was attending a ceremony to mark the arrival of the first jumbo jet to join Alia, which later became Royal Jordanian airlines.

The king's first marriage, to Dina Abdul Hamid, whom he had met in London when still a schoolboy, took place in 1955, shortly after his nineteenth birthday. Dina, seven years his senior, was an intellectual with a university education and a keen understanding of the politics of the Arab world. The marriage was encouraged by his mother,

Queen Zein, who admired Dina's intelligence and Hashemite credentials and was eager for her son to settle down. A daughter, Princess Alia, was born, but the marriage collapsed only eighteen months after the wedding. While Dina was on a holiday in Egypt, the king divorced her. For the next six years, Princess Dina was allowed to see her daughter only once. Many years later, Dina married a Palestinian commando who was also seven years younger than she.

In 1961, King Hussein married for the second time. His bride, Antoinette "Toni" Gardiner, was a nineteen-year-old English girl, the daughter of a lieutenant colonel serving in Jordan. They were introduced at a dance. Toni became a Muslim and adopted an Arab name, Muna al Hussein, meaning "Hussein's wish." Like Dina, Muna was made a princess, but not queen, and when Hussein announced the engagement on the radio, he described Muna as a Muslim, but not as an Arab. Her English background was left for a subsequent announcement. A year later a much-hoped-for son was born. Prince Abdullah was named after Hussein's slain grandfather. Another son followed, Prince Feisal, and twin daughters, Princess Zein and Princess Aisha. In addition, Alia, his daughter from his marriage to Princess Dina, was brought up by Princess Muna as one of her own family.

By the end of 1972, King Hussein had met and fallen in love with Alia Toukan, the daughter of a Jordanian diplomat. To the surprise of most people in Jordan, who were unaware of any problem in his marriage, the king divorced Princess Muna and married Alia, whom he made Queen of Jordan. In 1977, Queen Alia was killed in a helicopter crash while returning from visiting a hospital in the south of Jordan. The queen left behind two children, Princess Haya and Prince Ali, as well as an adopted daughter, Abir.

Abir as an infant had survived an air crash in which her mother was killed. She was found alive, cradled in her dead mother's arms. Alia was moved by the baby's plight and adopted her from her father, a Jordanian truck driver. Abir was brought up in the palace on equal footing with her royal siblings. In the five years of her marriage, Alia had become a popular and beloved queen. The king was grief-stricken by her death, and the nation was plunged into mourning. For a while he withdrew into seclusion.

When the king met Lisa Halaby, the attraction between the two was immediate. Marietta Tree, who was visiting in Jordan at the time, remembers being told by Lisa that the king had asked her to lunch. Later that day, returning from a trip to Petra, Mrs. Tree asked, "How was the lunch?" Lisa told her, "It lasted five hours. He showed me the palace, and we played with the children." One of her close friends told me that she detested the word "dated" when speaking of her romance with the king. They "courted" for six weeks, escaping from the ever-watchful eye of Amman society, sometimes on the king's motorcycle for jaunts in the country and sometimes by helicopter for private dinners at Aqaba, the beach resort on the Red Sea, where the king maintains a summer residence.

Lisa Halaby converted to Islam and took the name Noor al Hussein, which means "light of Hussein." They were married on June 15, 1978, and the new queen became stepmother to the king's eight children, adopting Abir, who was then seven, and the two small children of Queen Alia. Sarah Pillsbury said of her old friend, "She was always very bright and very mature. We were always very impressed with her. She got in touch with me about a year after the wedding, and we have kept in touch since then. I was struck by her dignity and her determination to be the best wife and queen. The king never said to her, 'Do this.

Do that.' She figured it out herself. Has she changed? None of us are the same people we were back then, and she's not, either." Another friend, the journalist Carinthia West, who attended the National Cathedral School with her, said, "Sure, it was hard for her in the beginning. She had no family. No buddies." It is a fact that there was a great deal of resentment toward the new queen at the beginning of her marriage, especially on the part of the fashionable ladies of Amman. There are indications also that jealousies occurred in the king's family over the new, fourth wife of the king. "It wasn't just because she's tall, blond, and American," a Jordanian woman told me. "It was because she became the queen." In the years that have followed, Queen Noor has had four children of her own. Prince Hamzah was born in 1980, Prince Hashim in 1981, Princess Iman in 1983, and Princess Raiyah in 1986.

When the queen goes about her daily duties, she travels in a motorcade, but there are no Daimlers, no Rollses, no Bentleys, no sirens, and no flags. This queen drives herself, in a jeep—a Mercedes jeep, but a jeep nonetheless. She chooses who is going to ride with her, and her companions change during the day so that she can talk privately with her attendants or her guests. Her jeep is in the middle of the motorcade, preceded and followed by military vans with soldiers.

On several occasions I rode in the jeep with the queen. She drives the way she speaks, carefully. Unlike the English princesses, who are always being stopped for speeding, she does not drive fast. She is sometimes recognized by passengers in other cars, who lean out their windows to wave at her. She always smiled and waved back. At a busy five-way intersection in the middle of the city, one of the soldiers in the vehicle ahead of the jeep hopped out to halt traffic in all directions so that the queen and her party could go through. "I don't like when they do that," she said. She stopped the jeep, shook her head, and waved the other cars through, sitting out the red light like any other driver. When the light turned green, she passed through the intersection. The traffic cop on duty smiled at her, and she waved back at him. "He knows me," she said.

After looking over the new facilities for the Jubilee School, she visited a school for girls, going from classroom to classroom, listening to children recite or perform, talking to as many of them as possible, giving her full attention to each conversation. About 50 percent of Jordan's population is under the age of fifteen. There is no bobbing and curtsying to her as there is to English royals making their official rounds in flowered hats. Rather, the queen extends her hand in the American manner and almost immediately engages in conversation. Her style of dress is extremely simple: Usually she wore a below-the-calf-length khaki skirt with a blue denim shirt and a blazer. She told me that when she was first married she was taken aside by an adviser and told that her duties would consist, for example, of cutting ribbons to open schools and buildings. She knew that her role would exceed such functions, but there was no precedent in the country for an activist queen. "I had always worked," she said. "My role has been a pioneering role."

When she is performing her official duties, she speaks only in Arabic. "It's my working language," she said. "I use no English when I am working with the people in the country, but I use both English and Arabic with people in the scientific fields." She now speaks the language fluently but says, "I will never be a great poet in Arabic. It's such a challenging language." With the king, who was educated in England at Harrow and Sandhurst, she speaks both languages, but they converse primarily in English. "My children are completely bilingual, more than I could ever be. I spoke only Arabic with my first child. I hope and pray they won't have to study Arabic as a second language. I want them to think in Arabic. They all go to Arabic schools. Their courses are taught in Arabic, except for English courses. Arithmetic and science are taught in both languages."

"Do they have accents?"

"They don't sound like foreigners speaking English," she replied.

Once, talking about her children, she said, "I was so lucky I was raised the way I was, and that I traveled and worked before I was married. I want my children to do the same before they marry."

"Will you send your children to school abroad?"

"I once said to the headmaster of my husband's school, 'I will send my children to the best school for each one of them when the time comes.' They will study abroad. Each is entitled to have some time to compete equally with everyone else. Within Jordan, they will always be the sons of the king. There will be those who will surround them with too much attention, judge them too easily, even take advantage of them. To really learn how to stand on their own feet, they need to get away."

Despite growing anti-American sentiment, which in some circles extends to the queen, she is in daily touch with her subjects. "The people on the street like her. They get excited when they see her. They don't look *up* to her. They look *to* her for help. They see her as the female, the softer figure whom they can reach out to for help. She has been here twelve years now. She has grown in her job," said

Dr. Sima Bahous, an assistant professor of journalism at Yarmouk University, north of Amman.

I went with Queen Noor to the village of Al Bassah, an hour's drive from the capital. It was the first visit ever paid to the village by a member of the royal family. Schoolchildren lined up on both sides of the road to greet her motorcade. Like a latter-day character out of Lesley Blanch's *The Wilder Shores of Love,* the queen walked through rows of clapping schoolboys and cadets to shake hands with the elders of the village. She entered a Bedouin tent and sat on a sofa that had been placed there for her. Opposite her on chairs sat the men of the village, who told her what they needed for the village. She replied in Arabic, promising them help, asking her aides to make notes, speaking in the same deliberate manner as when she speaks in English. Up the hill from the tent, women with covered heads watched from the porch of a house. When she finished with the men, she walked up the hill to the women. They crowded around her, several hundred of them, wanting to be near her. They held up babies. They kissed her hand. She addressed herself with special care to the problems of the women. "We are equal with the men and work together, plus raise our children," they told her. During the harvest, they said, they needed a kindergarten for their children while they worked in the fields. She promised to help them. She went into the olive groves and picked olives with the women, and then walked down into a green valley that looked biblical, where the villagers grew pomegranates and figs.

On the way back to the city, I drove in the jeep with the queen. High on a mountaintop in the distance was a beautiful sprawling estate looking down on the Dead Sea. It was the country house of Prince Muhammad, a brother of the king. "My husband and I were given land up there as a wedding present, but we never built," she said. "Maybe someday, something simple, a place to get away."

The king and queen maintain a large house in London as well as an estate in the English countryside, grand enough to have been lent to the Duke and Duchess of York to live in while their own country house was being built. But their main home is Al Nadwa, the cream-colored royal palace in Amman. As palaces go, Al Nadwa is more like a rich man's mansion than a monarch's royal residence. If all twelve of the king's children were home at the same time —an unlikely event—it would probably be a tight squeeze. A large estate set in the middle of the city, it is in a well-guarded compound with staff offices, guest residences, barracks, and several other palaces, one of which, the old palace of King Abdullah, the king's grandfather, is used by Queen Noor for her foundation and offices.

We sat in the English-looking garden under a white marquee, looking out over a lush green lawn. The marquee seemed to have permanent status in the garden, since the poles were covered with ivy. The lunch table was set for two. A butler wearing English butler clothes—dark jacket, striped trousers—carried the food on trays from the palace down a poplar-lined walkway to where we were sitting.

"This is my favorite room in the house," said the queen. "The garden is a recent thing. I put all this in. Gardening is something new for me. I wish I'd done it long before. It established an equilibrium with nature, putting my hands in the dirt, planting."

She looks as though she might have played field hockey in boarding school, but she complained about not getting enough exercise. "I do aerobics with a friend who comes here, and play tennis. We don't have a swimming pool."

Plans were drawn up for one several years ago, but for security reasons it was never built. She likes to dispel the image of luxury living behind the palace walls. "I like being able to say, 'We don't have a pool.' "

"Have there been difficulties between you and other women in the royal family?" I had heard there was a chilly relationship with a sister-in-law and a former sister-in-law.

She shrugged. "I suppose it is the same in every family," she answered.

"Do you see Queen Zein?" The king's mother, Queen Zein, lives in a large, well-guarded house on Jubaiha, the road in Amman where most of the embassies are located. For years Queen Zein was the central figure in the royal family. After King Abdullah's assassination, she was a powerful influence on her son when he became king.

"If there is a family wedding, part of the celebration will always take place at her house," replied the queen carefully. "She came to see me in the hospital each time one of the children was born."

Ever since her marriage, the queen has been gossiped about. She has been accused of extravagance in clothes and jewels. She has also been accused of having had plastic surgery on her face, but her friends insist that clothes and jewels are not where her interests lie. "She is passionately interested in what's going on," says Marietta Tree. While I was in Jordan, a report was printed in an American newspaper that said she had recently purchased an estate in Palm Beach, Florida. When I asked her about it, she just smiled and shook her head in exasperation. "I am becoming inured to criticism. When you're in my position, people are always going to talk about you." She told me of a story that went around about her several years ago in which she was accused of purchasing a ring of extraordinary value. "Everyone knew someone who had seen the bill of sale, but it could never be found. It happened to Raisa Gorbachev too. I work with a wide variety of people from all segments of life. I'll never be approved of by everybody."

In all the time that I spent with her, there was never once when I felt I could have crossed the boundaries into the verbal intimacies of Americans meeting abroad. Her guard is never relaxed. Her conversation is without levity. It is not that she is humorless; it is simply that her sky is so darkened with the winds of war and its consequences that there is no time for laughter in her life. She is always addressed as Your Majesty. As an American, I found it difficult to call another American Your Majesty, but there is no other form of address. There are those in the court who address the king as Sidi, an affectionate term meaning "sir" or "My Lord," and address the queen as Sitti, meaning "My Lady," but I never did.

"How many assassination attempts have there been on the king?" I asked. I had been told there had been twenty-seven during his thirty-eight-year reign.

She waved her hands in front of her face as if to dispel my question. "I don't know. I don't want to know. My husband has learned from experience to be wise and pre-scient. He gives each moment of his life a maximum en-ergy for good use. If we sealed ourselves off in a protective bubble, we wouldn't be able to reach out and touch and feel what people need. I feel they should be able to touch us. I'm willing to take the risk of being stampeded upon if it gives them hope. It runs against any security advice he has been given over the years. They feel he is not just a figurehead, or head of state in his office. He is there as a father to the people."

"Would you discuss the succession?" I asked her.

"At the moment, Prince Hassan, the king's brother, is the crown prince, so he is the king's successor. In this country, the succession has always been modified to accommodate. The monarchy should always be able to serve as a constructive and unifying force. The most important thing is that it serves the people of the country. For me, it's entirely in harmony with all I was raised to believe the role of the leader should be. It should not seek to protect its existence for its own sake."

When Prince Abdullah, the older son of Princess Muna, was born, in 1962, King Hussein named him as the crown prince, but since the country was in a constantly turbulent state, Hussein realized that a small child was not a reasonable successor. The king has two brothers. Prince Muhammad and Prince Hassan. Muhammad, who was next in line after the child Abdullah, was married to, and later divorced from, the international social figure Princess Firyal, who subsequently had a highly publicized liaison with the Greek shipping magnate Stavros Niarchos. After much consideration, the king bypassed Muhammad in favor of his younger brother, Prince Hassan, who is twelve years younger than the king. Oxford-educated and a brilliant public speaker, Hassan is considered the intellectual of the family. His wife, Princess Sarvath, is the daughter of a distinguished Pakistani leader and ambassador. Since the ratification of Hassan, the king has bypassed his two sons by the English Princess Muna and has named Prince Ali, his son by the Jordanian Queen Alia, as next in line after Prince Hassan. Prince Ali, now fifteen, attends Deerfield Academy in Massachusetts.

"I have heard it said that, because you are an American, you are becoming a liability to the king. Is that correct?"

She seemed surprised. "I haven't felt that. I have never felt it. I was born into an Arab-American family. My name, Halaby, is Arabic. I have returned to the Arab world. I am not aware that my Americanism is a liability."

Although most people in Amman dress in Western fashion, there is a growing group of Muslim fundamentalist women who have eschewed modern dress as a form of protest. "It has come out of the frustrations of the people," Sima Bahous had told me the day before. "Everybody wants an identity. It is more than a religious movement. If they unite behind a front, their voice will be heard."

"Do you feel threatened by the fundamentalists?" I asked the queen.

"I personally don't feel threatened, but I know that my work and what I have achieved could be threatened by them. Extremism will only feed off the economic inequalities. Traditionally, women in this area, even my mother-in-law, Queen Zein, wore their hair covered. It is part of the cultural tradition. As religious extremism started to develop, there came a form of dress that was devoid of color, that covered the body from head to toe. Over it is worn a headdress that is restrictive, an uglifying fashion psychologically, to defeminize, to desex, to make women totally unappealing, to negate their femininity. It is a symbol of submission. There is pressure brought to women to dress like that. I don't dress for the conservatives in society. At the same time, I don't dress the way Western women do, which would be immodest in this country."

"If war comes, do you fear losing your throne?"

"In the first place, I don't consider myself as having a throne. The only thing I would ever fear is if the peace and stability that the monarchy has offered to this country were destroyed, if all my husband struggled for, and what I have struggled for by his side, were lost. That is what I fear for. My happiness, satisfaction, and security do not come from the throne or the monarchy or having been privileged to carry the title of Queen of Jordan."

Her older son, Prince Hamzah, arrived from school and

crossed the lawn to greet his mother. Dressed in a black
T-shirt and light trousers, he looked like any American boy
of ten arriving home from school, ready for playtime. In a
garage on the opposite side of the palace, there were miniature Volkswagens and jeeps for the royal children, the kind
that run on gasoline. Hamzah was joined by the princes'
young American tutor. After greeting his mother and talking about the events of his school day, Hamzah pointed to
the far end of the garden and asked, "Can we make some
noise down there?"

The queen smiled and nodded to her son, and then
resumed the conversation. "People are beginning to realize
that we in Jordan don't conform to the worst stereotypes of
the oil rich, or the worst stereotypes of the terrorists. Each
Arab society is different from the others. For many in the
Arab world, Saddam is a patriot. He represents someone
who has stood up to the overwhelming forces of the West
for what he believes in. He is against Western interference
in Arab affairs. For many Arabs, whose history has been
marked by Western interference over many decades, his
tough stand is deemed to be courageous. Whatever happens, we shall follow King Hussein. For thirty-eight years,
his humanity, experience, and wisdom have been what the
people identify with."

In the background Prince Hamzah appeared from behind a tree, carrying a very realistic toy assault rifle. The
tutor could be seen hiding behind another tree. The queen
watched for a minute, shrugged, and said, "I guess he plays
war with the boys."

It had turned dark. "Will you turn on the garden
lights?" she called out to Prince Hamzah. Then her youngest child, Princess Raiyah, age four, arrived back at the
palace from a children's music class. Dressed in pink jeans

and a pink T-shirt, she raced to her mother. For several minutes they discussed the music class.

There was the beginning of a chill in the air. "The weather's going to change," she said. "This will be the last time I have lunch in the garden. It will soon be too cold to sit out like this. Sometimes there's even snow." She stood up. "Would you like to see the children's zoo?" she asked.

"If war comes, what will happen to Jordan?" I asked Sima Bahous.

"Some people think Jordan will suffer the most," she replied. "If it comes, the people in the streets will not be quiet. The youth of the country will not accept war without having a say in what will come about."

"Will the king survive?"

"War means change," she said. "Everything will be in danger. Not the king, who is popular, but the institution of monarchy."

On the night before I left Amman, the king and queen asked a small group of American journalists to dinner at the palace. On arriving there, each guest was given a seating plan showing where his or her place would be at the table. Thirty-five minutes after we had assembled and been served nonalcoholic drinks, the king and queen arrived in the reception room and, as a couple, moved around the room, greeting each guest. That night the queen wore tight black trousers and a loose-fitting black evening sweater. The king was wearing a dark business suit.

They did not sit at the head and foot of the long, narrow, elaborately set table. Instead, they sat opposite each other at the center of the table, so that during general conversation they were able to converse together. While we were served food passed by a staff of waiters, the king's plate was brought to him with food already on it. He ate almost nothing. Speaking in quiet tones, he held the attention of the entire table as he explained his role in trying to keep peace in the Middle East since August 2, when he had been awakened by King Fahd of Saudi Arabia at six o'clock in the morning to be told that the invasion of Kuwait had taken place. In the first forty-eight hours, he had gone off to mediate at the request of President Bush, President Mubarak, and King Fahd. He had been given assurances that there would be no condemnation of President Hussein, nothing to put him on the defensive. His efforts at peacekeeping, however, had been misunderstood, mistrusted, or rebuffed by former allies and friends. He seemed mired in personal melancholy, smoking cigarette after cigarette during the meal. Taking a cue from the king, a journalist seated to the left of the queen also lit up a cigarette. The queen mildly chastised the journalist for smoking, a chastisement clearly meant for the king.

Rising at the end of the dinner, the male reporters made a beeline for the queen, surrounding her to ask questions. From the sidelines, the king watched his wife at the center of the group of reporters and smiled proudly and affectionately. Lisa Halaby, Queen Noor al Hussein, had clearly come into her moment in time.

January 1991